BATTALION OF HEAVY & MEDIUM TANKS

HQ

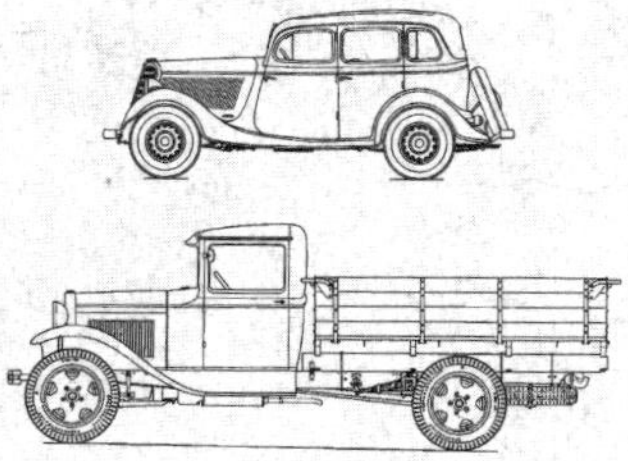

MAINTENANCE & RECOVERY SQUAD

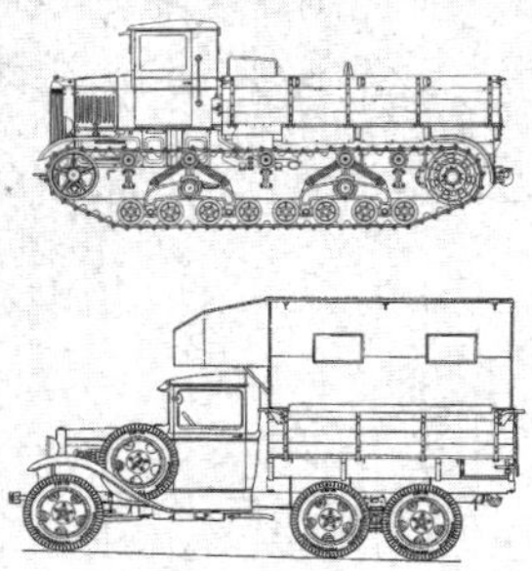

HEAVY TANK COMPANY

KV

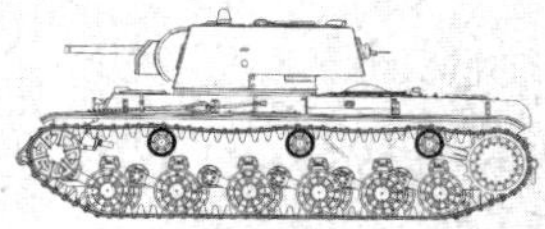

Company Commander's Tank

TANK PLATOON

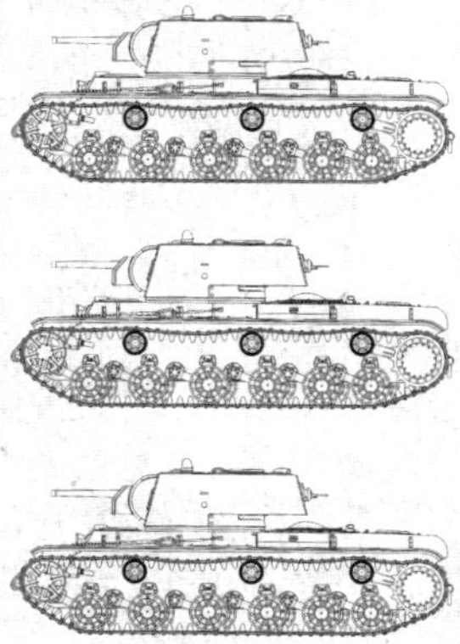

TANK PLATOON

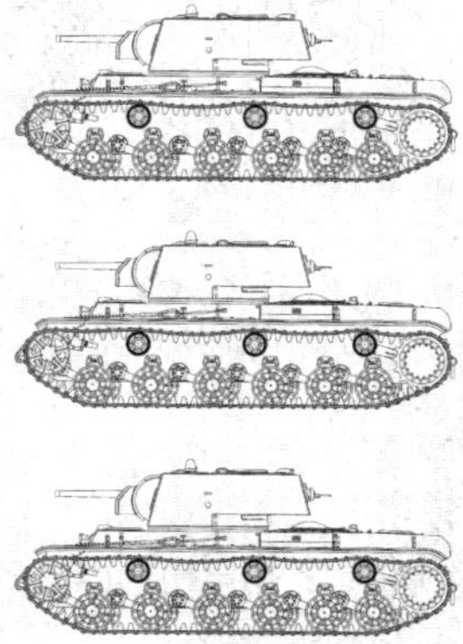

MEDIUM TANK COMPANY (3 PER BATTALION)

T-34

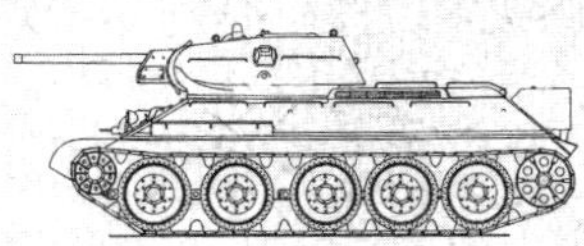

Company Commander's Tank

TANK PLATOON

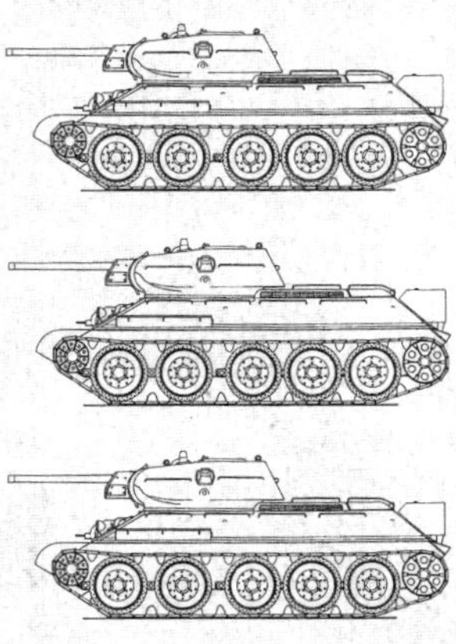

TANK PLATOON

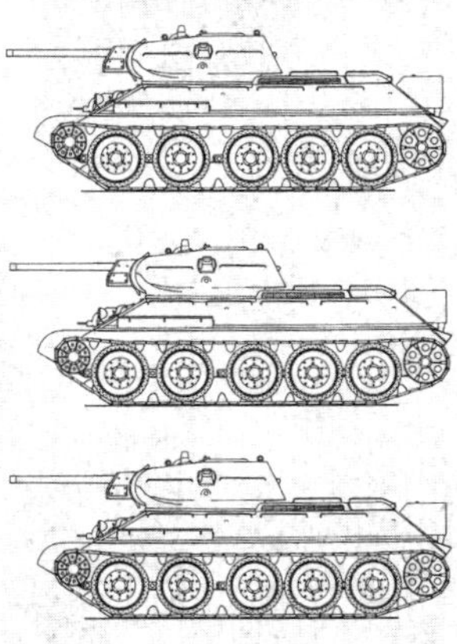

TANK PLATOON

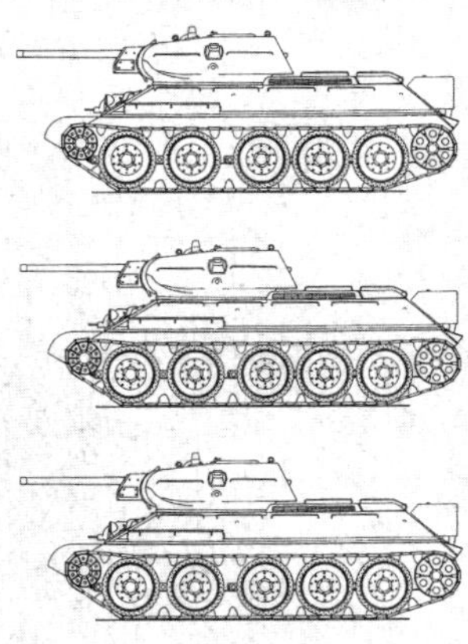

❶

❷

WORLD OF TANKS®

Andrei Ulanov and Dmitry Shein

THE T-34 GOES TO WAR

Lombardy Studios

WARGAMING.NET
LET'S BATTLE™

The T-34 Goes to War

Lombardy Studios
English Edition Series Managing Editor: Dana Lombardy
English Edition Production: Mark Schumann
Index: Cindy Coan

Wargaming.net
Director of Product Vision: Chris Keeling
Special Projects and Research Manager: Michael Buonagurio
English Edition Editor: Christopher J. Parker
Russian to English translation services by LanguageTran.com
Additional Translations: Egor Buzayev

Russian Edition
Series Development and Artistic Editor: M. Levykin
Edited by: G. Pernavsky
Cover Design: V. Petelin
Color Sidebars Authored by: A. Aksenov
Diagrams and Color Illustrations by: P. Shitkin
Layout Editor: I. Petrovskaya
Layout: R. Yeremeyev
Proofreaders: A. Baskakova and S. Kireyeva

The quality of some illustrations is that of the archival source material.

The book includes documentation, photography, and illustrations from the Central Archive of the Ministry of Defense of the Russian Federation (TsAMO RF), Russian State Military Archive (RGVA), the Russian State Archive of the Economy, the private collection of Yuri Pasholok, and the Nemirov 41 project.

The authors wish to express their deep gratitude for materials provided by Yu. I. Pasholok, A. Yu. Makarov, A. V. Isayev, and members of the military history forums RKKA and Nemirov 41—tankovyye srazheniya leta 1941 goda [Nemirov 41—tank battles of the summer of 1941], and the International Military Forum, without whose invaluable assistance this book could not have been written.

For worldwide distribution except in the CIS (countries of the former Soviet Union) contact:
Casemate Book Distributors, 1950 Lawrence Road, Havertown, PA 19083-1709
610-853-9131
www.casematepublishing.com

First North American Edition published by:
Lombardy Studios, 835 8th Avenue, Oakland, California 94606-3608 U.S.A.
www.WorldofTanksBooks.com

Library of Congress Control Number 2015953843

ISBN (Print) 978-1-940169-03-3 Copyright ©2017
ISBN (eBook) 978-1-940169-09-5 Copyright ©2017

Printed in China.

featuring the art and graphics of WORLD OF TANKS®

PUBLISHER'S PREFACE

This is the second book in the *World of Tanks* series that has been translated from the original Russian edition and made available in English. These books are an outgrowth of Wargaming.net's massive, multiplayer online game World of Tanks. At the time this book was published, World of Tanks had more than 80 million registered players worldwide.

There are two reasons why these books are important to readers interested in World War Two (the Great Patriotic War to Russians) and the armored fighting vehicles (AFV) that were the breakthrough weapons of that conflict:

- Russian documents, photos, and archival materials never before seen by outsiders were accessed to learn about the design, procurement, development, manufacturing, and combat employment of Soviet AFV before and during World War Two;
- English readers now get this information through the eyes and opinions of Russian researchers—which is why we added the obvious descriptor The Russian View to this series.

There are three categories of books: Combat Service (such as this T-34 book); Construction and Development; and Military Operations.

Andrei Ulanov and Dmitry Shein, the authors of this book about the T-34's pre-war development and combat service in 1941, uncovered fascinating facts and the mystery of why such a revolutionary design, far ahead of anything the invading German armies fielded, did so poorly in many of its first battles:

- The T-34's birth date of 19 December 1939, an advanced design intended to replace the numerous BT series as the "tank of independent mechanized units"
- Trials of the first two T-34 prototypes in January 1940 and subsequent field tests exposed flaws in the turret, vision devices, and sights; a radio that often failed; and a V-2 diesel engine that did not guarantee 100 hours of operational reliability
- Instead of 5–6 rounds per minute, the actual "deliverable" average rate of fire was only 2 rounds per minute, partly due to the restricted view from the tank
- Constant breakdowns occurred due to minor and major failures of the first mass-produced parts and systems
- The first "thirty-fours" did not reach Red Army front line units until April 1941, barely two months before the German Wehrmacht attacked the Soviet Union
- Rapid expansion of the Red Army armored force and a lack of manuals and training time led to poorly skilled tank commanders and T-34 crews in June 1941
- The most widely used German antitank gun—the small 37 mm PAK 36—proved lethal to the T-34 while leaving almost no significant mark of damage

This *World of Tanks* series provides English readers of World War Two history with a much better understanding and greater appreciation of Soviet AFV development and operations. I am extremely fortunate to be able to offer these innovative books for the first time in English.

Dana Lombardy
Lombardy Studios
March 2016

TABLE OF CONTENTS

AUTHORS' INTRODUCTION

"Legendary"—that is the label most often applied to the "thirty-four." It is called, "the best tank in the world," almost as often. Choice quotes appear in book after book. From Kleist we see "Their T-34 was the finest tank in the world;" from Mellenthin, "It was the most excellent example of an offensive weapon in the Second World War;" and from von Zenger und Etterlin, "The T-34 surpassed all other tanks. Its hull shape was ideal and served as the model for many later tanks." The West German magazine *Soldat un Technik* commented, "The T-34 was indisputably a masterpiece of military equipment." Hearing these laudatory odes, however, people are bothered by an insidious question: why is it that in 1941 the Red Army, which had 1,000 of these remarkable tanks that "so surpassed the German tanks and became a real nightmare for the German army's infantry and antitank defense," [1] failed to rout the enemy with "little bloodshed, on foreign soil," but retreated to Moscow and Leningrad instead? Why is it that newsreels showing "thirty-fours" driving through the streets of liberated cities flying red banners were only shot in 1942 and 1943, when the most acute phase of the crisis with Germany's armored blitzkrieg was already over? In any event, in 1942 Germany's generals had not yet lost battles due to "the superiority of the Russian T-34 tanks that sharply demonstrated their superiority from the first." [2] However, Soviet propaganda found a simple answer to this question that was plausible to all—there were too few of these new tanks. The treacherous enemy had committed a surprise attack with overwhelming numerical superiority, etc.

After the collapse of the Soviet Union, however, sources marked "For Official Use Only" and much more open Western encyclopedias became available—and the people of the former Soviet Union learned, to their surprise, that there had not been all that many German tanks, and there had been more than a few T-34s and KVs. The soap bubble of myth had burst—and, as usual, new answers that were just as "profound" and "pithy," and also were simple and understandable, crept in: "... but the Red Army was preparing an offensive and therefore was unable and did not prepare to defend itself;" "... but the Soviet people did not want to fight for such a merciless, bloodthirsty government; the Army abandoned the overwhelming miracle weapon it had been entrusted with and fled, hiding like cowards under fig trees and in homes;" "... Actually, the tanks only existed on paper;" and many variations and combinations of these explanations. However, the legend of a powerful and invulnerable tank fully satisfied those who first gave simple new answers to complex questions. [3] The legend remained—until now...

In this book, we want to talk about those who were eclipsed by the legend; the story of the real tank that has loomed larger than life and the real people who fought in it. This book is not about supermen or robots with burning engines in place of hearts who fearlessly take on countless hordes of enemies in a few miracle tanks—and blow them away with a few crushing shots from their high-power guns. [4] This is the story of those who were thrown into the war at its beginning on June 22, 1941; those who burned in tanks; those who went out in beat-up and broken-down vehicles or simply

A T-34 from an unknown Red Army unit on its way to the front line, August 5, 1941. This may be the only combat photo of a T-34 shot by a Soviet photographer.

abandoned their vehicles with dry fuel tanks, received new tanks, returned to battle to burn again—and, finally, forced the enemy to halt and then retreat. The story of those who unhesitatingly paid the highest price and bought Victory in the end.

• • •

Here, the authors would like to say a few words about the photographs used to illustrate the book. The first few months of the Great Patriotic War were an unprecedented disaster and called into question the very existence of the Soviet state. There are few genuine, unstaged photographs of "thirty-fours" in battle taken by Soviet photographers during the time of deep enemy breakthroughs, encirclements, confusion, panic, and chaos after the enemy had seized the field of battle following the tragic end of a fierce "defense to the last bullet, the last drop of blood, the last breath." Wehrmacht soldiers were much more likely to carry personal cameras than were Red Army soldiers.

The authors are far from uncritical in their admiration of the "invincible German military machine;" the problem is that, to our deep regret, most of the photographs illustrating the impact of the T-34 in the early months of the war show the invaders posing next to destroyed and broken-down Soviet tanks.

We would also like to make another important point about how the photographs we selected should be perceived. The Wehrmacht's most widely used antitank artillery system at the beginning of the Great Patriotic War was the 37 mm PaK 36 antitank gun. The shell it fired often proved lethal for the "thirty-fours;" visually, however, the damage

The second T-34 tank prototype during testing (showing the driver-mechanic's "compartment"). Front view.

it caused was not especially spectacular. It left no gaping breaches or fist-sized holes in its armor that would be visible from a distance. The number of tanks that burned or were blown up after being hit by small-caliber shells was also relatively small—no more than 20% of those destroyed during 1941–1942. As a result, the "thirty-fours" sometimes photographed by curious German lensmen in their gray uniforms show no conspicuous external damage. Nevertheless, the illusory "serviceability" of the tanks in the photographs does not support statements like, "The Red Army did not want to fight. Just look at the photographs of captured Soviet tanks abandoned by fleeing crews!" Analysis of German battle documents effectively refutes that idea.

A. Ulanov and D. Shein
2013

NOTES

1 Eike Middeldorf, *The Russian Campaign: Tactics and Weapons [Russkaya kampaniya: taktika i vooruzheniye].* St. Petersburg: OOO Izdatelstvo Poligon, Moscow: OOO Firma Izdatelstvo AST, 2000, p. 288.

2 H. Guderian, *Memoirs of a Soldier.* Smolensk: Rusich, 1999, p. 315.

3 "Therefore, Soviet historians should have directly and honestly written that the Red Army had 1500 tanks, and the German army had none. Not one. The number of 'tank' regiments, divisions, and groups is known; but the number of tanks is not. And that conclusion would have been entirely appriopriate for the classification system invented by Soviet 'historians,'"...because in the summer of 1941, the Wehrmacht did not have a single tank with specifications comparable to those of the T-34 or, especially, to the monstrous KV. (M. S. Solonin, *Screwing the Brains: The False History of the Great War [Mozgoimeniye: Fal'shivaya istoriya Velikoy voyny].* Moscow: Eksmo: Yauza, 2010)

4 "German tanks (up to 40 vehicles) broke through our defenses. They destroyed our one battery and headed towards the 12th Tank Division's command post. The situation was serious. General T. A. Mishanin quickly allocated three KV tanks and four T-34 tanks and ordered them to destroy the enemy that had broken through. I sent three KV tanks located at the corps command post to assist those seven. A tank battle erupted behind our lines. I watched as the German tanks with their black crosses darted between our enormous KVs, seeking safety. They attempted to maneuver in order to fire at our weak side armor. But it did not help: The KVs and T-34s nimbly fired their 76 mm guns at the enemy tanks... Six KVs and four T-34s destroyed all 40 German tanks without losses." (D. I. Ryabyshev, *The First Year of the War.* Moscow: Voyenizdat, 1990, p. 40)

The "Red Cavalry's steeds of steel": from left to right, BT-7, A-20, T-34 with L-11 gun, and T-34 with F-34 gun.

CHAPTER 1. **BIRTH OF THE LEGEND**

The history of the gradual transformation of the "iron horse of the Red Cavalry"—the BT tank, with tracks that could be removed so the tank ran on its wheels—into the legendary "thirty-four" has been described many times in contemporary literature, although in different ways: for example, whether the development of the fully tracked vehicle originated with the military or with factory designers.[1]

December 19, 1939, can be considered the T-34's official date of birth. On that day, the Defense Committee of the Council of People's Commissars of the USSR passed Decree No. 443ss "On the Acceptance of Tanks, Armored Vehicles, and Artillery Prime Movers into Service with the Workers' and Peasants' Red Army, and Their Production in 1940." The decree stated the following:

> ***1.*** *The following systems shall be accepted into service with the RKKA [Workers' and Peasants' Red Army]: ... The T-32 tank—a tracked vehicle with a V-2 diesel engine manufactured by Factory No. 183 of the People's Commissariat of Medium Machine Building, with the following modifications:*
> ***a)*** *Increase the thickness of the main armor plates to 45 mm;*
> ***b)*** *Improve visibility from the tank;*
> ***c)*** *Mount the following weapons on the T-32 tank:*
> ***1)*** *The 76 mm F-32 gun coaxially with a 7.62 mm machine gun;*
> ***2)*** *A separate 7.62 mm machine gun for the radio operator;*
> ***3)*** *A separate 7.62 mm machine gun;*
> ***4)*** *A 7.62 mm antiaircraft machine gun.*
> *Designate the tank the "T-34"...*

2. To ensure production of tanks, tractors, and armored cars in 1940, and development of the required capacities... the People's Commissar of Medium Machine Building (Comrade LIKHACHEV) shall undertake the following actions:
Factory No. 183 shall:

- **a)** *Organize production of T-34 tanks at the Komintern Kharkov Factory No. 183;*
- **b)** *Manufacture two T-34 prototypes by 15 January 1940 and produce a pilot batch of 10 vehicles by 15 September 1940;*
- **c)** *Produce at least 200 T-34 tanks in 1940;*
- **d)** *By 1 January 1941, increase the capacity of Factory No. 183 to produce 1600 T-34 tanks ...*

The Stalingrad Tractor Plant shall:

- **a)** *Organize production capacity at the Stalingrad Tractor Plant for annual production of 2,000 tanks per year in 1940;*
- **b)** *Produce 20 T-34 tanks in 1940;*
- **c)** *Set up a production line at the Stalingrad Tractor Plant to produce 1,000 T-34 tanks in 1941;*[2]

T-28 tanks of the 20th Heavy Tank Brigade disabled while attempting to break through the main sector of the Mannerheim Line.

As is evident from the decree, the initial output of the new tanks would be rather modest—220 vehicles per year from two factories. This cautious start-up can be partially explained by the fact that the customer—the Red Army's Armor Directorate—did not yet fully understand the role the new vehicle would play in the Army's armored vehicle system. In the fall of 1939, for example, not long before Decree No. 443ss was issued, Corps Commander D. G. Pavlov, Chief of the Red Army's Armor Directorate, wrote a report for the People's Commissar of Defense, K. V. Voroshilov, saying:

Considering that when production of the T-32, with its armor thickness of 45 mm, gets underway, the Army will have a high-quality, fast, and economical vehicle weighing no more than 23–24 tons that 37 mm antitank artillery will be unable to penetrate, I believe that beginning in 1941 production of the T-26 class of vehicle can be canceled, i.e., when mass production of the T-32 begins at the Stalingrad Tractor Plant, and the existing vehicles can be completely replaced by the new types: the T-20 will replace the BT; the T-32 will replace the T-26 and the T-28, and the heavy KV vehicles with diesel engines; and, if the SMK and the 100 are adopted, the RKKA will have a new class of vehicle in its inventory.

That is, the "thirty-four" was seen as replacing both the "infantry" T-26 and the improved T-28; and the BT—the "cavalry" tank and "tank of independent mechanized units"—would be replaced by the new BT-20.

However, the T-34's future changed significantly even before mass production began. Decree No. 443ss was adopted to the sound of battles rumbling in Finland. Even Finland's relatively few antitank guns convincingly demonstrated that the time of light tanks with anti-bullet armor had come to a decisive end. That left only two possible opinions.[3] The spring 1940 analysis of the lessons learned at such a high cost radically changed views on the role of the T-34 in the Red Army's armored vehicle system:

Based on the combat employment of previously existing and newly created units: the Commission considers separate tank battalions, rifle divisions, and mechanized infantry divisions; separate tank companies in rifle regiments; and tank regiments in rifle divisions to be completely impractical. These organizations result only in the complete dispersal of combat vehicles, cause them to be used improperly (including in the defense of headquarters and rear areas), make it impossible to repair them in a timely fashion, and sometimes prevent them from being used... The Commission proposes the following: that all tank battalions in rifle and motorized infantry divisions, separate light tank regiments and divisions, with the exception of the 1st and 2nd independent Order of the Red Banner Armies and cavalry divisions, be disbanded and tank brigades established... That any form of tank units other than tank brigades be strictly prohibited. When the need for tanks arises, they should be sent only as complete tank brigades... The tank brigade as a complete organization of tank forces proved itself in the fighting in Finland. The tank companies and battalions of infantry divisions, chemical battalions, and chemical brigades have not proven themselves as organizations for employing tanks in modern combat—they should be disbanded.

The Red Army's tank forces shall be organized as follows:

a) *T-28 tank brigades;*
b) *BT tank brigades;*
c) *T-26 tank brigades;*
d) *Tank brigades and motorized divisions (having at least as many tanks as their brigades);*
e) *Tank regiments in cavalry divisions (with tanks of a single type—the BT-2-5-7);*
f) *Tank battalions and rifle divisions of the 1st and 2nd Independent Order of the Red Banner Armies (with tanks of a single type—the T-26);*
g) *Separate tank battalions of amphibious tanks in infantry corps (with tanks of the same type: T-37 or T-38 or T-40)...*

Form KV company-battalions as the KV tanks are introduced into T-28 brigades in 1940.

As T-34 tanks are received by BT tank brigades, form T-34 company-battalions...

Thus, the T-34 was to replace the numerous BT, the "tank of independent mechanized units."

As that view of the role of the T-34 in the Red Army tank armament system crystalized, the country's top leadership followed suit, issuing the following decree regarding T-34 production volumes:

Project
Decree of the Defense Committee under
the Council of People's Commissars

Subsequent to Defense Committee Decree No. 443, dated 19 December 1939, establish the following tank program for Factory No. 183 for 1940:

BT-7M—860 928

T-34—400 300

T-34 spare parts in the amount of 4,000,000 rubles shall be delivered by the following dates:

	2nd quarter	3rd quarter	4th quarter	TOTAL
BT-7M	450	60		510
T-34	30 25	140 / 100	230 /175	400 / 300
T-34 spare parts		1,000,000	3,000,000	4,000,000

RGVA, f. 31811, op. 2, d. 1022, pp. 174–178. Cit. ex: A. Makarov, *Chronicles of the First 'Thirty-Fours,'* Tekhnika i vooruzheniye, No. 3, 2011, p. 17

However, the doubled production of T-34s, like the orderly system for forming armored forces based on tank brigades, was not to be long-lasting. In addition to the notion that separate tank companies and battalions were "impractical," the Finnish campaign revealed the unsatisfactory nature of the accepted standards for reinforcing the infantry with medium and heavy tanks: between December 17 and 19, 1939, the 20th Heavy Tank Brigade, which was equipped with T-28 tanks, fought bloody battles on the Karelian Isthmus with poor, almost non-existent coordination with the 50th Infantry Corps, in an unsuccessful attempt to break through Summa Hawtin fortified area of the Mannerheim Line, the main Finnish line of defense. The effectiveness of the simple, self-evident solution—increase the number of tank brigades assigned to the infantry corps—was highly suspect: in its order summarizing the unpleasant outcome of the Finnish campaign, the People's Commissariat of Defense zeroed in on the command staff's weak knowledge of the combat characteristics and capabilities of other combat arms, the poorly organized joint operations, and the clumsy employment of tanks and artillery.[4] When an infantry corps was assigned several tank brigades, in addition to fulfilling its own complex duties its command staff was given the task both of organizing joint operations between its own infantry and the tanks, and operations of the tank brigades with each other. No satisfactory solution of this difficult problem should have been expected.

T-34 tanks of the 8th Tank Division mired in a swamp on the eastern edge of Nemirov (N 50.105143, E 23.451149) during combat on June 24, 1941.◊

All photographs marked with a ◊, along with their annotations and coordinates, were provided by the Nemirov 41 Project.

The agenda included an item about organizing tank units larger than tank brigades, and a practical solution to the issue was not long in coming—in May 1940, the People's Commissariat of Defense had worked on creating tank divisions consisting of two tank regiments, an artillery regiment, and a motorized rifle regiment.[5] Each tank regiment included one battalion of heavy tanks, two battalions of medium tanks, and a battalion of flamethrower tanks. It was essentially equivalent to the existing heavy tank brigade, and the tank division became a permanent (not improvised "on the fly") and powerful resource for reinforcing infantry forces. The inclusion of a motorized infantry regiment in a tank division ostensibly made it possible to overcome the lack of coordination between infantry and tanks that had become apparent during the Finnish campaign—tanks would now have their "own" infantry, whose chief mission would be to support tanks in all types of combat.

However, the planned changes to the structure of the armored force were not limited to the formation of tank divisions. The Soviet General Staff's theoretical studies took place at a time when battles were shaking Western Europe and yielding a very unpleasant surprise: within a very short period of time, about a month, the French army, which had been considered one of Europe's most powerful armies (if not the most powerful), was defeated and British forces were evacuated back to Britain, having abandoned almost all of their heavy weapons on the beaches at Dunkirk; France signed an armistice about three weeks later. Germany's Wehrmacht had significantly, roughly, and visibly demonstrated its military might; it no longer had a major enemy on the ground in Europe other than the Red Army. Soviet staff officers analyzed the available information com-

T-34 and BT tanks of the 8th Tank Division caught in a peat bog on the eastern edge of Nemirov during combat on June 24, 1941. The crews of the trapped vehicles continued firing in place until the morning of June 25 (N 50.105143, E 23.451149).◊

ing from the battlefield[6] and stressed the importance of the factor that had contributed greatly to the resounding victory by German forces—Germany's use of massive tank units: tank corps that combined several tank divisions under a single command. It was a vivid illustration of the power of that type of unit, and the Soviet military leadership immediately raised the issue with the government of forming eight tank corps, each of which would consist of two tank divisions and one motorized division.

Thus, it was necessary in the shortest period possible to form 18 tank divisions (two of which should be independent divisions); that is, to equip with the new medium tanks 72 medium tank battalions (18 divisions with two regiments per division and two medium tank battalions per regiment, with each battalion having 50 tanks). More than 500 T-34s were needed to equip these units; considering the need for gradual replacement of the BT light tank brigades with T-34s, a total of approximately 8,000–9,000 T-34s were required. And there was no time left for the unhurried "startup" of mass production that was to stretch over several years and begin with a couple of hundred tanks per year…

On June 7, 1940, the Council of People's Commissars of the USSR and the Central Committee of the All-Union Communist Party (Bolshevik) issued Decree No. 976-368ss, "On Production of T-34 Tanks in 1940":

Emphasizing the importance of equipping the Red Army with T-34 tanks, the Council of People's Commissars of the USSR and the Central Committee of the All-

A T-34 undergoing field testing during the spring of 1940.

Union Communist Party (Bolshevik) decrees the following: require Comrade I. A. Likhachev, the People's Commissar of Medium Machine Building, to manufacture 600 T-34 tanks in 1940, of which:

Comintern Factory No. 183 shall manufacture 500
The Stalingrad Tractor Plant shall manufacture 100
with monthly production as follows:

	June	July	August	September	October	November	December
Factory No. 183	10	20	30	80	115	120	125
Stalingrad Tractor Plant					20	30	50

Fully implement a program to produce T-34 tanks with diesel engines. To accomplish that, increase production of V-2 engines at Factory No. 75 and produce 2000 engines by the end of 1940, with monthly production as follows:

	June	July	August	September	October	November	December
Factory No. 75:	210	230	260	300	320	330	350

Cit. ex: A. Makarov, *Chronicles of the First 'Thirty-Fours,'* Tekhnika i vooruzheniye, No. 5, 2011, p. 15. The initial order was tripled before even the first mass-produced tank had rolled off the production line.

NOTES

1 For example: Ya. L. Reznik, *Creating Armor: A Documentary Story [Sotvoreniye broni: Dokumental'naya povest'].* Moscow: Voyenizdat, 1983; M. N. Svirin, *Stalin's Armor Shield: History of the Soviet Tank, 1937–1943 [Bronevoy shchit Stalina: istoriya sovetskogo tanka 1937–1943].* Moscow: Eksmo, Yauza, 2006; et al.

2 Cit. ex: A. Makarov, *Chronicles of the First T-34s*, Tekhnika i vooruzheniye, No. 1, 2011, p. 12–13. The full text of the document is provided in the Appendix. Here and elsewhere, the original orthography of the documents quoted is retained.

3 "***Shtern:*** But we can't improve the BT-2.
Pavlov: The situation doesn't allow us to lose more than 3000 tanks.
Voroshilov: This tank needs to be taken out of the inventory.
Shtern: That means we may be sending units to their destruction."
RVGA, f. 4, op. 14, d. 2736, pp. 173–197. Cit. ex: *The Winter War: Correcting Mistakes (April–May 1940): Materials of commissions of the Main Military Council of the Red Army on best practices of the Finnish Campaign.* Moscow, St. Petersburg: Letniy Sad, 2004, p. 205.

4 Order No. 120 on Military and Political Training during the summer of the 1940 Training Year. RVGA, f. 4, op. 15, d. 30, pp. 336–356. Cit. ex: Russian Archive. *The Great Patriotic War: Orders of the People's Commissar of Defense of the USSR*, 1937–June 21, 1941, vol. 13 (2–1). Moscow: TERRA, 1994, p. 135.

5 M. I. Meltyukhov. *Stalin's Missed Opportunity [Upushchennyy shanc Stalina]. The Battle for Europe: 1930–1941.* Third edition, revised and expanded. Moscow: Veche, 2008. p. 259.

6 It should be noted that, in addition to the unquestionable value—freshness and relevance—of the information collected by the Soviet General Staff, it also suffered from a major drawback—a lack of complete accuracy. We need only recall the numerous references to the crushing of fortifications on the Maginot Line by German heavy tanks armed with 105 mm guns, the "collapsible" armored vehicles deliverable by glider that were supposedly in the inventory of German paratroopers, or the hordes of German motorcyclists crowding the highways of Holland, Belgium, and France.

CHAPTER 2. THE T-34: A CANDID PORTRAIT OF THE TANK DURING DEVELOPMENT

I knew you in diapers, when you were just a drawing.
You traveled a straight path, unswerving,
Flying a flag of "Secret," on the waves of science.
The chief designer let you run wild from design bureau to Quality Control—

But now you're in the tester's sights![1]

Among the many misconceptions that befall the average person, the idea is prominent that the heroes of stories, whether outstanding historical figures, entire groups of people (Panfilov's 28 guardsmen or the 300 Spartans, for example), or inanimate objects (famous tanks, ships, and aircraft), are great, epic and legendary, not just in a narrow sense clearly described in the pages of a heroic story, but "throughout all and in every particular detail." The myth of the T-34 has not escaped that fallacy. Accordingly, when speaking of the T-34, out of delight for its "overall nature" (praising it as the "finest tank in the world" and "the most remarkable example of an offensive weapon"), its champions immediately carry that over to particulars, strongly praising the logical slope of its armor; the hitherto unprecedented power of its gun; its broad tracks; its powerful, fireproof diesel engine; and so forth. As we stated in the preface, however, this begs the question of why the thousand tanks that stood head and shoulders above the enemy's equipment both "overall" and in terms of "particulars" failed to have a noticeable impact on how the drama of 1941 played out on the strategic, or, at least, the operational level...

Unfortunately, the reality was much more complicated than the beautiful legend. The first mention that the "best tank of the century" was not the very best appears in Defense Committee Decree No. 443ss—which we quoted in the first chapter. While approving the T-34 for service use, it required that "visibility from the tank" be improved.

There was virtually no time to modify the vehicle—on January 23, 1940, G. I. Kulik, Deputy Peoples' Commissar of Defense, issued a directive ordering operational trials of two T-34 prototypes to begin on January 25, 1940.[2] The trials, which were to determine

M. I. Koshkin—Chief Designer of Factory No. 183's design bureau.

A. A. Morozov—Chief Designer of Factory No. 183's design bureau after M. I. Koshkin's death.

the tanks readiness, began after a three-week delay on February 13, 1940, and lasted until almost the end of April.

An April 27, 1940, report on operational trials noted major deficiencies in addition to the traditional listing of successful design solutions ("The armor protection, weapons, and mobility of the T-34 tank under winter conditions significantly exceed those of tanks currently in the inventory"):

The following are the main shortcomings of the T-34 tank:

a) *Flaws in the turret hinder use of the weapons, vision devices and sights, and ammunition, preventing full usage of the gun system.*

b) *The problem of radio communications in the T-34 has not been resolved.*

c) *The vision equipment installed on the T-34 tank does not provide reliable and sufficient visibility.*

d) *Measures to prevent flammable liquid from entering the tank have not been satisfactorily implemented…*

The mass-produced V-2 diesel engine installed in the tank does not guarantee 100 hours of operation or operational reliability.[3]

The list of needed changes and improvements to the T-34's design extended over more than a dozen pages and contained a number of hard-hitting assessments:

The main clutch does not function properly... The ammunition rack on the prototypes is unusable... The driver's hatch should be designed to allow entry into and exit from the vehicle with the turret in any position… The tank's turret is cramped. The gun and sights are mounted in such a way that they are difficult to use—this affects accuracy and rate of fire from both the main gun and the machine guns. The angles of elevation and depression provided by the sights are completely unused, which increases the dead zones and reduces the range of the tank's main gun… The turret must be enlarged for the crew's convenience and ease of operation. Increase the size of the turret without altering the hull or the slope of the armor... The gun laying devices are difficult to use, and the knob on the TOD sight cannot be used at all… Prevent scraping of the hands when the elevation and traversing mechanisms are operated simultaneously… The aim changes when the latching mechanism is engaged or released; prevent that from happening… Reduce the effort required on the lever to operate the turret mechanism by hand... The vision blocks installed on the T-34 tank do not support observation and driving of the tank (with the hatches closed)… The vision block design is unacceptable… The design of the all-round vision block is unsuitable… The external protective lenses on the vision blocks and some of their mirrors fracture during firing.[4]

The commission also noted that

because the tank was tested under winter conditions, the following issues have not been checked:

a) *The thermal behavior of the engine under summer conditions.*

b) *Negotiation of natural and artificial obstacles under summer conditions.*
c) *Tank performance.*
d) *Reliable operation of tank mechanisms during long trips under summer road conditions.*

One T-34 tank needs to undergo test-range trials on these points, followed by proof firing and ballistic testing.[5]

The commission's conclusion was harsh: "The T-34 Tank cannot begin mass production unless the deficiencies noted are corrected."

Now that we have addressed some widespread historical myths, we would like to focus the reader's attention on a rather significant point. A very common misconception about the prewar Soviet Union was and remains the myth of the military's unlimited power and an extremely militarized country controlled from the top down: that as soon as the Red commanders in dusty helmets dreamed about something marvelous, ephemeral, and quasi-fictional in order to quickly bring about the world revolution, the economy, defying the boundaries of the possible and supplying inexhaustible bloody victims to the Moloch of the Gulag, would immediately assume a servile pose and ask, "What would you like, dear sir?" while offering the required numbers of technical wonders. However, the reality was strikingly different from this fantastic picture. The "dissenting opinion" appended to the troop test report by Factory No. 183 repre-

A T-34 during testing. A bottle with burning gasoline has been thrown on the engine compartment hatch.

sentative A. A. Morozov, who became chief designer of Factory No. 183 following the death of M. I. Koshkin, is revealing:

All parts of the main clutch functioned properly throughout the entire test... Only warping of the discs was observed during operation; the cause has not yet been determined... The existing 71-TK-3 radio cannot be moved to the bow of the tank... The factory cannot at present suggest a different design for the vision blocks... Although the all-round vision block does not provide a 360-degree view, it is an auxiliary vision instrument and does exactly what it is supposed to. Because the Commission has identified no other deficiencies with the vision block than the conclusion that it is unsuitable and the factory has no other design for it, we cannot offer a new vision block design for the 1940 program... The Commission's remark about expanding the turret is not specific.[6]

Instead of an obliging and fanciful "What would you like?" the factory recommended that its military customers avoid digging their feet in and be more willing to accept what the factories could give them.

But let's return to 1940. During the summer of 1940, tests to determine "engine thermal behavior, natural and artificial obstacle negotiation, tank performance, and tank-mechanism reliability under summer conditions" could not be carried out. On October 31, 1940, however, three mass-produced "thirty-fours" left Kharkov to drive the route Kharkov – Kubinka – Smolensk – Kiev – Kharkov. The tanks were required to travel two thirds of the 3,000 km route over dirt roads and off road. The tanks traveled 30% of the route at night and 30% over dirt roads and unbroken ground while in fighting order (with hatches closed). The test program was not limited just to travel—it again provided for testing of weapons, communications gear, and negotiation of natural and artificial obstacles, as well as for testing of the tank against antitank mines and for determining tightness "by pouring a flammable liquid over it."

The report on these tests is of considerable interest, both from the standpoint of comparing the advantages and disadvantages of the vehicle that had already begun mass production and from the standpoint of evaluating the changes made to the tank design to correct deficiencies noted during the tests conducted in April.

Live firing to solve fire missions revealed the following shortcomings:

1) *Cramped crew space in the fighting compartment caused by the small size of the turret.*[7]

It would have been hard to miss that—the turret that was developed initially for a tank armed with a 45 mm gun was obviously cramped after installation of the 76 mm gun, prompting a number of complaints from the crew. It is particularly noteworthy that no changes were made to the turret race ring between late April and late December 1940 (the "Report on Tests Conducted on Three T-34 Tanks During Extended Travel" was printed on December 20, 1940, and approved on December 24). It was only made larger on the T-34 armed with the 85 mm gun. Morozov's dissenting opinion became the Army's prevailing opinion.

... The tank loses momentum when shifting from 2nd gear to 3rd during the rainy conditions of fall and spring and snow during winter, causing it to slow abruptly on dirt roads and off road....

2) The ammunition stored in the fighting compartment floor is difficult to use.
3) There is a delay in shifting fire due to the inconvenient location of the turret traversing mechanism (manual and electric).
4) There is no visual communication between tanks when calculating a firing solution because the only instrument that provides all-round observation—the PT-6—is used only for sighting.
5) The TOD-6 sight cannot be used because the PT-6 overlaps its elevation scale.
6) Significant and slowly fluctuating oscillations by the tank during travel have a negative impact on accuracy of fire by the main gun and the machine gun.

These shortcomings reduce the rate of fire and increase the amount of time needed to calculate a firing solution.

Determination of the rate of fire of the 76 mm gun....

Maximum rate of fire—5–6 rounds per minute.

Particular attention should be paid to that last point. This is the number usually cited in reference sources (especially in publications from the Soviet era). However, the report clearly stated how the number was obtained:

Firing from a stationary position. The rounds were placed in the most conveniently located canisters. The rubber mat and cover were removed from the canisters.

... The mobility of the T-34 tank during autumn is unsatisfactory....

The results of the next test were much less optimistic—it determined the practical rate of fire from the move and from short halts:

> *The average deliverable rate of fire obtained was two rounds per minute. This rate of fire is insufficient....*

The first item on the list tells us that a large part of the report was devoted to the vision devices (and their unsatisfactory condition). Once again, the ammunition storage rack in the prototypes, which was described as "unsuitable," had not been significantly changed.

> ***The all-round vision block.***
> *Access to the vision block is very difficult, and observation is only possible in a limited sector no greater than 120 degrees... The limited field-of-view, complete inability to see the rest of the sector, and... the uncomfortable head position during observation make the vision block unsuitable for operation.*
> ***Turret vision blocks (side)***
> *The vision blocks are in an inconvenient location. Shortcomings include a large dead space (15.5 m), a small angle of view, inability to clean the protective glass without exiting the tank, and low position relative to the seat.*

Driver's vision blocks...

Significant shortcomings with the vision blocks when driving with the hatch closed were identified. After driving over a muddy dirt road and unbroken ground for 5–10 minutes, the vision blocks became covered with mud, completely blocking vision, resulting in a complete loss of vision. The wiper for the central vision block did not remove mud from the protective glass. It was very difficult to drive the tank with the hatch closed. The vision block protective lens shattered during firing...

By and large, the driver's vision blocks are unacceptable.

And we note again—eight months passed and the section concerning vision block deficiencies in the mass-produced tank was deleted from the carbon copy of the April report based on results of the operational trials on the two prototypes. And once again the factory design bureau's "dissenting opinion" prevailed over the Army's wishes.

But let us return to the report.

The overall conclusion drawn at this stage in the testing was a logical consequence of these findings:

The weapons, optics, and ammunition storage rack in the T-34 do not meet the requirements established for modern combat vehicles.

The main shortcomings are as follows:

a) *Cramped crew compartment;*

b) *Restricted vision from the tank;*

c) *Poorly designed ammunition storage rack.*

The following steps must be taken in order to properly position the weapons, firing devices, vision blocks, and crew:

Increase the overall size of the turret....

<...>

Vision blocks.

Replace the driver's vision block, which is clearly unacceptable, with a more modern design.

Install a vision block in the turret that provides all-round visibility from the tank.

Ammunition storage rack.

The ammunition storage rack for the 76 mm gun in canisters is unacceptable. The rounds must be stored such that all types are accessible simultaneously....

Somewhat fewer complaints were registered concerning the communications gear. Remarking on the successful placement of the radio in the tank hull rather than the turret (ignoring the factory's "dissenting opinion"), the testers stated that following the driving test *"The quality of the radio had deteriorated, and its range had dropped sharply."* They ascribed this to the poor quality of the radio's mount, damage sustained by the antennas during the test, and contamination with mud. The intercom was the only item that functioned properly.

Nor was everything rosy with the running gear. Although the tank was able to reach a maximum speed of 54 km/h, that speed was achieved on a flat asphalt highway—and as we know, tanks in combat generally travel over entirely different kinds of terrain.

Tank performance.

When shifting from 2nd to 3rd gear on difficult terrain, the tank loses so much inertia that it stops or the main clutch slips for an extended period. This makes it difficult to use 3rd gear over difficult terrain that should allow it.

This deficiency of the tank results in drastically reduced speeds when driving on country roads and off road during a rainy autumn and spring and during a snowy winter...

The sharp difference between the net travel speed and the speed while in motion results from frequent breakdowns of the main clutch and the tracks (track shoes breaking, pins coming out, etc.).

Conclusions.

Because 3rd gear, the gear most necessary for use under tactical conditions, cannot always be used, the tank's performance overall is considered unsatisfactory.

Travel speeds are low, which reduces the reliability of the main clutch and the running gear.

Mobility.

Conclusion.

The T-34's mobility during autumn is unsatisfactory for the following reasons:

The track shoe surface that engages the soil is not properly designed, and as a consequence the tracks slip on inclines even when the groundcover is only slightly damp. The effectiveness of the track shoe cleats is low.

The tracks are poorly secured on the support wheels....

The small number of support wheels causes reduced mobility on marshy terrain, despite the overall low ground pressure.

The ability of the T-34 tank to negotiate water obstacles should be considered completely satisfactory.[8]

The unreliability of the transmission and running gear reduced both the tank's speed and the distance traveled per day.

The maximum distance traveled in a day on highways was 255 km; over dirt roads it was 225 km.

These are the maximum distances obtained, because in most instances parts failures significantly reduced the distance traveled.

Conclusion.

The daily travel distance was limited by failures of parts, tracks, and the main clutch.

The data obtained for the daily travel distance fully supported the fuel and engine lubricant endurance.[9]

A rather shocking conclusion. It is difficult to imagine that the daily travel distance of a tank would be determined not by the amount of fuel and lubricant on board and the crew's skill and fatigue, but by the distance the tank could travel between breakdowns. The tests conducted during autumn produced even less favorable results than did the springtime operational tests—at least, the mobility of the T-34 was seen as fully satisfactory in April, and track attachment was satisfactory. To continue...

Operational reliability of tank assemblies.
Engine, fuel system, lubricants, cooling, and instrumentation.
Conclusions.

Engine reliability over the warranty period (100 hours) is satisfactory. The engine's warranty period is too short, especially for a vehicle this heavily armored. It needs to be increased to at least 250 hours.

Constant oil leaks and instrumentation malfunctions were a feature of the lubrication system, and the gauge connections were unsatisfactory.

Main clutch.

Operation of the main clutch and fan was generally unsatisfactory.

Note: the unreliability of the main clutch and fan is also noted in the conclusions of the Military Commission.

At the risk of boring the reader, we once again point to the conclusions reached in the April tests conducted on the T-34 and the "dissenting opinion" expressed by Morozov, who failed to detect the poor performance of the main clutch parts.

Transmission.

A "loss of neutral" (gears remaining engaged while the gearshift lever is in neutral) and difficulty shifting were repeatedly noticed when all vehicles were driven... [10]

The incorrect choice of gear ratios results in unsatisfactory tank performance and reduces its tactical value.

Difficult shifting and "loss of neutral" make it hard to control the tank and result in emergency stops.

The transmission and its drive mechanism must be completely redone.

Steering clutches:

The steering clutches and brakes with ferodo linings and cast iron shoes functioned satisfactorily.

Note: Operation of the transmission, steering clutches, and final drives could not be completely checked for reliability because the main clutch failed first, functioning as something of a safety device in the tank's powertrain.

Once again, assessments were being revised for the worse: the transmission was perceived as functioning reliably during the April tests; its design was satisfactory, and its gear ratios were considered correct. By December, the customer had lost faith that the transmission was functioning properly.

Finally, the report ended with a disappointing conclusion.

Maintenance.

Time trade-offs between net travel, maintenance, and stops due to malfunctions on all three tanks:

Type of work	Time		Notes:
	Hours	%	
Total time required	922 hours 56 minutes	100	
Net travel time	350 hours 47 minutes	38	
Repairs	414 hours	45	Done by a 2-man repair team
Correction of malfunctions en route	158 hours 9 minutes	17	Done by the crew

Conclusion.

The ratio between net travel time and time spent on repairs (38% and 62%) is indicative of the tank's poor engineering.

The volume and complexity of repairs mean that the crew cannot repair the tank and require the efforts of a repair and reconstruction brigade.

The occurrence of the above-listed repairs during the warranty period prevents the tank from operating separately from repair facilities, which is unacceptable for operation under field conditions.

Routine maintenance.

The large volume and extensive time expended for routine maintenance of the tanks due to the poor reliability of individual assemblies is unacceptable for field operations.

The version of the T-34 tank submitted for testing does not meet modern requirements for this class of tanks for the following reasons:

a) *The tank's firepower cannot be fully utilized due to the unsuitability of the vision devices, flaws in the installation of the weapons and optics, the cramped crew compartment, and the difficult-to-use ammunition storage rack.*

b) *The tank's performance characteristics were poorly chosen given the tank's adequate engine reserve capacity and maximum speed, which reduce its speed and mobility.*

c) *The tank cannot be employed tactically when separated from repair facilities due to the unreliability of its main assemblies—the main clutch and suspension.*

d) *The characteristics of the 71 TK-3 radio and its poor installation in the T-34 tank make the range and reliability of communications seen during testing unsatisfactory for a tank of this class.*

Far from singing enthusiastic praise about the "finest tank in the world," the report's conclusions were compounded by the fact that ordinary tank units completely lacked the resources to assign each tank section a maintenance team consisting of a tow truck on a 4-ton high-mobility ZiS-6 chassis, two 3-ton trucks with spare parts, and a bus for transporting the personnel of a trained factory repair team, much less to equip it with all of the necessary tools, materials, and spare parts (jumping ahead, we know that the situation with spare parts was not just bad, it was very bad). In addition, the ordinary tankers in line units were much less capable of dealing with breakdowns than were the hand-picked crews used during the factory tests.[11] The tragic summer of 1941, with its encirclements and retreats, meant that many tanks with minor malfunctions were just as irrecoverable as tanks hit by a shell or a bomb in combat.

The tank prior to ballistic testing at Mariupol during the spring of 1941.

After the fall road test, the "proving ground tests on two T-34 tank hulls with turrets" (as they were called on the official list) held in April 1941 at the Ilyich Mariupol Factory's test range brought more bad news. Perhaps for the first time in the history of Soviet tank manufacture, a test range received not empty, odd-shaped armor boxes and individual armor plates but tanks that were "almost real"—the chassis had drive wheels, track adjusting wheels, and road wheels with suspensions. The tracks were tight, the final drives were armored, and the driver-mechanic's hatches and the vision blocks were installed. The hulls had "almost completely real" turrets mounted on race rings, along with a mantlet and armor for the gun system, a traversing mechanism with a stop, hatches, vision blocks, and plugs in the firing ports intended for firing revolvers. Ballistic tests were conducted using a 37 mm antitank gun M1930 (a licensed Soviet copy of the German PaK 36 "door knocker" gun), a captured Polish 37 mm Bofors gun, a 45 mm gun, and a "three incher."

The tests lasted three weeks and gave the Soviet tank designers rich food for thought—which they did not always accept. The front armor plates creditably withstood a 76.2 mm armor-piercing shell fired from close range, but the sloped 40 mm side was defeated even by the 37 mm sharp-pointed armor-piercing projectile from a range of 175–250 m, revealing that the much vaunted "sound angle of slope" of the 40 mm side armor plate was noticeably worse at withstanding projectiles than was the 45 mm vertical armor plate on the lower side. Another unpleasant discovery was the identification of a significant hazard to the crew and the tank's mechanisms—armor plates defeated but not technically penetrated by a projectile:

The tank after ballistic testing.

It had previously been thought that a hull penetration smaller than a projectile's caliber would produce a single slug capable of killing or injuring only some of the crew or causing a small amount of localized damage within the tank that would not completely disable the tank. On the contrary, observations made during these tests established that shrapnel from a projectile's warhead that breaks apart when it passes through the armor enters the tank in addition to the cylindrical plug of armor. In addition, the slug frequently fractures into several pieces, and small pieces of shrapnel in addition to the slug spall off the armor. There were sometimes more than ten pieces of armor shrapnel and projectile fragments inside the hull when the hole was smaller than the projectile's caliber and most of the projectile remained outside the plate. Therefore, a hole smaller than the projectile's caliber is more dangerous for the crew inside the tank, its assemblies, etc., than previously thought; this type of defeat is relatively dangerous for the crew. Numerous cases of destruction within the hull caused by armor slugs were observed; for example, both of the soft carbon-steel side plates, which have a total thickness of 6 mm, were penetrated, as were oil tanks, radiators, fuel tanks, etc. These observations show that the slug travels at a high speed beyond the armor protection.

Let's illustrate the report's dry conclusions with vivid examples of armor failures from the firing log: when a projectile was fired from a 45 mm gun at the right turret plate,

It became stuck in base part 30-018.[12] *A slug penetrated the left side skirt in three places; the hole sizes were 120–100 mm, 50–120 mm, and 60–20 mm. The slug and shrapnel from the projectile were found within the left front fuel tank.*[13]

This meant the armor slug flew completely through the left compartment and defeated the side skirt on the opposite side. It is unlikely that the crew members in the path of shrapnel from the 10 cm hole in the metal side skirt would have survived. Strictly speaking, the projectile did not pass through the armor—it caught in the armor plate.

Testing continued, and the turret's right-side plate was hit with a Polish 37 mm Bofors projectile:

Hole smaller than projectile caliber. The diameter of the entrance hole was 40–32 mm, and the diameter of the exit hole was 37–40 mm. The projectile located in front of the plate was in fragments. Shrapnel between the upper and lower race rings caused a dent that prevented the turret from turning. The shrapnel damaged the traversing mechanism gear housing.[14]

Note that the projectile was in fragments in front of the plate, and the tank turret no longer turned, even though the projectile technically did not penetrate and did not even enter the race ring.

Now let's turn our attention to the upper right side plate, which was placed at the "sound angle of slope" of the 40 mm side armor plate. The vehicle was hit by a 45 mm projectile, producing

a 35–35 mm entrance hole and a 36–34 mm exit hole. A 60–70 mm slug penetrated the suspension spring housing. Along its flight path, the slug penetrated tanks, radiators, and other assemblies.[15]

Once again, there is a hole smaller than a projectile's diameter and a projectile that did not pass through the armor, yet deadly shrapnel spalled off behind the armor, destroying fuel tanks and radiators. Would the tank and crew be better off because the armor technically was not penetrated (the projectile failed to pass through the armor)?

Quite a few surprises resulted from cases where the armor was defeated without producing holes in the "armor's key assemblies." For example, it was learned that an armor-piercing projectile hitting the running gear could ricochet upward, penetrate the 15 mm upper side plate bottom, and enter the hull—which, naturally, was not observed during ballistic testing on the side of a hull without tracks mounted. It was also learned that the support wheels increased protection for the lower armor but left open the upper vertical part of the side, which was further weakened by milling for the joint with the upper side plate bottom. It was found that when a projectile struck a support wheel where the suspension arm passed through cut-outs in the side of the hull, it easily penetrated the armor through the wheel disk, the cut-out, and the suspension arm spring.

Three-inch high-explosive shells caused quite a headache—although the test reports record no penetration of 40–45 mm armor parts by a 76.2 mm HE shell:

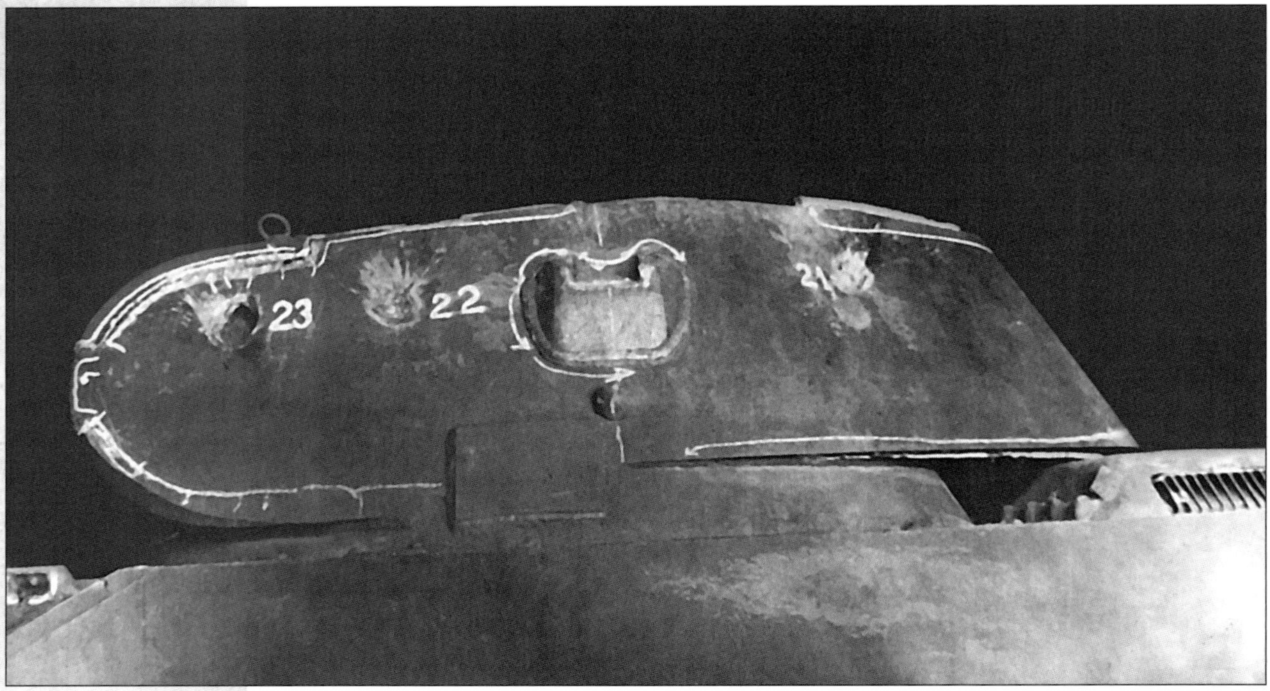

... Weld disintegration following a hit by the first 76 mm projectile to the side of the [welded] turret....

a 76 mm HE projectile striking the running gear or the side near the tracks and wheels (up to 100–200 mm) destroys the track, drive wheel, idler wheel, and support wheels, causing the tank to stop...

and it also destroyed the upper side plate bottom. Explosions of three-inch HE shells caused extensive cracking of welds:

After the first impact by a 76 mm projectile on the side of the turret, the welds were badly fractured, and after the fourth 76 mm projectile hit, all of the welds on the side of the turret had come apart. Individual parts (vision block bases, roof plates, turret access hatch) broke away when struck by 45 mm and 76 mm shells due to the low rigidity of the welded turret.

Even shells that did not penetrate the armor caused serious damage to the tank:

The final drive housing lacks sufficient armor protection. Both 37 mm and 45 mm projectiles penetrate the 25 mm armor protection of the final drive housings and the housings themselves, causing the vehicle to stop.

The rear turret plate is not properly attached: the thread is crushed, and the plate moves out of position.

The turret traversing mechanism housing, which is made of cast iron, is unsuitable. The housing cracks and splits when it strikes the walls of the turret; the housing attachment lugs come off, and the traversing mechanism shifts out of position.

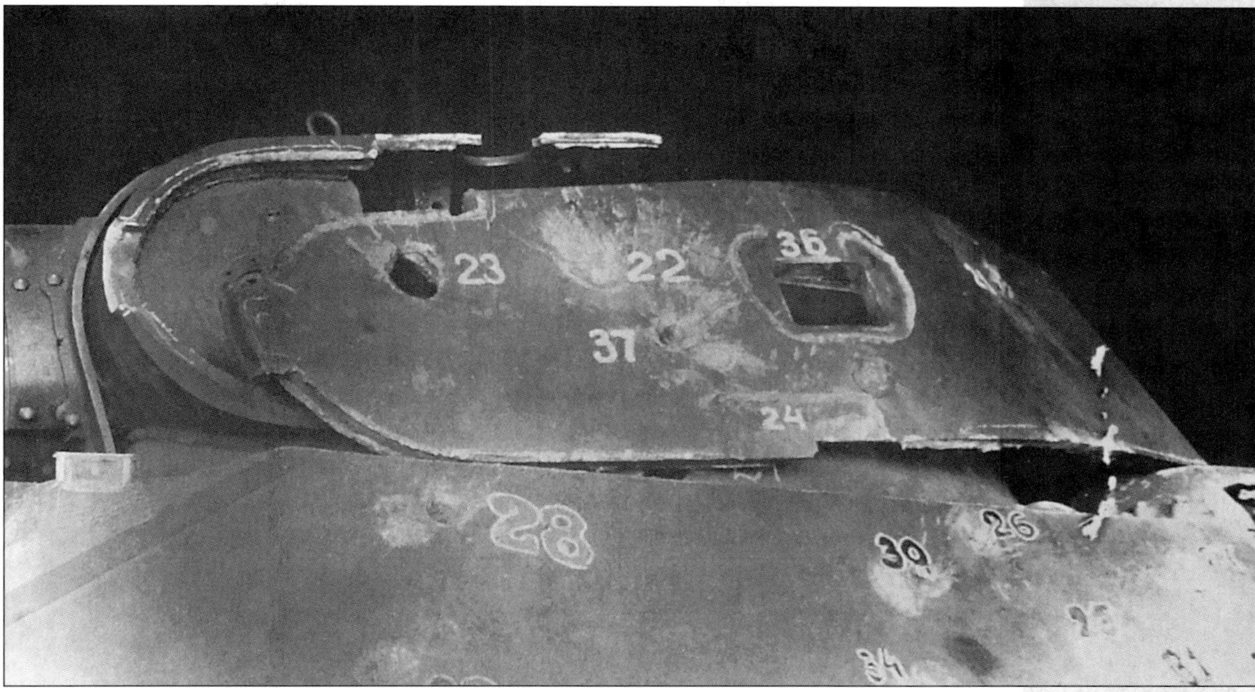

... After four 76 mm projectile hits, the side of the turret had come loose at all of its seams....

The upper access hatch has very weak hinges. The hinge pins broke in every test, and the hatch was thrown out of position. This left the top of the turret completely open.

The turret roof plates are too thin. As a result, their welds crack and separate.

The signal hatch and ventilation hatch hinges are weak, and they are not properly attached to the hatches.

Hits by 45 mm projectile on the armor caused the welds at the base of the vision blocks to fracture.[16]

Incidentally, the ability of the vision blocks themselves to withstand projectile impacts was not impressive:

Also, the covers, latches, and headrests of the vision blocks are not securely attached. The outside protective lenses of the vision blocks cracked when the turret was struck by 45 mm projectiles a substantial distance from the vision block, and even when the opposite side of the turret was struck.[17]

Ballistic testing in which bullets were fired at the vision blocks on the driver-mechanic's hatch revealed that the protective lens could be penetrated by bullet fragments that would injure his eyes.

That, however, was a trifle when compared with the demonstrated weakness of the driver-mechanic's hatch design—the first impact by a projectile damaged the hinges, and the second impact caused the hatch to fall inside the tank (accordingly, the test report stipulated that:

... The armor protection of the final drive housings is unsatisfactory. Both 37 mm and 45 mm projectiles penetrate the 25 mm armor protection of the final drive housings and the housings themselves, causing the vehicle to stop moving....

in general, the presence of a hatch in the bow significantly weakens the vehicle's frontal armor; therefore, when designing new models it is imperative that the bow plate not have a driver's hatch.

Here, we would like to call the reader's attention to another fine point. The T-34's armor underwent ballistic testing during the spring trials: two rounds were fired from a 6-ton, 37 mm Vickers gun and a 45 mm BT-7 gun from a range of 100 m. Shell impacts on the turret only dented the armor; they did not penetrate. A comparison between these results and the results of the spring 1941 tests could support an argument that sub-standard armor parts were provided for the tests in Mariupol, that, therefore, the Mariupol ballistic tests could be considered unrepresentative, and that the authors retrieved them from archived obscurity solely in order to cast a shadow on the T-34's reputation. Unfortunately, archival documents prevent us from blithely dismissing the results of the Mariupol tests:

To: Chairman of the Defense Committee
of the Council of People's Commissars
Marshal of the Soviet Union
Comrade K. Ye. Voroshilov
27 December 1940

Damage to the side and turret of a T-34 struck by 37 mm and 45 mm armor-piercing projectiles during testing in the spring of 1940.

I hearwith report as follows:

In September of this year, by order of the Deputy Chief of the Main Artillery Directorate and Chief of the Main Armored Forces Directorate (GABTU) of the Red Army, ballistic tests were conducted at the Research Artillery Firing Range (NIAP) on a T-34 tank turret to check whether its systems and armor are securely attached.[18]

The tests showed that the turret armor was penetrated at a 30° angle of incidence by a 45 mm armor-piercing, blunt-nosed projectile from a range of 160 m, whereas the armor had not been penetrated during tests previously performed under the same conditions at the factory from a range of 50 m.

The People's Defense Commissariat (of the GABTU) jointly with the 3rd Main Directorate of the People's Commissariat of Shipbuilding and the Chief Directorate of Special Machine Building of the People's Commissariat of Medium Machine Building established a commission for ballistic testing of parts and turrets in order to establish the strength of the armor in accordance with specifications.

Out of 180 turret sets manufactured by the Mariupol Factory, the commission tested three turrets taken from Factory No. 183 (of the People's Commissariat of Medium Machine Building) and six hull armor parts of the T-34 tank selected from current production at the Mariupol Factory (of the People's Commissariat of Shipbuilding).

A T-34 disabled near Dubno.

The tests yielded the following results:

a) *Six T-34 hull armor parts passed ballistic protection tests, but the damage (penetration by a 45 mm projectile) sustained by two parts resulted in shrapnel larger than stipulated by the specification.*

b) *Of the three turrets, one completely passed the tests and met the specifications. The two other turrets did not fully pass; individual parts were found to have uneven ballistic protection.*

For example, one part from these tanks was penetrated when struck by a 45 mm projectile at a 30° angle of incidence fired from a range of 50 m.

c) *The strength of the weld joints was unsatisfactory.*

The first projectile caused the welds to crack, and they were completely destroyed by subsequent impacts.

The reduced armor protection of these turret parts is due to improper heat treatment. The turret parts were tempered in a device that does not provide even cooling during tempering.

Based on the test results and inspection of armor-production technology and quality control, the Commission decided to leave the manufactured T-34 tank turret on the tanks and task Factory No. 183 (People's Commissariat of Medium Machine Building) and the Ilyich Factory (People's Commissariat of Shipbuilding) with a number of requirements intended to improve their manufacturing process and quality control so as to produce armor of uniform quality that meets the specification.

I hereby request that a commission be established to develop the basic specifications for tank armor.

Marshal of the Soviet Union G. Kulik. [19]

This was not the first time nor, alas, the last time we will see a sad story develop: product quality deteriorated noticeably in the transition from a one-off, carefully prepared prototype to mass production. Equally importantly, armor parts with lower ballistic protection were approved for installation on tanks. Furthermore, only one of the three turrets tested met the specification. Therefore, we have no reason to assume that armor parts with lower ballistic protection ended up being tested by unlucky happenstance in Mariupol and were the exception. On the contrary, there is every reason to believe that the tanks tested in Mariupol were fully representative of the majority of the "thirty-fours" produced prior to the war.

We believe that the documents quoted above suffice for an understanding of the situation—during the last year before the war, opinions about the T-34 in no way resembled a friendly chorus of praise or unmitigated enthusiasm for its sloped armor, powerful gun, diesel engine, and wide tracks. The first "thirty-fours" were still very "crude" machines. Nevertheless, orders continued being placed for the tank, it was still in production, and demand for it was growing. This phenomenon is not all that rare for military hardware, especially when the military customer is insistent about seeing large numbers of a new system by this evening or, better yet, by yesterday morning. The outcome of this kind of haste is completely foreseeable: the unsuccessful debut of the German Tigers at Leningrad is well known. Two out of four vehicles broke down immediately upon arrival; three broke down during the second attack; and a fourth vehicle burned up. [20] Then there was the Panther debut in the Battle of Kursk. The engines of two vehicles caught fire and burned while being driven from the railroad station, and another 44 (of the 200 present) broke down for technical reasons over five days of fighting. A similar fiasco occurred with the famous American B-29 Superfortress bombers during their first attack on Japan—18 of the 75 bombers assigned to take part in the attack were unable to get off the ground due to malfunctions and ill-prepared crews. One B-29 crashed on takeoff, one was shot down by antiaircraft fire, and engine fires downed another six. Only one bomb was dropped in the vicinity of the target, and it exploded 1.2 km from its aim point. A tarnished introduction did not prevent the Tigers and Panthers from becoming symbols of the German Panzerwaffe during World War II, nor did it stop the B-29 from becoming America's main strategic bomber in the Pacific.

Nor did the bleak results during prewar testing prevent the T-34 from becoming the most important tank of World War II. The Kharkov designers' focus on continuity with existing tanks completely justified itself. [21]

The decision to crank up production of the T-34 was very straightforward and hardly an example of the "totalitarian volunteerism of the powers that be": although the T-34 had a number of serious shortcomings, it also had many advantages. Chief among them from the standpoint of the Soviet leadership was the fact that mass production of a modern medium tank with ballistic protection was getting underway at factories that previously had mass-produced only light tanks. Before the advent of the T-34, the Red Army's sole medium tank was the T-28, which was produced by only one factory—the

A T-34 disabled in combat in Ukraine during June 1941. Despite its outward appearance, this tank had burned—the rubber tire on the front left road wheel is burned.

Leningrad Kirov Factory, which had switched to production of the heavy KV. The country could not patiently wait for engineers to design new tanks without flaws and for factories to master their production gradually—even a T-34 that was "crude," blind, and unreliable from the standpoint of its technical characteristics was much more attractive than older tanks with anti-bullet armor. And they were definitely better than no modern medium tank at all.

NOTES

1 From Vladimir Vysotsky's poem, "Test Pilot."

2 RGVA, f. 31811, op. 3, d. 2165, pp. 71–85. Cit. ex: A. Makarov, *Chronicles of the First T-34s*, Tekhnika i vooruzheniye, No. 1, 2011, p. 6.

3 RGVA, f. 31811, op. 3, d. 2165, pp. 71–85; RGVA, f. 31811, op. 3, d. 2115, pp. 39–48. Cit. ex: A. Makarov, *Chronicles of the First T-34s*, Tekhnika i vooruzheniye, No. 2, 2011, p. 9–10; No. 2, 2011, p. 20.

4 RGVA, f. 31811, op. 3, d. 2165, pp. 71–85; RGVA, f. 31811, op. 3, d. 2115, pp. 38–48. Cit. ex: A. Makarov, *Chronicles of the First T-34s*, Tekhnika i vooruzheniye, No. 2, 2011, p. 9–10; No. 2, 2011, pp. 20–23.

5 RGVA, f. 31811, op. 3, d. 2165, pp. 71–85; RGVA, f. 31811, op. 3, d. 2115, pp. 39–48. Cit. ex: A. Makarov, *Chronicles of the First T-34s*, Tekhnika i vooruzheniye, No. 2, 2011, p. 9–10; No. 2, 2011, p. 20.

6 RGVA, f. 31811, op. 3, d. 2165, pp. 71–85; Cit. ex: A. Makarov, *Chronicles of the First T-34s*, Tekhnika i vooruzheniye, No. 2, 2011, p. 9–10; No. 2, 2011, p. 23.

7 Cit. ex: RGVA, f. 31811, op. 3, d. 2116 (Report on long road test performed on three T-34 tanks).

8 ibid.

9 ibid.

10 Measurements showed that as much as 40 kg of effort was required to operate the gear shift lever and the steering clutch levers.

11 "... The crews were selected in such a way that they could take each other's place virtually without limit." (M. N. Svirin, *Stalin's Armor Shield: History of the Soviet Tank, 1937–1943 [Bronevoy shchit Stalina: istoriya sovetskogo tanka 1937–1943].* Moscow: Eksmo, Yauza, 2006, p. 198.)

12 Right side of turret.

13 TsAMO RF, f. 38 (GABTU), op. 11355 (Tank Directorate), d. 332 (Certificate issued by NII No. 48 Committee on proving ground tests performed on armored hulls), p. 109.

14 ibid., p. 113.

15 ibid., p. 120.

16 ibid., p. 77.

17 ibid., p. 78.

18 Here "systems" refers to the gun system.

19 TsAMO RF, f. 2 (People's Commissariat of Defense), op. 11569 (Secretariat), d. 300 (Draft decrees of the People's Council of Commissars of the USSR and the Defense Committee under the Council of People's Commissars; GABTU letters and correspondence with the Central Committee of the All-Union Communist Party (Bolshevik), the People's Council of Commissars of the USSR on the status of tank manufacturing, heavy tank prototype manufacture, the removal of T-27 tankettes, nonfulfillment by factories of the plan for supplying tanks and armored hulls for T-40s, and other issues), pp. 2–3.

20 We would especially like to mention the fact that the vehicle that burned on September 21 stood on neutral ground until it was blown up because it could not be recovered by German sappers—but Soviet forces showed no interest in it for several months; it was not examined by scouts, and no attempts were made to tow the latest German tank to the Soviet side. German forces treated the T-34 the same way during the summer of 1941—they "failed to notice" the very Soviet tanks that later were named as perhaps the main reason for the Wehrmacht's defeat in the campaign of 1941.

21 "In its overall layout, the T-34 is essentially a copy of the Christie tank and the BT. Although it is now called a classic tank, it is far from optimal because the volume protected by armor in that design is not great. However, the engineers in Kharkov undoubtedly acted correctly in selecting that design for the T-34, because changing the overall layout with the war imminent could have resulted in unexpected problems that would have been very difficult and perhaps impossible to overcome. Clearly, optimum (according to science) design decisions could not always taken for the 'champion' vehicle." (N. A. Astrov, light tank and self-propelled gun designer)

CHAPTER 3. **THE COMPLICATED PATH TO MASS PRODUCTION**

Two T-34s of the 10th Tank Division abandoned during an attempt at towing. (N 49.900015, E 24.849225)◊

... I love our sweeping plans,
Our long stride...[1]

As we mentioned in the first chapter, the estimated demand for the new vehicle reached almost 10,000 even before mass production actually began. In the summer of 1940, however, manufacturers could only dream about production in the thousands. Even the Kharkov Factory failed to meet the 1940 production plan for its "own" T-34. Out of the 500 vehicles the plan called for, it delivered only 115 to the Army. Not even orders from on high resulted in either the military equipment called for by the plan or sufficient quantities of the equipment needed to produce it being generated out of thin air. The joint decree adopted on June 7, 1945, by the People's Council of Commissars of the USSR and the Central Committee of the All-Union Communist Party (Bolshevik) "On T-34 Tank Production in 1940" scheduled production of 10 tanks by Factory No. 183 in June 1940. Five days later, the Armor Directorate's military representative at the Kharkov Locomotive Works made the following announcement:

The development of manufacturing processes has concluded. Work is underway to design and manufacture tools and dies.

Development of approximately 1,000 of the highest priority types of tools and dies should be done by 1 July. Currently, 537 have been developed. We have produced 250.

Shortages of tool steels constitute the main obstacle to the manufacture of tools at Factory No. 183, as well as at other factories partnered with it (the Stalingrad Tractor Plant, the Kharkov Tractor Plant, the Stalin Automotive Plant, and Samara Piston Factory No. 1).

Capital construction and reengineering of sections 100 and 700 are slow getting started.

Assembly of T-34 vehicles may be delayed: track band tires, radiators, fans, mirrors and triplex lenses, starters, coaxial ball mounts, etc.[2]

However, the situation at the Kharkov Locomotive Works had not changed significantly by the end of the month—in the "Summary of Preparations for Mass Production of the A-34 by June 25," the plant's military representative wrote:

1,400 types of high-priority tools and dies have been designed, and there have been no significant changes regarding their manufacture since the summary of 10 June. The Gorky Automotive Plant, Stalingrad Tractor Plant, Samara Piston Factory No. 1, and Kharkov Tractor Plant, which were to make more than 100 types of tools and dies, are delaying their manufacture, and none have been made yet.

Capital construction is not yet fully underway. The construction organizations do not have enough workers. Steps are being taken to hire workers in other areas. There is also a shortage of building supplies. The materials stipulated by government decision have not yet arrived.

A contract to obtain armor from the Mariupol Plant[3] *was concluded on 15 June. The Mariupol Plant has refused to manufacture the Degtyarev machine gun front protective plate and the final drive cover out of cast armor. The People's Commissariat needs to put pressure on the Mariupol Plant.*

The Stalingrad Tractor Plant has supplied none of the 90 types of items it was supposed to; 11,100 track shoes were supposed to have been delivered by 1 July. As of 25 June, they have delivered only 200.[4]

Not surprisingly, the plans for immediate production of the vehicle came apart at the seams: of the 10 vehicles planned for production in June and 20 in July 1940, the factory produced four in June and one in July.

Moreover, that poorly made vehicle immediately began to reveal its "balky nature."

After 38 hours of operation, the engine fan on vehicle No. 311-04-3, which had been supplied to the factory for crew training, failed (cracked blades). To correct this defect, a fan with sub-blades to reinforce the blades was produced.[5]

However, problems with the fan remained an "Achilles' heel" (one of many, unfortunately) on the vehicle until the very beginning of the war.

The gap between planned and actual vehicle production continued growing like an avalanche. In August 1940, the factory was supposed to produce 30 vehicles (a total of 60 since the year began); it actually produced only two (seven since the first of the year). The tank's path to mass production was strewn with very thorny roses.

A total of 24 vehicles have undergone a long road test; 18 vehicles underwent the test once, three vehicles twice, and three vehicles three times. The main defects, which caused the long road tests to be repeated, are as follows:

- ***a)*** *Engine replaced due to smoking and low oil pressure*
- ***b)*** *Main clutch not working properly (poor shifting)*
- ***c)*** *Difficulty shifting from first gear to second*
- ***d)*** *Oil leak in a final drive seal*
- ***e)*** *Steering clutch slippage*
- ***f)*** *Bulge in oil radiator tank*

Of the 24 vehicles that underwent a long road test, 12 were given a test run for the following defects:

- ***a)*** *Engine needing replacement*
- ***b)*** *Main clutch engages poorly*
- ***c)*** *Transmission gear teeth chipped*
- ***d)*** *Oil leak in a final drive seal*
- ***e)*** *Brake linings replaced (burned)*
- ***f)*** *Poorly adjusted steering clutch (will not execute a U-turn)...*[6]

We should mention that, contrary to the still-widespread myth about life in the prewar Soviet Union, the failure of the summer 1940 production program did not occasion the immediate involvement of the NKVD and result in bloody repressions among the tank builders. At either the Kharkov Locomotive Works or its contractors:

Manufacture of tools and dies at partner factories is proceeding poorly. For example:

Manufacturer	To be produced by Aug. 15, 1940, per People's Commissariat schedule	Actually produced by Aug. 15
Stalin Automotive Plant	63	4
Samara Piston Factory	19	—
Stalingrad Tractor Plant	87	16
Kharkov Tractor Plant	131	23

Abandoned T-34 and BT tanks.

A T-34 tank in the 8th Tank Division. This tank destroyed a 50 mm PaK 38 antitank gun along with its prime mover and was disabled by point-blank fire from le.FH.18 howitzers on June 25, 1941. (N 50.110448, E 23.64392)◊

> *According to executive order, Zaporozhstal should have produced 35 tons of high-speed turning tools and replacements. A total of 7 tons have been received as of 20 August 1940; Zaporozhstal refuses to allocate the rest.*
>
> *Tool manufacture at Factory No. 75 was proceeding very slowly. For example, of 386 tools for the A-34 that were to be produced by August, only 45 have been made as of August 20, 1940.*
>
> *Despite an order issued by the People's Commissariat of Medium Machine Building, Factory No. 75 refused to make flywheel rims, swivel studs, and several other items.*
>
> *The Kharkov Tractor Plant has refused to manufacture the tools scheduled by the People's Commissariat.*[7]

Things evidently changed for the better in September—the factory produced 37 vehicles of the planned 80; that is, they satisfied almost half their planned goal. However, this large but incomplete clearing of the backlog did not resolve the problem of the tank's many design flaws:

> *In September, 39 vehicles were taken on a long-distance test run; five of them completed a second long-distance test run, and 23 made a test run from one to three times. The following main defects were identified during the runs:*
>
> ***a)*** *The main clutch shifts poorly (not cleanly), causing the gears to clatter during shifting, and the carbonized layer on the gear faces is separating.*
>
> ***b)*** *Oil leaks through the end seal of the main transmission shaft.*
>
> ***c)*** *During testing, the gap between the ball and the ring groove of the final drive shift mechanism increased, causing the clutch to slip.*[8]

The September 1940 tally is also a good illustration of one of the many sources of confusion about the number of tanks produced: production of tanks by a factory meant acknowledgment that they had met the terms of an approved contract and their customer had paid for them, but it did not mean that the completed tanks had been immediately shipped to military units. Whereas in August 1940 the numbers of tanks produced and "shipped from the factory" coincided (although one of the vehicles released—the previously mentioned tank No. 311-04-3, whose fan had broken—had not actually left the factory), in September 1940 the factory shipped only two tanks (for a total of nine vehicles since the beginning of the year).

In October 1940, the Kharkov Locomotive Works produced only one tank against the plan, which called for 115 vehicles. The total number of tanks produced over a five-month period—45—did not suffice to equip even one medium tank battalion (50 tanks); only 10 tanks made it out of the factory, three of which were produced in October.[9] In October, 32 vehicles underwent a long driving test, and 17 of the vehicles produced in October and four produced in September broke down during a repeated test from one to four times. In addition, the tanks of September 15 and 16 were test driven from one to five times. In 13 vehicles, three or four cluster gears on the transmission output shaft seized up; 12 vehicles needed to have the main clutch discs replaced because of burrs and warpage; the end seals of the transmission output shaft leaked in 11 vehicles; engines needed replacing in three instances; track shoes had to be replaced four times; and so forth.[10] However, fracturing[11] in armor parts near welds was the most common defect, and this occurred on all vehicles without exception. The factory was unable to solve the problem on its own, meaning higher authorities needed to intervene.

> *When production of welded A-34 medium tanks at Factory No. 183 got underway, a large number were rejected due to cracks in welded parts. Comrade Redkin, Deputy People's Commissar of Shipbuilding, sent a telegram to NII-48 ordering that a team be sent to Factory No. 183 to determine the reasons for the cracks and provide technical assistance.*[122]

It remained at the Kharkov Locomotive Works from October 1 to November 16, 1940.

> *A detailed examination of the design drawings and welding practices resulted in... design and procedural changes to the drawings and the weld process sheet....*
>
> *Considering that the factory lacks experience welding with nonmagnetic electrodes and has no welders trained in their use, the team took the following actions:*
>
> *It generated welding procedures for assemblies to be welded using austenitic electrodes.*
>
> *Under the team's leadership and with its practical assistance, the factory completely set the factory up for production using coated electrodes in accordance with the specifications and procedures developed by the NII-48 team.*
>
> *It developed a program to train factory welders on how to weld with austenitic electrodes and provided instructions on how to test them.*
>
> *Fifty-two factory welders were trained in the use of austenitic electrodes. The trained welders were tested by a qualification committee, and all passed.*
>
> *With the team's proposals partially implemented, 40 hulls were produced under the team's leadership... Because the welds on the 40 hulls were satisfactory, the team's proposals were implemented for the factory's total output.*
>
> *On inspection, no cracks were found in the joints between the sides and the bow pieces and the upper side plate bottoms, whereas before conversion to welding with austenitic electrodes large numbers of cracks were present in almost every hull. Out of 40 hulls, just 18 small isolated fractures were found on the front glacis plates.*
>
> *These fractures occurred because the valve part is located in a very inconvenient spot for welding, and many different things are welded on and in its surface. In addition, it is welded across the entire hull. Such extensive welding stresses the part severely, causing fractures near the welds.*[133]

November 1940 was a turning point: although the factory was falling far short of meeting its target, it was beginning to produce tanks in larger batches—against its monthly plan of 120 vehicles (for a total of 375 tanks since the beginning of the year), the factory produced 38 vehicles (83 since the beginning of the year). Over the course of a month, the factory shipped 35 vehicles,[14] which made it possible to begin equipping medium tank battalions in tank divisions.

Other than the 83 vehicles that have been received, the following are in backlog:

- ***a)*** *For painting and final fit out—five vehicles*
- ***b)*** *Passed by the Quality Control department for paint but not provided for GABTU acceptance because the tracks were lacking—five vehicles*
- ***c)*** *Given driving test; main guns installed and checked—six vehicles*
- ***d)*** *Completed driving test; awaiting installation of weapons—eight vehicles*
- ***e)*** *Completed driving test; being prepared for installation of weapons—18 vehicles*
- ***f)*** *Completed factory driving test; being prepared for long-distance driving test—three vehicles*
- ***g)*** *Assembled but have not undergone driving test because the turrets are lacking—34 vehicles*
- ***h)*** *On assembly line—11 vehicles*

Total backlog—90 vehicles.

In December 1940, the Kharkov Locomotive Works produced 32 tanks (for a total of 115 since the beginning of the year); its target was 125 vehicles (500 since the beginning of the year). Another 85 vehicles had been:

> *assembled, tested, painted, and given their SPTA kits but not accepted by the GABTU due to a large amount of play in the turret (5 mm vice 3 mm), and some of the vehicles have cracks in the hull and turret armor. These issues have been referred to the Chief Directorate of Special Machine Building of the People's Commissariat of Medium Machine Building. In addition, some of the vehicles lack tracks because not enough tracks have been received from the Stalingrad Tractor Plant, or they arrived after a long delay and are currently being assembled, following which they will be given a test run. Twelve vehicles are ready to be painted and fitted out, but they lack tracks. L-11 systems have been mounted on 39 vehicles, but the system has been submitted to the Red Artillery Directorate's representative (all testing has been done)....*

The factory shipped 63 vehicles during December (for a total of 108 since the beginning of the year).[155]

In addition to the factory's failure to meet the production plan, the military's impression of the vehicle was significantly influenced both by the previously mentioned mixed results during the long-distance tests conducted on three tanks and the factory's slow progress in correcting the tank's flaws.

Report on T-34 tank reengineering inspection.

Defect type	Status	Handwritten notes on original report	Conclusion
Redo oil radiator	Not done	Beginning with 1,001st vehicle	New oil radiator designed to decrease temperature 40°. Implement as part of an overall upgrade.
Provide for centralized drainage of oil from the engine and oil pump	Not done	Beginning with 1,001st vehicle	Require Factory 75 to implement with V-2-K engine.
Make gear shifting easier	Not done	Beginning with 1,001st vehicle	Shifting of gears not improved on samples tested. By February 1, 1941, test new designs for improving gear shifting and find solution.
Eliminate burning of brake linings	Experimental cast-iron linings passed tests	Beginning with 1,001st vehicle	No later than February 1, 1941, decide on initiating mass production based on results of troop test run.
Reduce size of foot rest and design gas pedal to be like that in ZiS vehicle	Done beginning with 201st vehicle		
Develop ammunition storage rack to support convenient and rapid crew operation	Not done	Beginning with 751st vehicle with replacement	Ammunition storage rack made but not tested. Come to conclusion on storage rack suitability no later than 1 January 1941. Replace on tanks produced previously upon obtaining positive results.
Make sure all hull and turret hatches close tightly			Driver's hatch and stern hatch have been engineered to close tightly. Turret, access, and signal hatches engineered to close tightly beginning with tank 141.
Prevent injury to loader by breech lever	Done		Beginning with 201st vehicle. Install on all previously produced tanks.
Prevent all-round vision block from falling inside tank	Done		
Select vision block (artillery panoramic sight, periscopic sight, etc.). Develop to replace all-round vision block by 1 December 1940		Beginning with 1,001st vehicle with replacement	Beginning on 1 January 1941, do not install all-round vision block due to unsuitability. Do not design an all-round vision block to replace the current all-round vision block, because per Defense Commissariat Decree No. 428 a commander's cupola with all-round view must be installed beginning on February 1, 1941.
Main clutch operation unreliable due to plate warpage	Defect not completely corrected	Repair	Warranty kilometerage test performed on version with cast-iron plates negative due to rapid plate wear. Test conducted on version with thicker plates also negative. Sample tested with thin slotted plates performed significantly better (sample tested over a distance of 2,500 km). Factory to replace previously installed cast-iron plates on tanks that have been produced and that are in production with thin slotted steel plates by 1 February 1941. Test 2–3 clutches with thin slotted plates for greater safety factor by 15 January 1941. Upon receiving positive results, begin production on 1 February 1941.

Defect type	Status	Handwritten notes on original report	Conclusion
Warranty kilometerage test needed on modified engine fan		Beginning with 1,001st vehicle with replacement	Fan with friction coupling that was tested yielded an unsatisfactory result. Version tested with two sub-blades, thicker housing without covers, and friction mount tested. Lighter version with two sub-blades is in production. Factory does not yet have fan guaranteed for 3,000 km of tank operation.
Provide reliable accelerator rod return with hand and foot controls; eliminate sticking	Not done		Additional spring installed on vehicles to ensure reliable return of rod. Inspect action taken to ensure stable engine idle on prototype and implement by 1 February 1941.
Decrease seat width in turret. Make lighter	Not done	Beginning with 1,001st vehicle	Complete testing and submit conclusion by 1 January 1941; upon obtaining positive results, begin mass production on 1 February 1941.
Develop and test lift eyes that are convenient and quick to use by 1 December 1940	Not done	Shackles beginning with 1,001st vehicle	Build and test eyes (shackles) by 15 January 1941.
Provide gun depression limiter on stern	Not done		Turret rotation tests with gun depressed caused engine compartment cover to jam. Begin producing limiter by 1 February 1941.
Develop manhole hatch security lock mount on outside of vehicle	Not done		Begin mass production on 1 January 1941.
Include jacks of sufficient strength with vehicles and develop storage rack for them on vehicle (complete development by 1 December 1940)	Not done		A test conducted to raise the bow and stern of the vehicle with the two onboard jacks was positive, but they could not lift vehicle from the side. Include greater capacity jacks in the onboard kit after the upgraded vehicle enters mass production.
Provide means to determine fuel level in lower tanks (manufacture and test; develop prototype fuel gauge by 1 December 1940)	Not done		Undergoing testing; if results positive begin production on 1 February 1941.
Eliminate separation of screen over stern louvers when firing to the rear (test new version of screen by 1 December 1940)			Production of reinforced screen has begun. Ballistic testing not done.
Develop field repair toolkit (complete by 1 December 1940). Develop toolkit for repair depot use			Complete testing by 1 January 1941 and submit to Red Army Armor Directorate representative for approval.
Install vacuum tanks for drinking water (beginning with 201st vehicle)	Not done		Check suitability and install on previously produced tanks.

Defect type	Status	Handwritten notes on original report	Conclusion
Provide for storage of crew food and property in accordance with allowance list	Not done		Allowance list not provided by Red Army Armor Directorate.
Develop 15-day field spare parts kits - company - battalion - brigade within 15 days after receipt of report from troop road test	Not done		Factory has not yet received field commission's report.
Produce catalog, regulations, and maintenance instructions (submit catalog and regulations to Red Army Armored Force Directorate for approval by 1 December 1940; submit maintenance instructions by 1 January 1941)	Not done		Submit to the Red Army Armor Directorate for approval by 1 January 1941.

Director, Factory No. 183
Maksarev
Chief Engineer, Factory No. 183
Makhonin
Acting Chief Designer, Factory No. 183
Morozov
Representative
Chief Directorate of Special Machine Building,
People's Commissariat of Medium Machine Building
Masalskaya
Representative, Red Army Armor Directorate
Panov
Military Representative, Factory No. 183
Kozyrev
12/28/1940[166]

The requirements listed do not give us the impression that the military's requirements are "trumped up" or excessive; the vague statement that most of the changes would be made "after the 1,001st vehicle" inspired little optimism, given that the lead factory had only produced 115 tanks that year. It brings to mind the Russian proverb: "He who expects a great deal from a promise has three years to wait." Under the circumstances, the salient question was whether the Red Army needed the T-34 tank at all as it existed in late 1940. And the answer to that question is not as straightforward as the current myth about the "tank of the century" would lead us to believe. For example, a January 29, 1941, letter from the director of Factory No. 183 to GABTU chief

This T-34 crushed a German light field howitzer but was captured by the enemy when it was no longer able to move.

A T-34 of an unknown unit. Summer 1941.

The 8th Tank Division T-34 that destroyed a German gun on June 25, 1941.
This vehicle is also shown in the photograph on page 43.

K. A. Korobkov and Goreglyad, Deputy People's Commissar of Medium Machine Building, expressing the factory's conclusion about the long-distance driving test conducted on three T-34 tanks, explicitly stated the following:

> *We consider the Commission's remarks on the results of tests conducted on T-34 tanks* ***suggesting that the factory stop manufacturing the tanks*** *with thick armor that the Red Army needs in large numbers to be unfounded and incorrect.*

The letter was signed by factory Director Maksarev and Chief Designer Morozov, as well as Portnoy and Kolesnikov, two factory employees who participated in the T-34 long-distance driving tests.[177] As an example of an opposing opinion, a letter was appended from Engineer Colonel Panov, an officer in the GABTU's Armor Directorate, which put forward the military's "quintessential" desires. Fortunately, the prevailing opinion among the top Soviet military and political leadership was that the design that Panov's letter called "an improved T-34 tank" was actually a new tank. Therefore, mass production was not interrupted, and the factory continued manufacturing T-34s and prepared to begin producing the "improved" T-34 that the factory's design bureau was hard at work on.

Meanwhile, the "*decision by the Chief Directorate of Special Machine Building of the People's Commissariat of Medium Machine Building*" mentioned in the December report on fulfillment of the Armored Forces Directorate's order by Factory No. 183 was captured in the January 10, 1941, report from a conference of representatives called by the People's Commissar of Medium Machine Building. The conference was attended by People's Commissar of Medium Machine Building Malyshev and his deputy Goreglyad; Factory No. 183's director Maksarev, its chief designer Morozov, design bureau director Kucherenko, and lead engineer Masalskaya; Armored Forces Directorate chief Fedorenko; GABTU Armor Directorate chief Korobkov; Factory No. 183's military repre-

T-34 and BT tanks of the 14th Tank Division stuck in the Chernogostnitsa River, July 1941.

sentative Kozyrev; and Chief Directorate of Special Machine Building chief engineer Khlamov, among others. The decisions of the conference were approved by Malyshev, Fedorenko, and Deputy People's Commissar of Defense Marshal Kulik. The conference directed the following after hearing a presentation by Factory No. 183's director about hulls and turrets with cracks in the welds between armor plates and excessive play on the turret ring:

1. *Factory No. 183 shall be allowed to ship the manufactured hulls and turrets with fractures that have been accepted by the Military Representative in accordance with the T-34 specifications and formalized in certificates prepared by the factory and the Military Representative.*
2. *In order to further improve vehicle quality and make the specifications for the T-34 tougher:*

... Cracks shall not be acceptable in the crucial parts of the hull and the turret.

T-34s at Factory No. 183 and the Stalingrad Tractor Plant shall be considered acceptable as follows:

- **a)** *Between 25 January and 15 February 1941, hulls and turrets with no more than 10 fractures measuring a maximum of 30 mm and having no more than two fractures per part;*
- **b)** *Between 16 January and 1 May, vehicles with no more than 2–3 fractures on armor parts no longer than 30 mm;*
- **c)** *After 1 May 1941, T-34 tanks with fractures shall not be accepted, and for each occurrence of fracturing the issue of acceptance shall be decided by the People's Commissariat of Medium Machine Building and the Red Army's GABTU based on a submission by the Military Representative and the factory's Director...*

The 8th Tank Division T-34 that destroyed a 50 mm German antitank gun in combat on June 25, 1941.
This vehicle also appears in the photos on pages 43 and 54.

The Red Army's Armor Directorate shall thoroughly monitor the behavior of cracks in armor parts on tanks in service...[188]

3. *Factory No. 183 shall consider the possibility of accepting and shipping up to 800 assembled tanks, turrets, and traversing mechanisms with a total play in the turret race ring... of up to 5.5 mm.*
4. *Factory Director Comrade Maksarev shall:*
   - **a)** *Ensure the production of 500 T-34 tanks with a maximum play of no more than 4 mm by selecting traversing mechanism parts and more carefully installing the race ring;*
   - **b)** *Immediately begin developing a traversing mechanism and turret race ring design that ensures a total play of no more than 3 mm beginning with tank number 1,000.*[199]

After receiving the "green light" to produce "doubtful" tanks, the factory's output in January 1941 reached a record level: the factory produced 85 T-34 tanks of the line and 81 radio tanks—for a total of 166 vehicles. The factory shipped 36 tanks of the line and 51 radio tanks (a total of 87 vehicles). Unfortunately,

31 of the 135 vehicles assembled in January 1941 counted against the 1940 backlog.[20]

In other words, a "breakthrough" was made at the expense of the 1940 backlog, the fate of which was decided at the conference with Malyshev.

In February 1941, the Kharkov Locomotive Works released 69 tanks of the line and 16 radio tanks (for a total of 85 vehicles)—about half its output of the previous month. The factory shipped 96 tanks (50 tanks of the line and 46 radio tanks).[21] It is noteworthy that the operational reports for January and February 1941 lacked approved monthly and annual production goals—the 1941 contract for tank production had not yet been signed with the factory. Therefore, it was simply that no goals had yet been issued.

The goals for 1941 appeared in the March operational report: during that year, the factory was to manufacture 932 tanks of the line and 668 radio tanks, for a total of 1600 vehicles. During the first quarter of 1941, the factory was to manufacture 300 tanks (117 tanks of the line and 183 radio tanks), including 100 tanks in March (32 tanks of the line and 68 radio tanks). In March 1941, the factory actually produced 134 tanks (54 tanks of the line and the 80 radio tanks), making the total since the beginning of the year 385 vehicles (208 tanks of the line and 177 radio tanks).[222] For the first time since production of the T-34 began, it was starting to look like the Kharkov Locomotive Works was more or less meeting its targets. In addition, in March 1941 the Comintern Factory stopped mounting L-11 guns on tanks and switched entirely to producing tanks fitted with the F-34 gun. In 1941, a total of 268 "thirty-fours" with the L-11 gun were produced, of which 103 were radio vehicles and 165 were tanks of the line.

April and May 1941 brought no unpleasant surprises: the factory was supposed to produce 125 tanks in April, and it released 140 (120 tanks of the line and 20 radio tanks).[23] In May, the plan called for 120 tanks, and the factory released 121 (56 tanks of the line and 65 radio tanks). The total number of tanks shipped from the factory from the time production began until late May 1941 was 640 vehicles (388 tanks of the line and 252 radio tanks). By June, only 12 vehicles remained at the plant.[24]

Unfortunately, efforts to correct the shortcomings noted as early as 1940 had not yielded positive results even by the summer of 1941. In late April 1941, for example, the factory issued the following report about work that had been done to correct design flaws:

Report on correction of deficiencies noted during testing of new samples of tank-automotive weapons between 20 March and 20 April 1941

Deficiencies	Steps taken to correct in order of action taken
Unsatisfactory vision block design	Cast driver hatches with new vision blocks tested. Test results positive. Drawings were sent to the Armor Directorate for approval, following which hatch production will begin. Prismatic vision blocks were tested in place of vision blocks with mirrors. Preliminary results positive. In place of planned drop-forged drivers hatches, cast hatches of same size put into production. They will be tested after manufacture.
Poor fan	Three fans currently undergoing testing Fan with special blade braces instead of sub-blades tested for 2,020 km Mass-produced fan with additional ring on housing similar to A-7M underwent 1,800 km test run Fan seated on clutch flywheel underwent 1,460 km test run No deficiencies found in any fan; tests continuing.
Poor track	Factory No. 183 has corrected defects discovered in track that underwent 2,800 km test run in March. Corrected drawings sent to Stalingrad Tractor Plant for mass production.
Poor air cleaner performance	Several versions tested on test stand. Version that tested best sent to Leningrad for state testing, where it also tested well (with a result of 95%).
Large amount of play in race ring	Tests conducted on new race ring did not yield positive results. New development work underway.

...[25]

In fact, no new driver's hatch with improved vision blocks, new track, or new air filter had made it into production by June 22, 1941. Moreover, in response to the much-cited [326] May 15, 1941, letter from Deputy People's Commmisar of Medium Machine Building Goreglyad that concluded with the words:

I consider it necessary to put an end to the excessive name-calling about the quality of the T-34 tank,

a note was immediately prepared regarding correction of the T-34's main deficiencies. It stated that production of new track shoes was not scheduled to get underway at the Kharkov Locomotive Works until June 15; mass production had not begun on a new driver's hatch because Factory No. 183 had refused to manufacture a hatch with three-layer armor; production had not begun on an improved ammunition rack; the fan was guaranteed for 1,500 km; and weld quality was still poor. [327]

The beginning of the war had no impact on the T-34 production rhythm that the Kharkov Locomotive Works had achieved with so much difficulty: according to the June operational summary, 170 tanks (82 tanks of the line and 88 radio tanks) were produced against a monthly plan of 130 vehicles (40 tanks of the line and 82 radio tanks). In June 1941, the Kharkov Locomotive Works shipped 147 "thirty-fours" (51 tanks of the line and 96 radio tanks); 35 vehicles remained at the factory. [328]

By July 1941, however, the planned production volume had begun growing rapidly: the April operational summary showed a total T-34 production volume at the Kharkov Locomotive Works of 2,580 vehicles (1,524 tanks of the line and 1,056 radio tanks), and the monthly production plan increased to 225 vehicles (135 tanks of the line and 90 radio tanks). The factory almost met the higher target: in June, it produced 209 tanks (127 tanks of the line and 82 radio tanks); it shipped 248 vehicles. [269]

The Kharkov Locomotive Works exceeded its August target of 250 tanks by producing 266 vehicles and shipping 255. [30] The September 1941 operational summary underscored production of T-34s at the lead factory prior to evacuation: the monthly plan of 300 vehicles had not been met. The factory had produced 228 tanks (164 tanks of the line and 64 radio tanks). A total of 1,485 vehicles (876 tanks of the line and 609 radio tanks) had been shipped since tank production began. The September operational summary concluded with the following statement:

For October, the factory planned to assemble 160 tanks, 130 at the Comintern Kharkov factory and 30 at Nizhny Tagil. [31]

However, this target was not met: the Kharkov plant produced only 41 vehicles in October 1941.

Matters were looking even worse at the second factory assigned to produce the T-34, the Stalingrad Tractor Plant. According to a report by the GABTU military representative, Military Engineer Second Class Levin, at the November 1940 military representatives conference:

It didn't give us [the Army] anything. Prior to 1939, however, the factory was only preparing to implement the tank program during wartime....[32]

And, as they should have expected, it couldn't produce a medium tank with anti-projectile armor "on the fly." Recall that Defense Committee Decree No. 443ss ordered the Stalingrad Tractor Plant to manufacture 20 T-34 tanks in 1940,[33] and the plan (revised in accordance with the decree "On Production the T-34 Tanks in 1940," dated June 7, 1940) called for the manufacture of 100 T-34 tanks in 1940—20 in October, 30 in November, and 50 in December.[34] However, the first two Stalingrad-produced vehicles did not undergo factory tests until the third week in November, while an additional four vehicles were being prepared for factory tests and five were being assembled. The Stalingrad Tractor Plant did not provide the People's Commissariat of Defense with a single tank before 1941.

The reason for this bleak picture was simple and mundane. It had nothing to do with the conception that the tanks were designed by unbroken enemies of the people and assembled by enslaved prisoners under the bloodthirsty eyes of human-looking ghouls in pink-banded uniform caps who were just looking for people to mop the prison floor with and, ideally, would do it for no reason at all. The real explanation was that, although the Soviet Union was industrializing at an accelerated pace, it was still playing catch-up with the world's leading industrial countries. For example, this is how a Soviet intelligence report produced in the spring of 1941 described Germany's tank industry:

The war has accelerated tank production. The Alkett Factory in Berlin, which was producing 30–40 tanks per month in late 1939, scaled up to manufacture 100 tanks per month in 1940.[35]

The largest tank-producing factories are the following: Alkett and Daimler-Benz in Berlin, Krupp in Mardeburg and Essen, Miag in Braunshweig, eskomoravská Kolben-Dan k in Prague, and Škoda in Plzen.

The system of cooperation among factories enabled enterprises to specialize in producing specific assemblies or parts for tanks, which significantly increased the capacity of the tank industry.

For example, armored hull production was concentrated at Edelstahl (Hanover), Mittelstahl (Brandenburg), and at the Krupp factories in Essen.

Tank engines and transmissions were supplied by Maybach and Daimler-Benz.

A current feature of Germany's tank industry is its comparitively even distribution across the country.

The average capacity of Germany's main tank factories varies from 70 to 80 tanks per month.

The total production capacity of the 18 factories we currently know about in Germany (including the Protektorate and the Governate-General) is estimated at 950–1,000 tanks per month.

Given the ability to rapidly start producing tanks at the existing automotive plants (15–20 factories) and ramp up production at factories already manufacturing tanks, ***we can assume that Germany is capable of manufacturing as many as 18,000 to 20,000 tanks per year.***

By using the French tank factories in occupied France, Germany will be capable of producing as many as 10,000 additional tanks per year.

Chief, Intelligence Directorate,
Red Army General Staff
Lieutenant General Golikov.[36]

Here we should note that under the provisions of the Treaty of Versailles, Germany was prohibited from developing and producing any tanks at all. However, the Germans were able to convert their substantial capacity for manufacture and design to produce modern military hardware without great difficulty. And we should not blame the Kama Tank School in the USSR for being virtually the "cradle of the Panzerwaffe," where Soviet military theoreticians trained herds of ignorant Guderians and Hoepners in the proper use of tanks, and Soviet designers collapsed with laughter at the German Grosstraktors. After all, the Americans were able to make a similar leap: beginning with just 400 tanks and having virtually no significant tradition of tank production, between June 1940 and August 30, 1945, American industry produced 103,096 tanks and self-propelled guns[377] of their own design. Meanwhile, American industry produced 4,772 tanks in December 1942—a wartime world record for monthly production. If we add the 113,560 wheeled combat vehicles and halftracks (note that we are speaking specifically about combat vehicles, and not about support vehicles, i.e., we are talking about armored cars, halftrack armored personnel carriers, self-propelled guns, and antiaircraft machine guns on half-track chassis, and not about trucks, prime movers, or mobile repair shops), then it is clear that the Americans were capable of supplying tanks both for their own army and for the USSR and Britain. The production triumphs of the Soviet Union could not have been achieved without broader advances such as the campaign against illiteracy...

N*ote: During World War 2 Germany was able to produce 18,000–20,000 modern powerful tanks with armor capable of standing up to the 45 mm gun (which was described rather modestly in October 1940 as being capable of penetrating 40 mm of "modern armor" from a range of 150 m at a 30° angle of incidence*[389]*—which no longer met the basic requirement for armor-piercing projectiles: "to penetrate caliber armor at a 30° angle of incidence without breaking apart or exploding prematurely"*[40]*). Under those circumstances, the order for 600 "thirty-fours" in 1940 and 2500 in 1941 could hardly be ascribed to "Red militarism," nor is it a clear indication that Stalin was surreptitiously striving to rule the world.*

But let us return to 1940.

At the Stalingrad Tractor Plant, the T-34 production engineering program that was drawn up in early 1940 calling for production preparations to be finished and mass production to begin in October 1940 was in danger of falling apart almost immediately:

Factory No. 183 was to give the Stalingrad Tractor Plant all of the drawings for the pilot batch in February 1940. When the factory failed to meet this deadline, new deadlines were established: 15 March 1940 and 5 May 1940. However, it missed those deadlines also. Of the 3,500 drawings that were required by 20 April 1940, the Stalingrad Tractor Plant has received only 1,400.[388]

Naturally, it was somewhat difficult for the plant to get ready for mass production without drawings of the item

A group of 32nd Tank Division T-34s, June 25, 1941, Yazuv Stary.

it was to manufacture. Most of the plant's manufacturing processes had been already developed when a large number of problems emerged:

> *In addition to the equipment on hand at the Stalingrad Tractor Plant, 250–260 machine tools of different types need to be purchased.... The plant has received only 23 of the 253 machine tools listed on the attached requisition.*[41] *Orders have been placed for 37 machine tools. The program for production of parts for the T-34 in June that was sent to the shops over the signature of the plant's chief engineer has not been fulfilled, because it does not have the appropriate production equipment, metal, etc. The final assembly shop (building) was equipped with crane rails and completed in 1931 for production of T-26 tanks. The changeover for production of a new item requires that the following high-priority work be done: a brick wall needs to be built; the crane rails and hoist need to be refurbished; and a conveyor and at least three or four 30-ton cranes need to be installed. Construction has begun on the final assembly shop (demolition of the old foundations under the conveyer, laying of new foundations), but the work is proceeding slowly. The needed material... is lacking. Of the 10 cranes needed... the plant has a contract with the Kirov Factory for delivery of two cranes in the fourth quarter of this year.*
>
> *The machine shop is a bottleneck. I suggested to the Director that we operate the shop in two shifts at full capacity, cancel orders for other parts being worked on with the machine shop's machine tools, and test newly arrived equipment and install it temporarily in assembly areas that have been freed up until construction of the shop is complete.*[42]

Note that mass production of T-34 tanks at the Stalingrad Tractor Plant had not yet begun (and would not begin for a long time yet), but the suggestion had already been made for the machine shop to stop working on other orders. We might reasonably ask the question: "Why not work on tanks, spare parts, tractors, and trucks all at the same time?" But let's continue:

Conversion to dual-shift operation of the factory means that we now need to buy 376 machine tools instead of 282. Orders have been submitted for 144 machine tools. The factory has received 27. Not one of the vertical boring mills required has been received. Castings are being rejected at a rate of 70%. The steel foundry continues to operate satisfactorily. The casting process is being worked out very slowly but is essentially at a standstill. Machine Shop No. 2 has rejected a large number of parts in the partial delivery from the steel foundry. Examples include the following:

Inner brake drum—74 castings delivered, 10 acceptable

Strap—92 castings delivered, 2 acceptable

Hub—175 castings delivered, 3 acceptable

Disk—6 castings delivered, zero acceptable

<...>

Factory equipment delivery rates are unacceptable. In all, we need to have 402 machine tools; as of 19 August 1940 we have received 57. 242 are on order. In early August, the factory received an encoded telegram from the People's Commissariat of Machine Building calling for production of 15 to 34 tanks by 15 September 1940. Machine Shop No. 2 needs to supply 480 items for assembly of the first 15 vehicles. As of 19 August 1940, 140 items have been manufactured, 180 are being worked on, and work has not yet begun on the 160 most difficult and massive, which require a large number of machine tool hours for each part.[43]

The order of the People's Commissariat of Medium Machine Building for the Stalingrad Tractor Plant to produce 15 T-34 vehicles by 15 September has not been satisfied... the reason has been hit-or-miss operation and the production by fits and starts. The Stalingrad Tractor Plant has on hand six hulls with turrets, five engines, transmission parts, steering clutches, track idlers, and suspension arms. Vehicle assembly is being hindered by the lack of parts manufactured for the tanks by the Stalingrad Tractor Plant itself and by its partners. Machine Shop No. 2 has a high reject rate, primarily due to underskilled machine tool operators. The shop mostly employs young workers who recently finished the factory apprenticeship school....[42]

Factory management had readied three vehicles for factory road tests by the October holidays; the tests did not take place due to the lack of tanks, pipes, and other small parts from the extrusion shop. Factory road tests on these vehicles is expected to occur about 15 or 16 November. None of the earmarked 25 L-11 guns has yet been received.

The All-Union Association for the Import of Tools and Machine Tools should deliver 80 machine tools to the Stalingrad Tractor Plant. On Nov. 11, 35 machine tools were approved (for import) with deliveries to take place as follows:

12 machine tools—1940

2 machine tools—1st quarter of 1941

10 machine tools—2nd and 3rd quarters of 1941

11 machine tools—1942

For the 1941 program, 36 turning mills are needed. With some turning mills transferred to other shops, Machine Shop No. 2 has only 16 mills on hand. Import orders have been placed for 30 turning mills, but their delivery date (late 1941) means the program will not be fulfilled.[45]

Bottlenecks occurred often in what would appear to be completely smooth-operating areas:

To: Chief, Red Army Armor Directorate
Comrade Korobkov
29 May 1941

In accordance with Comintern Plant order 129/34,[46] *the phrase "The vehicle may be tilted at the appropriate angle" has been deleted in the section "General requirements for installation of the [gun] system" (p. 100) of the specification for the T-34.*

The Stalingrad Tractor Plant is currently checking installation of the F-34 gun on the tank in a hollow near the factory rather than on a test range. The test is not being conducted on a level pad. Instead, the vehicle is tilted at an angle to the horizon (up or down, so that when the gun is fired with an elevation of 30 degrees its barrel is horizontal).

Deletion of this phrase in the specification would require placing the vehicle on a horizontal surface, which is can only be done on a test range.

The nearest test range is located 80 km from the factory, and we believe that an additional travel distance of 160 km (for firing) is unacceptable.

Chief Engineer Demyanovich, Stalingrad Tractor Plant
Chief Designer Verner
GABTU Representative at the Stalingrad Tractor Plant
Military Engineer 2nd Class Levin[47]

Practice is the test of truth. The Stalingrad Tractor Plant's "practice," that is, delivery of T-34 tanks, looked like this: in 1940, the plant did not deliver a single T-34.

The first two tanks were produced in January 1941 (they were not shipped from the factory).[48] In February 1941, the Stalingrad Tractor Plant produced 28 tanks (as before, none were shipped).[49] In March 1941, it produced 45 tanks under a plan calling for 30 (the first 30 Stalingrad "thirty-fours" hit the field in early March).[50] In April, it produced 63 tanks under a plan calling for 55 (44 were shipped from the factory).[51] In May, it produced 70 "thirty-fours" against a plan calling for 60 (82 vehicles were shipped).[52] In the "stormy month of June," 86 tanks instead of the planned 75 were produced (with 90 shipped).[53]

An 8th Tank Division T-34 abandoned after a battle on June 24, 1941, on the northeast outskirts of Nemirov. (N 50.106817, E 23.445361)◊

NOTES

1 From V. V. Mayakovsky's poem "Good [Khorosho]," (1927).

2 TsAMO RF, f. 38 (GABTU), op. 11355 (Tank Directorate), d. 32 (Report of the Red Army GABTU's military representative on Factory No. 183's completion of orders for manufacture of tanks and equipment), pp. 12–13.
Here we would like to mention that the June 12, 1940, summary says, "Steps must be taken immediately to start producing starters. The experimental ST-700 starter tested poorly and is not suitable for use." That was easier said than done, however, and the December report on the long road tests performed on three T-34s stated: "The ST-700 starters and RC-371 starter relays are unreliable... Given their existing installation and manufacturing defects, the ST-700 starter and RC-371 relay are not suitable for use on T-34 tanks."

3 The Mariupol Plant is the Ilyich Mariupol Plant of the People's Commissariat of Shipbuilding.

4 TsAMO RF, f. 38 (GABTU), op. 11355 (Tank Directorate), d. 32 (Report of the Red Army GABTU on Factory No. 183's completion of orders for manufacture of tanks and equipment), p. 17.

5 Ibid., p. 19 (reverse side).

6 Ibid., p. 38, "Situation report on completion of a Red Army Armor Directorate order during August 1941 by Factory No. 183."

7 Ibid., pp. 49–50, "Correspondence about the preparations for production of A-34 at Factory No. 183 as of 20 August 1940."

8 Ibid., p. 59, "Situation report on completion of a Red Army Armor Directorate order during September 1940 by Factory No. 183."

9 Here, the attentive reader may experience a cognitive dissonance: how could it be that nine vehicles had been shipped prior to October, and another three in October, but the total number of tanks shipped was ten? The riddle is simply solved, however: two vehicles that the factory had previously shipped for testing were returned for preventive maintenance and fitting out, with the intent of turning them over to military units later. Therefore, they were not included among the total shipped from the factory to avoid counting them twice.

10 TsAMO RF, f. 38 (GABTU), op. 11355 (Tank Directorate), d. 32 (Report of the Red Army GABTU on Factory No. 183's completion of orders for manufacture of tanks and equipment), p. 83, "Situation report on completion of a Red Army Armor Directorate order during October 1940 by Factory No. 183."

11 "...'fracture' is understood to mean a crack that extends to one third the thickness of an armor part." (Notation on document).

12 TsAMO RF, f. 38 (GABTU), op. 11355 (Tank Directorate), d. 157 (Reports of NII-48 and factories regarding tests conducted on tanks and tank equipment, and correspondence with the factories and NII-48 on the subject), pp. 132–137, "Team report on technical assistance provided to Comintern Factory No. 183 (Kharkov) with regard to welding of the A-34."

13 Ibid.

14 TsAMO RF, f. 11355 (GABTU), op. 11355 (Tank Directorate), d. 32 (Report of the Red Army GABTU on Factory No. 183's completion of orders for manufacture of tanks and equipment), p. 151, "Situation report on completion of a Red Army Armor Directorate order during August 1940 by Factory No. 183."

15 TsAMO RF, f. 38 (GABTU), op. 11355 (Tank Directorate), d. 32 (Report of the Red Army GABTU on Factory No. 183's completion of orders for manufacture of tanks and equipment), p. 202, "Situ-

ation report on completion of a Red Army Armor Directorate order during December 1940 by Factory No. 183."

16 TsAMO RF, f. 38 (GABTU), op. 11355 (Tank Directorate), d. 41 (Report of the Red Army GABTU on manufacture of T-34 tank prototypes by factories; specifications for the T-34 tank with torsion-bar suspension; conclusion of Factory No. 183 regarding tests performed on the experimental driver's hatch and hatch cover with vision blocks), pp. 190–193, "Report on T-34 tank reengineering inspection."

17 Ibid., pp. 160–162, "Letter concerning report on tests performed on three T-34 tanks."

18 To implement this in the military units that received the first "thirty-fours," a GABTU committee met in the spring and gathered valuable information about the status of the T-34 tanks. For more details, see Chapter 4.

19 TsAMO RF, f. 38 (GABTU), op. 11355 (Tank Directorate), d. 41 (Report of the Red Army GABTU on manufacture of T-34 tank prototypes by factories; specifications for the T-34 tank with torsion-bar suspension; conclusion of Factory No. 183 regarding tests performed on the experimental driver's hatch and hatch cover with vision blocks), pp. 47–49, "Report of conference hosted by People's Commissariat of Medium Machine Building, Comrade Malyshev."

20 TsAMO RF, f. 38 (GABTU) op. 11355 (Tank Directorate), d. 32 (Report of the Red Army GABTU on Factory No. 183's completion of orders for manufacture of tanks and equipment), p. 204, "Situation report on completion of a Red Army Armor Directorate order during January 1941 by Factory No. 183."

21 Ibid., p. 205, "Situation report on completion of a Red Army Armor Directorate order during February 1941 by Factory No. 183."

22 Ibid., p. 212, "Situation report on completion of a Red Army Armor Directorate order during March 1941 by Factory No. 183."

23 Ibid., p. 218, "Situation report on completion of a Red Army Armor Directorate order during May 1941 by Factory No. 183."

24 Ibid., p. 220, "Situation report on completion of a Red Army Armor Directorate order during May 1941 by Factory No. 183."

25 TsAMO RF, f. 38 (GABTU), op. 11355 (Tank Directorate), d. 41 ("Report of the Red Army GABTU on manufacture of T-34 tank prototypes by factories; specifications for the T-34 tank with torsion-bar suspension; conclusion of Factory No. 183 regarding tests performed on the experimental driver's hatch and hatch cover with vision blocks"), pp. 353–354, "Report on correction of deficiencies noted during testing of new models of wheeled and armored systems between 20 March and 20 April 1941."

26 For example: I. Zheltov, M. Pavlov, I. Pavlov, A. Sergeyev, A. Solyankin, *The Unknown T-34 [Neizvestnyy T-34].* Moscow: OOO "Exprint Publishing Center," 2001, pp. 30–32.

27 TsAMO RF, f. 38 (GABTU) op. 11355 (Tank Directorate), d. 279 (Reports of Red Army GABTU military representatives regarding the manufacture of tanks at factories, and correspondence on the subject between GABTU and the factories), pp. 7, 8, 8a. Complete copies of the documents are provided in the Appendix.

28 TsAMO RF, f. 38 (GABTU) op. 11355 (Tank Directorate), d. 32 (Report of the Red Army GABTU on Factory No. 183's completion of orders for manufacture of tanks and equipment), p. 222, "Situation report on completion of a Red Army Armor Directorate order during June 1941 by Factory No. 183."

This is the tank shown stuck in a building on pages 96 and 97. It was successfully started and driven under its own power to a vacant platform in Nemirov. (N 50.104077, E 23.441257)◊

29 Ibid., p. 228, "Situation report on completion of a Red Army Armor Directorate order during July 1941 by Factory No. 183."

30 Ibid., p. 229, "Situation report on completion of a Red Army Armor Directorate order during August 1941 by Factory No. 183."

31 Ibid., p. 234, "Situation report on Factory No. 183's completion of Workers' and Peasants' Armored Force Directorate order dated September 1941."

32 TsAMO RF, f. 38 (GABTU), op. 11355 (Tank Directorate), d. 225 (GABTU reports, references, and explanatory notes on completion of delivery plans by tank factories and spare parts for them), sheets 24–25, "Report on military representatives conference of the Armor Directorate of the Red Army GABTU, 18–20 November 1940."

33 RGAE [Russian State Archive of the Economy], f. 8418, op. 28, d. 92.

34 TsAMO RF, f. 38, op. 11355, d. 13, p. 41, "Report on completion of planned orders of the Red Army Armor Directorate by factories in 1940."

35 Soviet automotive acquisition specialists who visited some German armored vehicle factories in the fall of 1939 wrote this about Alkett: "The Alkett factory is located in northern Berlin. The factory is one of Germany's first-class tank manufacturers. The factory is new. It opened in 1935–1936. All of its equipment and appliances are new. The factory manufactures Mark III medium tanks… The factory's Mark III medium tank production program called for producing 30 tanks in September and 60 tanks in October; it is ramping up to produce 100 tanks per month. When operating at full capacity (in three shifts), it could produce 150 tanks per month." RGVA, f. 31811, op. 2, d. 916, cit. ex: "Museum Memorial 'History of the T-34 Tank.'" Historical Document Collection No. 2.

36 TsAMO RF, op. 7237, d. 2, pp. 21–50. Cit. ex: Col. "1941" in 2 vols. Moscow: International Foundation "Democracy," 1998, Vol. 1, pp. 752–753.

37 During the years of the Great Patriotic War, the USSR produced 98,300 tanks and self-propelled guns.

38 TsAMO RF, f. 38, op. 11355, d. 30, p. 5, "Letter on preparations for production of the A-34 vehicle."

39 TsAMO RF, f. 81 (GAU KA), op. 12104 (Field Artillery Directorate), d. 9 (Artillery Research Proving Ground reports on tests of armor-piercing projectiles), pp. 284, 288, "Letter from the Deputy People's Commissar of Defense concerning results of tests conducted on armor-piercing projectiles."

40 M. G. Yefimov, *Artillery Projectile Course.* Moscow, Leningrad: Gosoboronizdat, 1939, p. 111, "Approved by the All-Union Committee for Higher Education of the People's Council of Commissars of the USSR for use as a textbook by military academies and defense industry institutions of higher education."

41 Here we would like to mention that the following machine tools were among those ordered by the Stalingrad Tank Plant as being **required** for production of T-34s:

- 13 Heidenreich & Harbek, 11 Beringer, and 1 Fr. Braun screw-cutting lathes;
- 35 Niles boring lathes;
- 11 Hirschold multiple-tool turning lathes;
- 18 Heineman turret lathes;
- 2 MAAG gear cutters;
- 6 Rheinecker, 3 Lorenz, and 1 Pfauter gear shapers;
- 1 Schmalz universal grinders;
- 1 Wotan internal grinders;
- 3 F. Werner spline grinders;
- 1 Glisson tool and cutter grinder.

This background puts the various speculations about the support Stalin's USSR provided for Nazi aggression in a very different light.

42 TsAMO RF, f. 38 (GABTU), op. 11355 (Tank Directorate), d. 30 (Summary of preparations for T-34 production, June 19, 1940), pp. 107–108.

43 Ibid., pp. 84–85.

44 Ibid., pp. 107–108.

45 TsAMO RF, f. 38 (GABTU), op. 11355 (Tank Directorate), d. 30 (Summary of Preparations for T-34 Production, 20 November, 1940), pp. 162–164.

46 The Comintern Kharkov Locomotive Plant No. 183.

47 TsAMO RF, f. 38 (GABTU), op. 11355 (Tank Directorate), d. 233 (Dispatches of ABTU military representatives on factory operations to produce and test tanks and equipment; Armor Directorate contracts with factories and bulletins on tank and equipment deliveries), p. 355.

48 TsAMO RF, f. 38 (GABTU), op. 11355 (Tank Directorate), d. 30 (Dispatches, information, and summaries concerning tank production), p. 184, "Report on Red Army Armored Force Directorate orders completed from 20–31 January 1941."

49 Ibid., p. 185, "Report on Red Army Armored Force Directorate orders completed from 20–31 January 1941."

50 Ibid., p. 187, "Report on Red Army Armored Force Directorate orders completed from 20–31 January 1941."

[51] Ibid., p. 193, "Information on the Stalingrad Tractor Plant's completion of an order under Red Army Armor Directorate contract No. B-1-222, dated March 8, 1941, in April 1941."

[52] Ibid., p. 195, "Information on the Stalingrad Tractor Plant's completion of an order under Red Army Armor Directorate contract No. B-1-222, dated March 8, 1941, in May 1941."

[53] Ibid., p. 196, "Information on the Stalingrad Tractor Plant's completion of an order under Red Army Armor Directorate contract No. B-1-222, dated March 8, 1941, in June 1941."

CHAPTER 4. **SKILLFUL HANDS**

A T-34 tank of the 5th Tank Division near Alitus.◊

Hard in training, easy in battle.[1]

Even the best tank is incapable of fighting by itself, without a crew. It is "the three tankers, three happy friends—a combat vehicle's crew"—that usually determines how well a tank acquits itself in actual combat. And if the crew is made up of highly capable individuals whose skills have been honed on tank ranges and training grounds and who have received excellent combat and political training, it will succeed.

Unfortunately, the Red Army's tank crews in June 1941 did not meet expectations, to put it mildly.

One of the main problems was the rapid increase, sparked by the growing threat of war, in the number of tank troops. Whereas in early 1938 the Red Army had almost

5,000 tanks and just over 90,000 personnel,[2] by June 22 the total number of tanks and tankettes in the Red Army's inventory exceeded 25,000,[3] and that armada was being manned and serviced by 650,000 tankers. However, that was merely the number listed in the plans—the actual number was just under half a million. Of tanker officers alone, 81,280 were needed by January 1, 1941 (there were 65,012 on the roster)—almost as many officers as there had been soldiers in the tank force in early 1938.[4]

The Soviet leadership could not solve the personnel problem with a snap of the fingers, or by ordering up an army of clone tank crewmen. And whereas in the upper ranks the problem could be solved by promoting officers from lower levels, the situation with the middle and, especially, the lower command slots was much worse. A smart battalion commander could take over a regiment, and one who was really on the ball might even attempt to handle a brigade. However, the difference between conscript soldiers/NCOs and even junior officers of technical troops went much deeper, and it was usually not possible to overcome this gap even with a dashing cavalry charge. Moreover, the situation became a vicious circle—the shortage of junior commanders resulted in poor training for the rank and file, and the best representatives from their slender ranks would later have to supplement the cadres of these junior-most commanders.

In order to examine how tankers were trained in practice, we need to understand exactly where the first "thirty-fours" were sent and how many there were. The first units to receive the new medium tanks were the 4th and 8th Mechanized Corps of the Kiev Special Military District: the "Summary of Requirements and Material Supplies of Corps as of 11/10/1940" reserved 50 T-34s for the 4th Mechanized Corps and 30 for the 8th Mechanized Corps.[5] Tanks were sent to the 8th Tank Division of the 4th Mechanized Corps (20 vehicles on November 20, 10 on November 28, and another 20 on December 17) and to the 12th Division of the 8th Mechanized Corps (30 vehicles on December 9[6]), and they were listed in the inventory of these units as of January 1, 1941.[7]

And as we said in Chapter 2, a commission from the GABTU inspected the tanks in March 1941. The documents produced by the commission are of particular interest to us primarily because its members scrupulously recorded the number of hours the vehicles were operated. And, to put it bluntly, that number is not impressive:

> *The vehicles inspected in the Kiev and Baltic Special Military Districts were kept in a storage park and, on average, had been operated 7–10 hours per vehicle.*[8]

And whereas the small amount of time (as of mid-March) that tanks in the Baltic Special Military District had been operated could be ascribed to the recent (in February) receipt of new "thirty-fours," the Kiev District could not use that as an excuse three or four months after having received their tanks. Of the tanks inspected, the undisputed recordholder was a tank of the 15th Tank Regiment in the Kiev Special Military District's 8th Tank Division, which had been operated 29 hours and 30 minutes; not far away, however, was another tank of the same regiment, which had "run up" 29 hours and 15 minutes, and two vehicles of the 16th Tank Regiment, which had logged 28 hours and 30 minutes and 25 hours and 30 minutes, respectively. Alas, many not only had not exceeded 20 hours of operation, they had not even come close, and a tank that had logged from 4 to 6 hours was nothing out of the ordinary.[9] To put it mildly, an "aver-

A T-34 of the 12th Tank Division, June 1941.

age of 7–10 hours of operation" was far from sufficient for crew training: according to the 1940 tank driver training course, just learning to drive a medium tank required five hours of practice, and all crew members were supposed to take the course—which meant that a driver training course for an entire crew required 20 hours. And that did not include training on tactics, firing the gun (firing tanks from a halt and from the move on a training range, which also put hours on the vehicle), or training on how to fight as a platoon/company/battalion—it only included starting and stopping, shifting gears, making turns, driving a tank under the simplest field conditions, and negotiating the simplest obstacles.[10]

As of the date the report was written—March 29, 1941—the T-34 tanks produced by the Stalingrad Tractor Plant had been operated as follows:

	Engine operation hours						Total vehicles inspected
Production month	**0–5**	**5–10**	**10–15**	**15–20**	**20–25**	**Over 25**	
August 1940	1	3	1	1		2	8
September 1940	10	13	4		1	2	30
October 1940	17	7					24
November 1940	22	1		1			24
December 1940	15	6	1				22
Total	65	30	6	2	1	4	108

Table compiled from TsAMO RF data, f. 38 (GABTU), op. 11355 (Tank Directorate), d. 24 ("Report of the Armor Directorate on Inspection of Fracture Behavior in T-34 Armor Parts in Service in the Kiev and Baltic Special Military Districts, correspondence with NN regarding drawings"), sheets 55–83.

T-34s from the 32nd Tank Division, June 25, 1941, Yazuv Stary. The tanks shown in the photograph on page 63 appear in the background. (N 49.994835, E 23.422396)◊

In addition to tank units, several military educational institutions were able to obtain T-34 tanks in 1940: as of January 1, 1941, the Moscow Academy of Mechanization and Motorization had three T-34s (and another two tanks were supposed to be coming); the Leningrad Officer Advanced Course had three vehicles (another two tanks were waiting to be sent); schools in Kazan had two "thirty-fours" (they were expecting an additional tank); the Orlov Armor School had one T-34 (they were expecting 15 more); the Kiev Tank Technical School had three tanks (and were expecting delivery of an additional two tanks); and the Kharkov School had five "thirty-fours" (11 more were anticipated).[11]

At the end of March 1941, about two thirds of the "thirty-fours" inspected had been operated for five hours or less—that usually meant that a vehicle's engine had only been run while the tank was moving onto the station platform, moving off the platform, and being driven from the railway station to the unit.

The next recipient of T-34s was the 7th Tank Division of the 6th Mechanized Corps of the Western Special Military District, which was sent 30 tanks in January 1941. Another 30 tanks were shipped to the 8th Tank Division of the 4th Mechanized Corps of the Kiev Special Military District;[12] two T-34s went to the Kiev Tank School; and nine were issued to the Kharkov Tank School and 15 to the Orlov Tank School.[13]

In February 1941, the list of units that were beginning to train on the T-34 expanded again: 30 T-34s were sent to the 5th Tank Division of the 3rd Mechanized Corps of the Baltic Special Military District. Another 20 tanks were sent to the 7th Division of the 6th Mechanized Corps of the Western Specialized Military District; 20 vehicles to the 8th Division of the 4th Mechanized Corps and the 12th Division of the 8th Mechanized Corps of the Kiev Special Military District; two T-34s to the Kharkov Tank School, and two to the Moscow Academy of Mechanization and Motorization.[14]

In March 1941, "thirty-fours" began going to the Odessa Military District—the 11th Tank Division of the 2nd Mechanized Corps received 30 vehicles. In addition, 20 T-34s were sent to the 5th Tank Division in the Baltic and 40 to the 8th Division of the 4th Mechanized Corps (the first Stalingrad vehicles delivered to a military unit). The 10th

Tank Division of the 15th Mechanized Corps of the Kiev District got 20 vehicles. Another 22 tanks were sent to Darnitsa; the authors have no information about what subsequently happened to them (some Kiev Special Military District tank units in Darnitsa were not deployed, and the tanks sent to Darnitsa are on a separate line in the Stalingrad Tank Factory purchase orders completed before the war began).[185]

As T-34 production ramped up, tank deliveries to the Army increased. In April 1941, another 20 Kharkov "thirty-fours" went to the 11th Tank Division of the 2nd Mechanized Corps of the Odessa District;[186] 102 Kharkov T-34s were sent to the 8th Tank Division of the 4th Mechanized Corps;[187] and 20 Stalingrad "thirty-fours" augmented the 12th Division of the 8th Mechanized Corps of the Kiev District; 24 Stalingrad tanks went to the 7th Division of the 6th Mechanized Corps of the Western District;[188] and one vehicle produced by the Kharkov Locomotive Works was sent to the Leningrad Officer Advanced Course.[19]

It should be noted that in late May and early April 1941 all mechanized corps—both "old" corps, those formed in the summer of 1940, and "new" ones that began forming in the spring of 1941—compiled fairly detailed notes on how their formation, inventories, combat training, and numerical strength were progressing. We will return to them a little later in order to understand how units trained on the "thirty-fours." Meanwhile, we will finish reviewing the history of tank deliveries to units prior to the war.

May 1941 set a record for the number of T-34s delivered to units and military training institutions: eighty-two Stalingrad and 72 Kharkov "thirty-fours" (a total of 154 vehicles) went to the 4th Tank Division of the 6th Mechanized Corps of the Western District and 100 Kharkov tanks to the Kiev Special Military District (58 "thirty-fours" to the 32nd Tank Division of the 4th Mechanized Corps, 52 to the 37th Tank Division of the 15th

WSMD: Western Special Military District

KSMD: Kiev Special Military District

OMD: Odessa Military District

BSMD: Baltic Special Military District

Mechanized Corps). In addition, military training institutions received 29 vehicles (the Ulyanovsk and 2nd Saratov Tank Technical School each got 10 "thirty-fours"; the Kiev Tank Technical School received six; the Kazan advanced course for commanders got one, and the Leningrad Officer Advanced Course got two), and one tank was transferred to Artillery Factory No. 92 in Gorky.[20]

Finally, during the three prewar weeks of the "stormy June," 18 Kharkov and 58 Stalingrad tanks were sent to the Western Special Military District, destined for Belostok (the 5th Tank Division of the 6th Mechanized Corps) and Grodno (the 29th Tank Division of the 11th Mechanized Corps).[21]

Reducing all of this information into a bar chart showing how numbers of "thirty-fours" in unit inventories changed with time gives us approximately the following picture: the chart clearly illustrates two serious problems that would have a noticeable impact on the Red Army's employment of armor in the first battles of the Great Patriotic War. First of all, the latest tanks were distributed very unevenly across the military districts. And if the meager number of T-34s in the Odessa Military District and their passivity in the early days of the war can be fully justified given their main enemy—Romanian forces—the 50 "thirty-fours" in the Baltic Military District facing Army Group North and, initially, two Wehrmacht tank groups do not inspire optimism.[22] Second, the chart showing how the unit inventories of T-34s changed with time lets us solve the "mystery of 1941" and answer the question of why just under 1,000 new tanks in the hands of the regular peacetime army disappeared without delaying the blitzkrieg juggernaut: most of the "thirty-fours" arrived in the units too late, and the tankers did not have enough time to learn how to use the equipment entrusted to them. What happened in the Western Special Military District is a particularly clear example of this: in early May it had 72 T-34s, and by the beginning of the war it had just under 370!

But first things first. As we mentioned above, in late April or early May 1941 all of the Red Army's mechanized corps prepared progress reports on their formation, inventory of combat and support equipment, and military training. Let us examine these documents in the order in which the mechanized corps received the new "thirty-fours." We will begin with the 4th Mechanized Corps, which began receiving T-34s in late 1940 (by May 1—the date of the progress report—the corps' 8th Tank Division had 140 T-34s, and its 32nd Tank Division had 102). Major General Andrei Andreyevich Vlasov, former commander of the 32nd, 20th, and 2nd Shock Armies and later of the Russian Army of Liberation, what can you tell us about the status of the mechanized corps with which you were entrusted?

The command staff for the corps and the corps' units and divisions have essentially been formed. By and large, the corps has been assembled. Final formation has been delayed because the units do not yet have their full complement of officers and matériel has been extremely slow in arriving. This is especially true for the 32nd Tank Division.

The 32nd Tank Division has the following shortages:
Officers: 984 personnel
NCOs: 1,268 personnel
Junior enlisted: 1,080 personnel

A captured 12th Tank Division T-34. The vehicle is ready for shipping to Germany for testing. The vehicle's factory number is 0405-7.

Not all of the matériel for the divisions and corps units per TO&E has been received. This is especially true for the 32nd Tank Division. The main types of matériel (tanks, repair shops, fuel trucks) have been extremely slow to arrive.

All of the corps' units have been moved to Lvov.

The units in the barracks are in very tight conditions and do not have enough storage parks, garages, vegetable storage facilities, or classrooms. For the most part, the equipment is kept in open storage parks…

Tactical proficiency of units and staffs

8th Division

Staff training

The division staff is tactically trained and performs well. It is capable of directing troops in all types of combat.

The tactical training and performance of the regimental staffs is fully satisfactory.

The tactical training and performance of the battalion staffs are mediocre; these staffs do not have enough experience to direct their subunits.

The staffs' tactical performance deficiencies are as follows:

a) *Shortage of staff officers;*

b) *Tactical training of several staff officers is low:*

c) *Practical experience in directing subordinate units is low;*

Attached personnel are untrained and will require 2–3 months of training.

32nd Division

The division's units are carrying out individual soldier training. On 15 May, they will begin tank crew, section, and gun crew training. The units have begun mastering their equipment and weapons. The units are not up to par tactically and are unprepared for combat. The staffs are not fully manned.[233]

We would like to call the reader's attention to the status of the 32nd Tank Division, in particular. "*The units are unready for combat, and the staffs are not fully manned*" (so we can imagine how well they performed)—and vehicles were in "open storage parks," i.e., more than 100 "thirty-fours" were canvas covered, under the open sky.[244] Sending these tanks into combat trained as described could not have been expected to have a noticeable impact. The units had tanks, but, admittedly, they may as well not have had them; their crews had just begun learning how to use them, and the platoons, companies, battalions, and regiments were not even close to becoming a cohesive fighting unit—it was early days yet. The division was not yet ready for those kinds of exercises. And with 102 tanks, the 32nd Division had approximately 10% of all the T-34s in the border military districts!

The situation in the 8th Tank Division was also quite far from the impeccable revolutionary "order and discipline in the armor forces." A report on the division's status clearly described the problem that was almost the scourge of the Red Army at the beginning of the war: although higher level staffs were well trained, the staffs of lower-level units were undermanned and poorly trained. But a division's staff could not split up into eight staffs and take over for the battalion staffs. Therefore, even the most reasonable, timely, competent, and appropriate decisions by higher-level staffs were at risk of not being implemented (or not carried out in a timely fashion or properly) because lower-level staffs were poorly trained. Even the most "reasonable, timely, competent decisions" on each individual issue cannot depend on the division commander (not to mention higher ranking commanders) personally surveying his division's entire battlefield, personally crawling on his belly over every square meter to determine trafficability for his tanks, or slowly and thoughtfully observing the enemy's location through binoculars from under every bush. He must make decisions based on information he receives from his subordinates. Even from those whose "*training is mediocre.*"

But let's talk about the training of the 4th Mechanized Corps' personnel in more detail by examining who trained whom and how and what they were trained on. We will begin by looking at the corps' personnel strength:

Personnel category	Authorized strength	Number on hand	
		8th Tank Division	32nd Tank Division
Top officers	2	1	2
Senior officers	56	41	27
Junior officers	621	534	110
Support personnel	231	179	19
Administrative personnel	110	79	35
Medical personnel	69	29	7
Political personnel	154	114	62
NCOs	2,166	1,883	897
Enlisted soldiers	6,426	6,629	5,339
Total	9,835	9,489	6,498

Table compiled from TsAMO RF data, f. 38, op. 11353, d. 896, p. 98

We are immediately struck by the disastrous (it would be difficult to describe it differently) state of the 32nd Tank Division's junior officers, NCOs, and support personnel—these are the individuals responsible for training personnel in servicing the newest equipment and repairing it as needed. We can also speak of the division's "overabundance" of enlisted personnel in comparison with the number of officers: the division's enlisted strength was above 80%, whereas the junior officer slots were manned at less than 20%, and the NCO slots were manned at approximately 40%, i.e., every junior officer had to do the work of five, and NCOs the work of "two and a half." And even if the officers of the 32nd Tank Division could accomplish such a feat, any complaint about the quality of the training would obviously be uncalled for...

No fewer "marvelous discoveries" also await us in the data on the educational level of the 4th Mechanized Corps' personnel:

Education	8th Tank Division	32nd Tank Division
Higher	199	148
Secondary	1,462	808
Grades 9–7	1,994	570
Grade 6–3	4,670	4,551
Semi-literate	1,050	421
Illiterate	114	—

Table compiled from TsAMO RF data, f. 38, op. 11353, d. 896, p. 99

Here, we should take note of two points. First, the majority of tank division personnel—the support troops—did not even have a secondary education, not having gone beyond sixth grade; moreover, the total number of those with a secondary or higher education was much lower than the total number of officers in the division. That is, quite a few of the officers had a ninth grade education at best, and some had not gone beyond sixth grade. Second, the number of semi-literate and illiterate soldiers in the "old" (summer of 1940) 8th Tank Division was comparable to the number of those who had completed secondary school. Needless to say, neither the first factor nor the second helped the pace of military training or contributed to its success.

Now that we have addressed who needed training and who was to do it, let us proceed to the next two questions: how were they to carry out the training, and what were they to be trained on?

Classrooms and instructional aids in the 4th Mechanized Corps

	8th Tank Division	32nd Tank Division
Commander training classroom	4	—
Tactical classrooms	7	1
Rifleman classrooms	3	—
Technical classrooms	19	2
Radio classrooms	15	4
Tactical/rifleman/technical classrooms	5	6
Gas compounds	2	—
Obstacle courses	2	—
Sport fields	8	—
Rifle ranges	5	—
Training grounds	—	—
Firing range	1 (jointly with the 34th Division)	—
Tank training ground	—	—

Table compiled from TsAMO RF data, f. 38, op. 11353, d. 896, p. 106

Information about training grounds and firing ranges of 4th Mechanized Corps units.

8th Tank Division

Live fire exercises will be conducted in accordance with Kiev Special Military District Order No. 12 41 at the 26th Tank Brigade's firing range located 5 km northeast of Grudek-Yagelyonsky. The land for the training ground was conveyed by decree of the Lvov Regional Executive Committee.

The firing range must be reserved for the exclusive use of the 4th Mechanized Corps, because it includes the 32nd Tank Division, which was moved to Lvov and which has no training ground or firing range.

The 8th Motorized Rifle Regiment occupies 37 hectares near the firing range; the land belonged to a landowner and is currently being used by individual peasant farmers. The firing range is located west of Yasnisk. The conveyance of the land resulted from a petition to the Lvov Regional Administrative Committee.

A group of T-34s from the 32nd Tank Division, Yazuv Stary.
The photograph on page 61 shows these same vehicles.

We would like to draw the reader's attention to something once again: this is an "old" tank division that was formed in the summer of 1940. It did not move anywhere; it was formed in Lvov. A little under a year had passed since the division was formed, and it still had no tank range. No land had been allocated for training grounds, and for a firing range the division's motorized rifle regiment was using land that previously belonged to a landowner and was now used by individual peasant farmers.

The 32nd Tank Division also does not have a training ground or firing range.

KV and T-34 tanks equipped with large-caliber guns do not have a training ground. They must use a firing line on the Lvov artillery range near Bzhezina Velka.

The units lack the following: firing tables for the 122 mm howitzer M1938 and the L-10 and L-11 tank guns.

Technical manual for the 122 mm howitzer M1938 and the 152 mm howitzer M1938.

Technical manual for the L-10 and L-11 tank guns.

Turret and turret pantograph simulators.[25]

Would it be easy for such poorly trained and undereducated NCOs to train semi-literate or even completely illiterate soldiers on how to maintain tank weapons, especially since they lacked training aids? Would it be possible to check the quality of their training when they do not have a training ground on which to practice firing and even lack firing tables? Could they have honed their skill in driving tanks while buttoned up under simulated combat conditions without tank ranges? But these are rhetorical questions.

There is, however, another point that we should pay close attention to. It concerns the way equipment was allocated among mothballed vehicles and vehicles used for training. The 8th Tank Division, which had 140 T-34s on May 1, kept 85 of them in

A stuck T-34 from an unknown unit, summer of 1941.

mothball storage and used 47 for training. Another eight tanks were inoperable: five were down for routine maintenance, and three were out for intermediate overhaul.[26] The number of nonfunctioning tanks is not surprising if we consider that the division may have had only 46 "thirty-fours" in storage parks, with another 94 vehicles stored in the open,[277] and remember that the division had received tanks between December 1940 and March 1941 (meaning the tanks had been standing under the open sky during the cold of winter and the melting snows of spring), and if we also consider the status of the personnel, who were undergoing training on the new equipment "by the seat of their pants" because they lacked manuals and handbooks. But at the same time, we need to remember that, given the small number of tanks in the training pool and the abundance of trainees, one can either train a few people and do it well or train a lot of people and do it poorly.

There were also potential problems with the nonfunctioning tanks: the factory received complaints about tanks that had broken down due to design defects and sent out improved assemblies and parts to replace them. And nobody was working with the tanks in long-term storage. On June 18, four days before the war began, Major General Morgunov, chief the Kiev Special Military District's Armor Directorate, sent a letter to the Red Army's Armor Directorate:

> *The manufacturers are doing nothing to prevent possible damage occurring on vehicles that are in mothballs and not being operated. I hereby request that you instruct the Kirov Factory and Factory No. 183 to take the steps necessary to prevent the above indicated damage from occurring on the KV and T-34 tanks that were produced first. The numbers of vehicles needing an upgrade in military unit 5427 are as follows: KV – 52, and T-34 – 100.*[28]

Few of the deficiencies noted in the 4th Mechanized Corps report are unique to it—on the contrary, the spring reports of other mechanized corps look like carbon copies of the 4th's. Here is the report of the 8th Mechanized Corps of the Kiev Special Military District, which received T-34s at the same time as the 4th and which had 100 T-34s in its 12th Tank Division by May 1, 1941:

> *Equipment on hand.*
> ***12th Tank Division:***
> *KV tanks at 91%*
> *T-34 tanks at 47%*
> *BT tanks at 486%*[289]
> *T-26 tanks at 186%.*
> *The presence of a large number of non-TO&E vehicles of various types and the lack of the required number of TO&E heavy and medium tanks reduces the striking power of the mechanized corps and hinders mastery of the new tank types by personnel.*
> *Repair equipment and spare parts.*
> *Repair equipment in the 12th Tank Division is at 50%. The division lacks sufficient spare parts in wartime reserve and for immediate use on KV and T-34 tanks, wheeled vehicles, tractors, and motorcycles.*

Storage parks.

The 12th Tank Division has no storage parks for KV and T-34 tanks. The dimensions of the existing storage parks are unsuitable for combat vehicles and are used for wheeled vehicles....

POL [petroleum, oil, lubricants] in wartime reserve.

12th Tank Division:

Diesel fuel sufficient for 3 fuelings;

B-70 gasoline sufficient for 3 fuelings;

Grade 2 gasoline sufficient for 4 fuelings.

Tank trucks:

Fuel trucks – 43%;

Water and tank trucks – 20%.

Squad rooms, apartments, and warehouses.

The 12th Tank Division has 100% of the squad rooms needed, but housing of personnel in a two-tier bunk system is cramped; and because there are no free rooms, the needed number of classrooms, Lenin Rooms, company offices, and storerooms cannot be provided.

Manning levels

The 12th Division is manned as follows:

Officers – 80%

NCOs – 84%

Enlisted – 103%

Junior officer manning is understrength by 28%; support by 27%. 23rd Tank Division junior officer manning level – 86%. 24th Tank Division junior and senior officer manning level – 63%. Support and other officers – 70%.

Training aids, classrooms, miniature ranges

Training devices, visual aids, regulations and instructions, especially for tank equipment and guns: units of the corps are at 50–60%.

Combat training

The corps began its normal winter training cycle on 1 November 1940.

The corps' units were trained in accordance with People's Defense Commissariat Order No. 30, KOVO No. 025, and the military training programs approved by the People's Defense Commissar.

The following factors had an impact on the normal course of combat training during the winter:

Officer shortages and turnover

Shortage of vehicle parking spaces

Shortage of spare parts and assemblies required for planned maintenance of combat and support vehicles

Shortage of units for training on T-34s and KVs

Shortage of classrooms, visual aids, regulations, and instructions

Ill-timed and insufficient provision of POL to meet immediate needs. Units have received only 50% of the required quantity of POL, and that disrupts tactical field exercises with vehicles (in March, exercises in the 12th Tank Division were interrupted).

T-34 and BT-7 tanks. Unknown unit, summer of 1941.◊

Results of spring inspection of combat and political training

The 12th Tank Division was not inspected in April; during the commission's inspection of the 8th Mechanized Corps in February the division was rated "satisfactory."

Availability of training grounds and firing ranges

The 12th Tank Division has one tank range and one firing range; it lacks a tank training ground.[30]

We would like to bring something to the reader's attention once again: here we have an "old" tank division that was formed almost a year before the report from which we quoted was written. Its problems were virtually identical to those of the 8th Tank Division of the 4th Mechanized Corps: officer shortages and turnover; cramped quarters without room for classrooms; and shortages of training manuals, training grounds, and fuel for exercises. By the way, why did the division receive only a "satisfactory" rating in February 1941?

The division is short a large number of officers—282, i.e., 21%. The positions affected are as follows: platoon commanders—41, company commanders—25. The division has a large shortage of NCOs—521, i.e., 21.6%. The division is understrength by 896 men. The significant shortage of junior officers and NCOs and the excessive numbers of enlisted soldiers cause the officers to be overworked, which greatly hinders the normal progression of combat training.... The results of a test on elementary infantry tactics administered to 15 officers of the 2nd Battalion of the 12th Motorized Rifle Regiment were as follows:

Good: 1 officer – 7%
Fair: 2 officers – 13%
Poor: 12 officers – 80%

The results of a test on tactical training taken by a group of officers from the 3rd Battalion of the 24th Tank Regiment were as follows:

Fair: 6 officers – 46%
Weak: 7 officers – 54%.

The majority of officers in these battalions are graduates of various short courses. Many of the officers of the 12th Motorized Rifle Regiment said that they have never read Part II of the Infantry Field Manual[31] *or Chapter 36 of the Field Service Manual. The knowledgeability of officers of the 3rd Battalion of the 24th Tank Regiment does not extend beyond Part I of the Armor Field Manual. They have read none of the other manuals. They do not read military journals. The 24th Tank Regiment was allocated one copy of the journal "Military Thought" and three copies of the "Armor Journal." Officer training is low in general, especially on tactics.*

Individual infantry training in the tank battalions has not been conducted at all, and many officers believe that it is not required for tank units.

Military Technician 2nd Class S. led exercises on the topic "The Soldier in Offensive Combat" in the 24th Tank Regiment's motor battalion. S. himself is poorly trained in infantry tactics. He is unable to give the unit an assignment. The choice of location for the exercise was poor. No firing line was indicated when conducting an attack. Platoon training was performed instead of individual soldier training. The charges by the soldiers were slow. They did not know how to take standing and prone firing positions with rifles; they did not select a firing position; and they did not prepare their weapons for combat.

Lieutenant R. led an exercise in the 2nd Battalion of the 24th Tank Regiment on the topic "Observation Outside the Tank" (from an observation post). No observation post was set up. The soldiers were unable to choose a location, and they were poorly skilled in the use of binoculars. They were unable to crawl. Observers practiced poor concealment when relieved. The observation post was not set up to transmit the results of observations. The exercise was conducted poorly in general.

Junior Lieutenant A. of the 12th Motorized Rifle Regiment's 6th Company led an exercise on the topic "The Soldier in Defensive Combat." It was organized as a two-part exercise. The soldiers displayed poor skills in digging trenches in the snow, camouflaged themselves poorly, opened fire without being commanded to do so by their squad leaders, and counterattacked individually.

Junior Lieutenant A. of the 4th Company led an exercise on the topic "The Soldier in Offensive Combat." A. himself is poorly trained in infantry tactics. The soldiers carried out unskillful charges; they did not dig in on the firing lines; they selected a poor location for firing; they did not use their sights; and they attacked without bayonets.

Overall, tactical training in the division's units was conducted unsatisfactorily.

Training on tank weapons in the 24th Tank Regiment was satisfactory. However, the NCOs were deficient in the use of technical skills and clear military language. For example, while training cadets on the "Recoil Mechanism and Recuperator Structure," Sergeant B. in the 1st Platoon of the 2nd Company of the regimental school used the wrong names for parts and vague wording, and he explained the recuperator spring design incorrectly....

During firing, tank crews are unable to accurately observe where their rounds struck; therefore, they do not adjust fire. Some tank commanders are unable to quickly determine the cause of a weapons jam and correct it. For example, the commander of tank 3 failed to complete the exercise because he could not correct a simple jam during firing and returned to the starting position without firing.[32]

We note that the "third wave" of mechanized corps had already begun forming on February 1, 1941, when the 12th Tank Division's inspection report was signed. That is, the problem of too few officers and unsatisfactory officer training did not develop suddenly, out of the blue, as a result of a large-scale reassignment of officers to the newly formed mechanized corps. And although the division was "old," it could not have been expected to "shine" on the battlefield.

A T-34 from the 8th Tank Division, disabled and burned in combat on June 24, 1941, in Nemirov. (N 50.104416, E 23.439186)◊

Manning of the 8th Mechanized Corps

	Authorized strength	Present in the 12th Tank Division
Top officers	2	2
Senior officers	222	159
Junior officers	455	379
Engineer personnel	2	2
Support personnel	233	194
Other officers	340	244
NCOs	2,172	1,834
Enlisted soldiers	6,449	6,737

Table compiled from TsAMO RF data, f. 38, op. 11353, d. 896, p. 132

Educational levels of 8th Mechanized Corps personnel

	12th Tank Division			
Education	Officers	NCOs	Enlisted	Total
Higher	25	29	40	94
Secondary	265	445	567	1277
Grades 7–9	504	884	2,833	4,421
Grades 3–6	153	437	2,836	3,426
Grades 1–3	33	39	461	533

Table compiled from TsAMO RF data, f. 38, op. 11353, d. 896, p. 132

In comparison with the 4th Mechanized Corps, the situation in the 12th Tank Division could be considered quite satisfactory: most soldiers in that division fell in the 7–9 grade group. However, they were led by commanders (junior and senior officers and above, i.e., junior lieutenant and above) with educations in the 1–3 and 3–6 grade groups.

To this we would add that, of the 100 "thirty-fours" in the 12th Tank Division, 96 vehicles were first-category vehicles and four were third-category.[33] You will recall that:

Defense Commissariat Order No. 12-16 of 1940 and the Regulation on Accounting and Reporting established the following quality categories for all equipment in the Red Army:

1st category—new, never operated, meets specifications, and suitable for use as intended.

2nd category—previously operated, fully functional, and suitable for use as intended. This category includes equipment in need of first-echelon maintenance (routine maintenance).

3rd category—needing repair in district shops (intermediate overhaul).

4th category—needing repair in central shops and factories (major overhaul).[344]

That means the 96 first-category tanks were new vehicles that ***had never been operated***; if they had been used for training, it was only as visual aids, and it is very questionable that they had been used for even that purpose.[355]

In wrapping up our review of the state of affairs in the Kiev Special Military District, we would like to include a few relatively large but highly useful numerical tables. The following table gives a breakdown of the social position of armor soldiers in the Kiev Special Military District as of January 1, 1941:

		Social position						Highest education level			
			Peasants								
Personnel category	Total	Blue-collar workers	Col-lective farmers	Self-employed farmers	White-collar workers	Students	Other	Higher	Second-ary	Grades 7–9	Grades 1–3
Officers	10,288							377	3129	4106	2676
NCOs	16,351	7178	4359	36	4063	672	43	422	3292	5991	6646
First-year enlisted	52,123	20,308	21,432	155	7540	2570	118	646	5059	13,793	32,625
Second-year enlisted	26,407	9842	10,919	64	4714	839	29	366	3264	7918	14,859
Third-year enlisted	274	129	77	4	61	1	2	1	23	82	168
Total enlisted	**86,769**	**33,631**	**35,194**	**238**	**13,661**	**3882**	**163**	**1098**	**9251**	**25,811**	**50,609**

Table compiled from TsAMO RF data, f. 131, op. 12951, d. 9, p. 33

Recall that the table describes the state of affairs on January 1, 1941, i.e., before the "spring" wave of mechanized corps began forming. It is evident from the table that the majority of the corps' officers had not finished secondary school, and its NCOs and enlisted personnel had not completed elementary school.

Further, almost twice as many recruits were conscripted in 1940 as there were soldiers in their second year of service. Considering the need to retain experienced soldiers in the service, we must recognize that the number of experienced enlisted personnel who could be made junior commanders was quite small. And that, in turn, presaged the promotion of first-year soldiers to NCO rank whose knowledgeability, experience, and qualifications differed little from those of the men they were to command and teach the intricacies of soldiering.

The next table summarizes the military and special education of armor commanders in the Kiev Special Military District by duty assignment as of January 1, 1941.

Duty assignment	Total	Military academies	Institutes	Officer advanced courses	Military schools	Other educational institutions	No military education
Division and brigade commanders	15	6	—	9	—	—	—
Division and brigade chiefs of staff	17	11	—	5	1	—	—
Regimental commanders	37	6	—	20	7	3	—
Regimental chiefs of staff	36	7	—	17	7	4	1
Battalion commanders	235	9	2	101	104	17	2
Battalion chiefs of staff	202	—	—	65	108	29	—
Company (squadron, battery) commanders	807	2	—	161	471	168	5
Platoon commanders	2959	—	1	106	1154	1642	56
Engineers	77	34	2	12	22	6	1
Technicians	830	6	—	31	402	349	43

Table compiled from TsAMO RF data, f. 131, op. 12951, d. 9, p. 60 and p. 60 reverse side

This table primarily illustrates the acute problem at the "grassroots" level of command—more than half of the armor platoon commanders were graduates of "other training establishments." In one case it was "courses for junior lieutenants and their equivalent" (1591 officers out of 1642). This meant they had not received a full course of special military education; however, these were the people who would have to directly organize combat training in lower-level units, supervise it, and monitor the depth and quality of the training.

Beyond that, a comparison of the "Company Commanders" and the "Platoon Commanders" line points to the underlying problem with the Army's growth that was still "dormant" on January 1, 1941: the lines from company commander up show a normal staff structure—at first, graduates of military schools predominate among commanders; then, as we go up the duty chain, the number of advanced officer school graduates increases, and, as it should be, slots are occupied by graduates of military academies (the table shows that there were two military academy graduates even among company commanders: one was a graduate of a mechanization and motorization academy, and one had graduated from an artillery academy). However, graduates of junior lieutenant courses would not be sent to a military school as they moved to higher positions—it was thought that the junior lieutenants's courses gave them the minimum knowledge and skills needed. Accordingly, as the graduates of "junior lieutenant courses and their equivalent" move to higher positions without undergoing additional training, they receive opportunities to become company commanders. And that was already occurring in the spring of 1941 as the "spring" wave of mechanized corps was being formed.

We would like to illustrate the situation before the war began with the following table showing the armor personnel strength in the Kiev Special Military District as of June 1, 1941:

Category	As of January 1, 1941	As of June 1, 1941	Change
Officers	10,288	16,748	6460
NCOs	16,351	32,465	16,114
First-year enlisted	52,123	143,740	91,617
Second-year enlisted	26,407	53,617	27,210
Third-year enlisted	274	358	84
Total enlisted	**86,769**	**197,741**	**110,972**

Table compiled from TsAMO RF data, f. 131, op. 12951, d. 9, sheets 33, 70

Within half a year, the number of armor officers had increased by 50% and the number of NCOs doubled, whereas the number of first-year recruits, who were most in need of training and monitoring, had almost tripled. The number of "old-timers" also failed to grow in proportion to the number of first-year soldiers (doubling as opposed to tripling). This situation clearly did not help solve the complex problems of training the personnel of the rapidly growing armor forces and assimilating the new tanks.

Next to receive T-34s were the 5th Tank Division of the 3rd Mechanized Corps of the Baltic Special Military District and the 7th Tank Division of the 6th Mechanized Corps of the Western Special Military District. Once again, these were "old" divisions formed in the summer of 1940. And, again, the reports on these divisions closely resemble those of the 4th Mechanized Corps and the 12th Tank Division that we reviewed above:

I enclose herewith a report on the equipment, gun armament and munitions, POL, training manuals, and classrooms in the inventory of the 3rd Mechanized Corps as of 25 April 1941.

As is apparent from the accompanying numerical data, the corps is seriously short of combat and support vehicles, which significantly reduces its fighting strength and

An 8th Tank Division T-34 that became stuck in a building during a retreat near Nemirov. (N 50.104001, E 23.442619)◊

striking power. The corps is ready for deployment with the matériel it currently has on hand.

The corps is currently experiencing a great deal of turnover, both in the junior ranks and among senior officers, which adversely affects the performance of its units as a whole. Decisive action is needed to stabilize the command staff.

The overall rating of the command staff is no better than satisfactory, and the ratings of platoon and company commanders are even lower, especially in motorized rifle regiments, because the platoons are led by junior commanders.

Vehicle parks and parking equipment of the 3rd Mechanized Corps

Most of the corps equipment is located in the open. Only the 84th Motorized Rifle Division and the 2nd Tank Division have partially covered parking. The most unfavorable (visible to outsiders) location of vehicle parks is in the 5th Tank Division, where the equipment is in an open area with a railroad and the Alitus Station on one side and the Alitus-Orany Highway on the other. Moreover, both the railway and the highway pass close to the vehicle park. None of the parks for storage and maintenance of vehicles in the corps' units have the equipment required by regulation for vehicle servicing and operation. All units have water and oil heaters that they constructed themselves, but rapid fueling of vehicles is hampered by the lack of the necessary quantity of fueling equipment (buckets, funnels)....

Classroom Availability

The 5th Tank Division has seven classrooms for weapons training, eight for mechanical training, 11 radio communications classrooms, and two classrooms for tank gunnery training.

Personnel Strength of the 5th Tank Division

Soldier category	Authorized strength	Number on hand
Top officers	2	2
Senior officers	52	52
Junior officers	625	525
Political officers	160	146
Administrative staff	107	82
Technical staff	235	194
Medical staff	69	51
Legal staff	4	3
NCOs	2,172	1,626
Enlisted	6,449	7,193

Table compiled from TsAMO RF data, f. 38, op. 11353, d. 898, p. 153

Training Equipment and Manuals

Manuals and visual aids in 5th Tank Division units are available in the following percentages: mechanical training 20%, weapons training 30%, tactical and topographical training 15%, physical training—with projectiles 10%, CW training 10%, engineer training 25%.

Training Grounds and Firing Ranges

The division's situation with regard to firing ranges has deteriorated with its current stationing in one location (Alitus). The division mainly uses the Oransky training ground, where units of the 29th Lithuanian Corps go for field training. The training ground is 40 km distant from the division's location. Other than small parcels of land, there are no training sites.[366]

And again we have a familiar picture—a definite shortage of junior officers and NCOs, who were overburdened by an excess of enlisted soldiers.

Educational Levels of the 5th Tank Division

Category	Higher	Secondary	Incomplete secondary	Elementary
Top officers	2	—	—	—
Top officers	6	10	29	7
Junior officers	1	154	209	161
Political officers	2	42	57	45
Administrative staff	—	19	31	32
Technical staff	4	47	84	59
Medical staff	18	20	13	—
Legal staff	2	1	—	—
NCOs	49	282	542	753
Enlisted	59	729	1,618	4,787

Table compiled from TsAMO RF data, f. 38, op. 11353, d. 898, p. 153

Once again, the picture looks familiar—a majority of the NCOs had received an elementary school education and had to train enlisted soldiers "educated" at the same level, without textbooks. It is not difficult to predict the poor quality of the training.

Number of Hours Drivers of the 5th Tank Division Spent Driving as of April 24, 1941

	Up to 2 hours	Up to 3 hours	Up to 5 hours	Up to 10 hours	Over 10 hours	Total
Driver-mechanics	210	94	57	52	151	564

Table compiled from TsAMO RF data, f. 38, op. 11353, d. 898, p. 164

Most driver-mechanics had practiced driving for no more than three hours. The division had only received its "thirty-fours" in February, of course. Nevertheless, the amount of driving experience the driver-mechanics had received inspires no optimism, especially when we consider that 44 of the 50 T-34s were in mothballs, and the training pool was allocated only six vehicles[37] for 50 crews to use in honing their driving skills. We might, of course, cheer ourselves up by assuming that only the best crews with extensive driving experience were assigned to T-34s, but there is good reason to doubt this favorable picture: in April 1941, representatives of the Kirov Factory inspected the KV tanks belonging to the 2nd Tank Division—"neighbors" of the 3rd Mechanized Corps' 5th Tank Division. Although the 3rd Tank Regiment, whose vehicles were inspected, had 90 driver-mechanics with over 10 hours experience driving the 27 KVs present, the report submitted by the Kiev Factory representatives stated: "The drivers receive very little practical driving experience. Some drivers have driven 300 m in a KV...."[388] It is difficult to imagine that the driving experience of the 3rd Mechanized Corps' driver-mechanics amounted to a few hundred meters, whereas the T-34s were driven "all out," with each driver accumulating dozens of hours of practical driving time.

We should consider a couple of numbers before reviewing the report on the 6th Mechanized Corps of the Western Special Military District. As of early May 1941, the corps had 70 T-34 tanks (all in the 7th Tank Division), of which 70 were deemed first category vehicles.[399] That is, all of the "thirty-fours" were firmly in mothballs. And in the rest of the report, the 6th Mechanized Corps in no wise stood out from other similar units. In the 7th Tank Division:

> *The vehicles are stored under canvas in the open. The training ground (Zelenoye) has too few dugouts and devices for use in firing on moving targets. There are no [division] classrooms due to lack of space. There is a shortage of training manuals: there are no instructions for the T-34 and KV tanks or the new weapons. Nor do they have the Infantry Field Manual, Part II; the Armor Field Manual, Part II; or the Staff Field Service Manual. The new rear service manual is missing. There are no visual aids for the new weapons models.*[40]

The story here is the same as before: the vehicles were mothballed and standing in the open, and their crews could not be fully trained because they lacked manuals.

The following table lists the 7th Tank Division's personnel strength:

Category	Authorized strength	Number on hand
Senior officers	2	2
Junior officers	83	77
NCOs	943	801
Engineer personnel	32	19
Technical staff	181	156
NCOs	2,171	1,844
Enlisted	6,465	6,671

Table compiled from TsAMO RF data, f. 38, op. 11353, d. 899, pp. 126–127

Everything is familiar here, too: the division had a shortage of NCOs and junior officers and an excess of enlisted soldiers. No data is available on the educational levels of the 7th Tank Division's officers; in general, tank regiments in mechanized corps with 585 men had 12 junior officers who had received a higher education, 148 with a secondary school education, 265 in the 7–9 grade group, and 155 in the 1–6 grade group. Of NCOs and enlisted personnel, these numbers were 250, 876, 2392, and 3768, respectively.[41] Once again, the picture looks very familiar—officers and NCOs with nominal educations had to train enlisted soldiers who were even less well educated with an acute shortage of training manuals, and they could only look at the new tanks—provided the top brass accepted the responsibility.

To that we should add that crews "rotated" in order to get at least some experience driving the new tanks. For example, the 7th Tank Division reported on a practical driving exercise with 12 KV tanks by listing the amount of time driver-mechanics spent operating the vehicles; out of 12 KV driver-mechanics, two had 6 hours of practice each driving a T-34[42]—but in the "stormy month of June" they went to battle as KV crews! The precious service life of the new equipment was not used efficiently.

We could quote from reports on all of the other units that received the newest equipment, but it would add nothing to picture we have painted. The month and a half that passed between early May and the war's beginning was obviously not time enough to correct so many major lapses, problems, and shortcomings. Under the circumstances, the accelerated "pumping up" of the border military districts with the latest equipment during the April–June 1941 timeframe unfortunately afforded the invaders interesting backdrops for the "dramatically heroic" photographs they sent back to the fatherland.

The assimilation of the new tanks was also complicated by the fact that it was necessary to do it literally blind, by touch, using the "educated guess method": the operating instructions and field repair manuals for the new tanks that the units complained about lacking simply did not exist. The Kubinka R&D Tank Proving Ground was not tasked with developing maintenance and field repair manuals for the T-34, KV, and T-40 tanks until early 1941, and they were given a November 1941 deadline for completing them. Monthly reports by the Scientific Institute for Armored Equipment (NIBT), the research and development institute responsible for testing armored vehicles, showed steady progress being made in drafting the manual for field repair and maintenance. The June 3, 1941, list of NIBT operations for June predicted that the T-40 manual would

A T-34 and a BT from an unknown unit, summer of 1941.

be 40% finished by July 1, and the manuals for the T-34 and KV would be 30% complete.[43] The commanders of the combat units that had received the new tanks could only report a disconcerting reality:

Units have experienced numerous mishaps with the diesel engines in the A-7M and A-34 vehicles and the Voroshilovets tractors due to failure to follow the basic rules for operation and maintenance of the V-2 engines.

For example, cylinder heads and sometimes engine blocks cracked during the winter of 1940–41.

During a 4-month period in 1941, the cylinders in 24 engines melted or partially melted.

The main reason for engines cracking was the failure of maintenance personnel to check the water system.

Water was removed from engines while cold, contrary to operating instructions.

The melting and partial melting of cylinders occurred for the following reasons:

Engine started with the oil valve closed.

Engine started without prelubricating the engine and achieving the required pressure.

Engine operated at elevated RPMs after starting and vehicle driven without warming up the engine.

Oil not drained out of the oil system from the tank to the oil pump in winter after cutting off the engine.

Engine operated on fuels that do not meet specifications. For example, a Voroshilovets tractor in unit 7816 was fueled with motor oil.

Low level of maintenance personnel training due to the lack of the correct number of instruction manuals, descriptions, and visual aids for diesel engines.[44]

Use of the wrong kind of oil for fuel, however, was only the beginning. There were worse incidents, like the one on May 23, 1941, in the 6th Mechanized Corps of the Western Special Military District, when tankers caused the breakdown of five T-34 tanks at once to the point where they needed major repair by attempting to run them on gasoline instead of diesel fuel[45]—which, incidentally, is an excellent illustration of how well one of the Red Army's most powerful mechanized corps was prepared for battle one month before the war.

In fairness, we should mention that sometimes the fuel and oil themselves turned out to be "wrong for the system":

SECRET
6 May 1941
To: Chief, Red Army Amor Directorate,
Military Engineer 1st Class Korobkov
Dep. People's Commissar of Medium Machine
Building Goreglyad

I have received a letter from a sergeant serving with unit 4141[46] *and several dispatches from factory inspectors with military units in the cities of Stryi, Lvov, and Zlochev, among others, informing me of difficulty starting and operating the V-2-34,*

V-2-K, and the V2-V diesel engines[477] *due to failure to follow operating instructions and maintain the engines.*

Almost all of the diesel engines in Stryi were run using Drogobych gas oil, which does not meet specifications. The constituents of Drogobych gas oil include:

a) *A high percentage of paraffin compounds*
b) *Water and mechanical impurities*
c) *A high percentage of ash and gum.*

When the unit located in Zlochevsk fueled diesel engines, filtration screens were used to filter the fuel instead of silk fabric (as required by the specifications), and in some cases fuel tanks were filled without the use of filtration.

In drawing your attention to these facts, I request that you take immediate steps to instruct the units in the proper fueling of diesel engines and prevent the use of fuels that do not meet the specifications stipulated in the instructions for care of diesel engines.

Chief Engineer Nevyazhsky, Factory No. 75[478]

Still, it should be noted that unsuitable grades of Drogobych gas oil did not excuse gross violations of fueling regulations.

The units intensified combat training as the new equipment arrived—and the numerous tanks that were used for training naturally began to break down, and design flaws that had been "dormant" while they were in storage began to emerge:

To: Military Engineer 2nd Class Kozyrev,
District Engineer of GABTU,
Factory No. 183
10 June 1941

By 20 June 1941, report the causes of breakdowns and actions taken by the factory in response to the following complaints by military units:

Vehicle type	Unit	District	Date of breakdown
T-34 – 4 vehicles	Armor school	Kharkov	17 May 1941
T-34 – 3 vehicles	Armor school	Kharkov	21 May 1941
T-34	7th Tank Regiment, 4th Tank Division, 6th Mechanized Corps	Western Special	12 May 1941
T-34	7th Tank Regiment, 4th Tank Division, 6th Mechanized Corps	Western Special	16 May 1941
T-34 – 26 vehicles	7th Tank Regiment, 4th Tank Division, 6th Mechanized Corps	Western Special	17 May 1941
T-34	11th Tank Division, 2nd Mechanized Corps	Odessa	16 May 1941
T-34	11th Tank Division, 2nd Mechanized Corps	Odessa	23 May 1941

T-34 tanks captured by the enemy while being transported by rail.

Illustrations from the German manual of infantry tactics for use against tanks. It shows how to disable a tank by placing a grenade cluster on the protective screen over the engine compartment and how to blow up the engine with a single hand grenade

Abbildung 18.

Eine solche geballte Ladung wirkt nicht auf die Panzerung oder Gleisketten mittlerer und schwerer Panzerkampfwagen, doch kann der Schalldruck einer auf Turmdeckel oder auf Bugfront gelegten Ladung die Besatzung vorübergehend betäuben.

38. Da häufig bei fahrenden Panzerkampfwagen die Entlüftungsklappen auf der Heckabdeckung geöffnet sind, bietet sich nach Zerstörung des Drahtgitters mit Stiefel oder Werkzeugen die Möglichkeit, den Motor durch hineingeworfene Handgranaten zu beschädigen bzw. in Brand zu setzen. (Siehe Abb. 19a u. b.)

Zur Zerstörung der Waffen werden Stiel- und Eihandgranaten sinngemäß nach Ziff. 36 verwendet.

b) Brandmittel.

39. Das Inbrandsetzen von Panzerkampfwagen ist schwierig und in der Regel nur möglich, wenn Panzerkampfwagen bereits durch andere Mittel kampfunfähig

Abbildung 19 a und b.

Take urgent action to repair the vehicles listed.

I also call your attention to the frequent instances of transmission gear tooth failure and warping of the third and fourth gear vertical transmission driveshafts and request urgent action to remedy the problems."[49]

As of June 1, 1941, the Red Army's armor forces had 892 T-34 tanks (832 of them in border districts). Of those, 845 "thirty-fours" belonged to the first category of "new tanks that have never been operated, meet the specifications, and are entirely suitable for use as intended." And only 46 tanks fell in the second category of "vehicles that have been (or currently are) in operation, are fully functional, and are suitable for use as intended. This category includes equipment in need of first-echelon maintenance (routine maintenance)." One additional "thirty-four" fell in the third category and was undergoing intermediate overhaul in a district shop.[50]

That essentially meant that at most 50 "thirty-fours" were used for combat training. How many crews could have been trained on the new tanks using just that many tanks? At best, two or three per tank—engine life did not allow for more. In 1941, the engine was barely able to run for 100 hours on a test stand, and in the unskilled hands of an inexperienced driver-mechanic it would have had a much shorter lifespan. And a replacement could not be counted on—diesel engine production was a bottleneck. After a year and a half, industry had provided only 85 spare engines, and by June 1941 all that the depots had left were the receipts saying they had been received. Most of the crews for the new tanks had to master the equipment entrusted to them after the war began—and not under "simulated combat conditions," but while real bombs were falling and shells flying. The outcome of this training for the new tanks, which were like fruit that had not yet ripened, and their inexperienced crews was exactly what one might expect—for example, the 8th Mechanized Corps of the Kiev Special Military District, which had 100 "thirty-fours" when the war began, left 5 on post and another 40 by the side of the road when they broke down. But the tankers under Major General Ryabyshev were relatively lucky—the T-34s underwent their very first driving test on the dusty roads of Ukraine and not under the antitank guns of German divisions.

However, the difficulties with mastering the new tanks were just one of the major problems that Soviet tankers faced.

One man in the field is no warrior—this proverb applies as well to tank crews as to the knights of old. Even if a knight has great strength and powerful armor, and instead of a horse carrying him into battle he has a firebreathing 500 hp engine, eventually the enemy's "flaming arrows" of armor-piercing shells will snap his tracks and pierce his turret, and the enemy will haul his defeated wonder-tank back home to measure the thickness of its armor. In real combat, therefore, as opposed to a fairytale battle, sappers need to clear a path through minefields; aircraft need to provide cover for tanks on the move, as well as columns of trucks carrying food and shells for them; artillerymen need to be ready to fire on enemy antitank guns; and infantrymen need to stay close to the tanks and make sure that intrepid enemy soldiers do not leap onto them with grenades or cans of gasoline. And ideally, of course, a tank attacks not alone, but in company with other tanks, and the more the better. There are many "need to's"—but such are the rules of the brutal game called "war."

In the summer of 1941, however, the only "need to" available was the one that called for having a large number of tanks on the battlefield—that, and courageous crews. The situation with logistics, air cover, and artillery, and infantry support was much worse. The surprise enemy attack meant the Soviet mechanized corps did not have time to receive the support equipment owed them by the national economy in time of war. Without civilian trucks and tractors, infantry and artillery units could not keep up with the tanks and remained behind the lines—and attempts to break through German defenses with tanks alone, without infantry support and suppressive fire on the enemy's howitzer and antitank artillery, usually ended sadly for the even most "impenetrable" tanks. Poor understanding of their equipment prevented crews from fixing even minor malfunctions themselves, and the disastrous shortage of spare parts and repair equipment meant that many tanks broke down before they even reached the enemy and could not be repaired. And then there were the disabled tanks that could have been towed away, repaired, and returned to battle—had the field of battle not remained in enemy hands. Added to this was the shortage of fuel and armor-piercing shells for the new tanks and—most importantly—the inability to fight on equal terms with the army that then was the world's best.

NOTES

1 A. V. Suvorov.

2 TsAMO RF, f. 16, op. 2154, d. 4, pp. 35–44. Cit. ex: *Collection: "The Year 1941": In 2 vols.* Moscow: International Foundation "Democracy," 1998, Vol. 2, p 537.

3 *Strength of the Armed Forces of the USSR during the Great Patriotic War (1941–1945). Statisticheskiy sbornik, No. 1 (June 22, 1941).* Moscow: Institute of General History, Ministry of Defense, Russian Federation, 1994, p. 135.

4 TsAMO RF, f. 38 (GABTU), op. 11353 (Red Army Armor and Mechanized Force Command Staff), d. 979 (References, diagrams, and reports of the Red Army armor and mechanized force staff concerning armies, units, and institutions; matériel production, technical condition, state of repair, and losses; shipments; authorized personnel strength; current personnel strength and losses; and number of officers with higher education during 1941–1944), pp. 26, 27.

5 TsAMO RF, f. 38 (GABTU), op. 11353 (Armor and Mechanized Force Command Staff), d. 865 (Reports and information about the numbers and condition of matériel in units), pp. 135, 136.

6 TsAMO RF, f. 38 (GABTU), op. 11355 (Tank Directorate), d. 13 (Armor Directorate plans for distribution of combat vehicles by district; reports and information from military representatives on completion of planned armored vehicle orders by factories and numbers of tanks in the Red Army by year of production), p. 136, "Report on T-34 tank shipments to districts as of 9 April 1941."

7 TsAMO RF, f. 38 (GABTU), op. 11353 (Red Army Armor and Mechanized Force Command Staff), d. 865 (Reports and information about the numbers and condition of matériel in units), pp. 147, 148.

8 TsAMO RF, f. 38 (GABTU), op. 11355 (GABTU), op. 11355 (Tank Directorate), d. 24 (Report of inspection of fracture behavior in T-34 armor parts in service in the Kiev and Baltic Special Military Districts; correspondence with NN regarding drawings), p. 38.

9 TsAMO RF, f. 38 (GABTU), op. 11355 (Tank Directorate), d. 24 (Report of inspection of fracture behavior in T-34 armor parts in service in the Kiev and Baltic Special Military Districts, correspondence with NN regarding drawings), pp. 55–83.

10 *Tank Drivers Training Course.* Moscow: Voyenizdat, 1941, pp. 8–12.

11 TsAMO RF, f. 38 (GABTU), op. 11355 (Tank Directorate), d. 13 (Armor Directorate plans for distribution of combat vehicles by district; reports and information from military representatives on completion of planned armored vehicle orders by factories and numbers of tanks in the Red Army by year of production), p. 51–52, "Letter of explanation for the 1941 combat vehicle distribution plan."

12 Ibid., p. 136, "Report on T-34 tank shipments to districts as of 9 April 1941."

13 TsAMO RF, f. 38 (GABTU), op. 11353 (Armor and Mechanized Force Command Staff), d. 908 (GABTU report on completion of planned orders for weapons and equipment), p. 12, "List of arms and equipment shipped during January 1941."

14 Ibid., p. 26, "List of arms and equipment shipped during February 1941.

15 Ibid., p. 41 "Information on shipments of weapons and equipment during March 1941; TsAMO RF, f. 38 (GABTU), op. 11355 (Tank Directorate), d. 13 (Armor Directorate plans for distribution of combat vehicles by district; reports and information from military representatives on completion of planned armored vehicle orders by factories and numbers of tanks in the Red Army by year of production), p. 136, "Summary of shipments of T-34 tanks to districts as of 9 April 1941."

16 TsAMO RF, f. 38 (GABTU), op. 11355 (Tank Directorate), d. 32 (Report of the GABTU Military Representative on factory No. 183's completion of orders for manufacture of tanks and equipment), p. 214 (reverse side), "Report on tank shipments during 1–10 April 1941."

17 TsAMO RF, f. 38 (GABTU), op. 11353 (Armor and Mechanized Force Command Staff), d. 920 (GABTU summaries on number of combat and support vehicles shipped from factories), pp. 16, 21 (reverse side), 23, 25, 26.

18 TsAMO RF, f. 38 (GABTU), op. 11355 (Tank Directorate), d. 30 ("Dispatches, information, and summaries of Stalingrad Tractor Plant concerning tank production"), p. 190 (reverse side), "Information on tank shipments during 1–10 April 1941."

19 TsAMO RF, f. 38 (GABTU), op. 11353 (Armor and Mechanized Force Command Staff), d. 920 (GABTU summaries regarding number of combat and support vehicles shipped from factories), p. 25, "Reference about combat and support vehicles shipped from 21–29 April 1941."

20 TsAMO RF, f. 38 (GABTU), op. 11353 (Armor and Mechanized Force Command Staff), d. 920 (GABTU summaries regarding number of combat and support vehicles shipped from factories), pp. 27–31; TsAMO RF, f. 38 (GABTU), op. 11355 (Tank Directorate), d. 264 (Information and summaries of the armor directorate about planned deliveries of combat vehicles and spare parts, and about armor systems at factories and warehouses), pp. 51, 55.

21 TsAMO RF, f. 38 (GABTU), op. 11355 (Tank Directorate), d. 264 (Armor Directorate information and summaries about planned deliveries of combat vehicles and spare parts, and about armor systems at factories and warehouses), pp. 62–63.

22 Hoth's 3rd Panzer Group initiated battle in the Baltic Special Military District's area of responsibility after moving into the Western Special Military District's area at the start of the war.

23 TsAMO RF, f. 38 (GABTU), op. 11353 (Red Army Armor and Mechanized Force Command Staff), d. 896 (Reports, dispatches, and summaries of the Kiev Special Military District, and units concerning matériel numbers, status, operation, and repair, authorized and present personnel strength, formation progress, inventory, and combat readiness of units), pp. 40–42.

24 To be absolutely precise and to the point, 13 of the 32nd Tank Division's T-34s were stored under roof, and the remainder were in the open. TsAMO RF, f. 38 (GABTU), op. 11353 (Red Army Armor and Mechanized Force Command Staff), d. 896 (Reports, dispatches, and summaries of the Kiev Special Military District and units concerning matériel numbers, status, operation, and repair, authorized and present personnel strength, formation progress, inventory, and combat readiness of units), p. 86.

25 TsAMO RF, f. 38 (GABTU), op. 11353 (Red Army Armor and Mechanized Force Command Staff), d. 896 (Reports, dispatches, and summaries of the Kiev Special Military District and units concerning matériel numbers, status, operation, and repair, authorized and present personnel strength, formation progress, inventory, and combat readiness of units), pp. 107–108.

26 Ibid., p. 52.

27 Ibid., p. 87.

28 See the Appendix for a complete copy.

29 Relative to authorized strength.

30 TsAMO RF, f. 38 (GABTU), op. 11353 (Red Army armor and mechanized force command staff), d. 896 (Reports, dispatches, and summaries of the Kiev Special Military District and units concerning matériel numbers, status, operation, and repair, authorized and present personnel strength, formation progress, inventory, and combat readiness of units), pp. 112–122.

31 Part one of the Infantry Field Manual regulates the actions of individual soldiers, squads, platoons, and companies. Part two of the Infantry Field Manual regulates the actions of battalions and regiments.

32 TsAMO RF, f. 131 (Kiev Special Military District), op. 12980 (Armored Force Directorate), d. 3 (Reports of the district's units regarding the status of military and political training in units), pp. 72–81.

33 TsAMO RF, f. 38 (GABTU), op. 11353 (Red Army Armor and Mechanized Force Command Staff), d. 896 (Reports, dispatches, and summaries of the Kiev Special Military District and units concerning matériel numbers, status, operation, and repair, authorized and present personnel strength, formation progress, inventory, and combat readiness of units), p. 125.

34 "Historical and statistical study of the qualitative and quantitative condition of the Red Army's tank fleet prior to the Great Patriotic War," Voyenno-istoricheskiy zhurnal, No. 11, 1993.

35 See document 11 in the Appendix.

36 TsAMO RF, f. 38 (GABTU), op. 11353 (Red Army Armor and Mechanized Force Command Staff), d. 898 (Reports, dispatches, and summaries of the Moscow Military District, the Baltic Special Military District, and units concerning matériel numbers, status, operation, and repair, authorized and present personnel strength, formation progress, inventory, and combat readiness of units), pp. 156–162.

37 Ibid., p. 195.

38 TsAMO RF, f. 38 (GABTU), op. 11355 (Tank Directorate), d. 15 (Reports, dispatches, and summaries of GABTU military representatives regarding factory operations to produce KV tanks), p. 132 (reverse side).

39 TsAMO RF, f. 38 (GABTU), op. 11353 (Red Army Armor and Mechanized Force Command Staff), d. 899 (Reports, dispatches, and summaries of the Western Special Military District, Orlov Military District, and units concerning matériel numbers, status, operation, and repair, authorized and present personnel strength, formation progress, inventory, and combat readiness of units), p. 33.

40 Ibid., pp. 101–103.

41 Ibid., p. 124.

42 TsAMO RF, f. 38 (GABTU), op. 11355 (Tank Directorate), d. 15 (Reports, dispatches, and summaries of GABTU military representatives regarding factory operations to produce KV tanks), p. 187.

43 TsAMO RF, f. 38 (GABTU) op. 11355 (Tank Directorate), d. 12 (Plans, reports, dispatches, and certificates of the Red Army GABTU and measurement station regarding the progress of testing performed on armor equipment, inventory, and condition of vehicles, tractors, and trailers), pp. 47, 307.

44 TsAMO RF, f. 38 (GABTU), op. 11355 (Tank Directorate), d. 138 (Reports and correspondence of GABTU regional engineers concerning deliveries and engine tests), p. 118.

45 M. N. Svirin, *The Tank Might of the USSR [Tankovaya moshch' SSSR].* Moscow: Yauza, Eksmo, 2009, p. 333.

46 10th Tank Division, 15th Mechanized Corps. The full text of the letter is provided in the Appendix.

47 Installed on the T-34, KV, and Voroshilovets, respectively.

48 TsAMO RF, f. 38 (GABTU), op. 11355 (Tank Directorate), d. 138 (Reports and correspondence of GABTU regional engineers concerning deliveries and engine tests), p. 110.

49 TsAMO RF, f. 38 (GABTU), op. 11355 (Tank Directorate), d. 233 (Dispatches of GABTU military representatives on factory operations to produce and test tanks and equipment; Armor Directorate contracts with factories and bulletins on tank and equipment deliveries), p. 334.

50 *Strength of the Armed Forces of the USSR during the Great Patriotic War (1941–1945). Statisticheskiy sbornik, No. 1 (June 22, 1941).* Moscow: Institute of General History, Ministry of Defense, Russian Federation, 1994, p. 132.

A T-34 stuck in a marshy meadow, summer of 1941.

CHAPTER 5. **BAPTISM BY FIRE**

An inch of foreign land we do not desire,
But we'll not give up a mile of ours.[1]

At dawn on June 22, 1941, to the accompaniment of exploding bombs and shells, angular gray vehicles with black and white crosses on their armor crossed the Soviet-German border. Their crews genuinely believed that the Führer's genius would bring them another quick and easy victory, because the backward Bolshevist industry could offer nothing to equal the best creations of Aryan engineers. Toward them from military garrisons and field camps rolled 450 battle-gray tanks, and their crews also were convinced that the Red Army of the world's first worker and peasants's state would crush the invading enemy with "little bloodshed and a mighty blow,"[2] and then finish "on foreign soil" what he had started. Few then, in the first hours of the war, could have imagined that the conflict would drag on for four long, bloody years.[3] Moreover, few could have guessed what the next few days would bring.

Before describing scenes of battle, the authors would like to say a few words about the sources that we drew on for our research. The heavy military defeats suffered by the Red Army at the beginning of the war, the destruction of many encircled units (often with all of their documents), and the chaos and confusion caused by the sudden-

Illustrations from the German manual of infantry tactics for use against tanks. Destruction of a tank gun by throwing a grenade with a weight attached over it.

Abbildung 2.

ness of the enemy's attack and the rapid advance of German forces meant that reports covering combat operations are very superficial, terse, fragmented, and frequently not very reliable; and many battles involving the new tanks were not described at all. For example, the archive of the 6th Mechanized Corps—one of the Red Army's most powerful—includes the following documents: servicemember evaluations, autobiographies, specifications, service records; officer duty rosters for the corps, the 4th Tank Division, and the 7th and 8th Tank Regiments; and support staff officer rosters (communications, chemical defense, etc.) for the corps, the 4th Motorcycle Regiment, the 185th Independent Communications Battalion, and the 41st Engineer Battalion.

All other documents of the 6th Mechanized Corps and its headquarters were lost when the corps was encircled. All of the other documentary materials we consulted are originals or copies of official records that were sent to various authorities, which have retained them to the present day. The holdings of the 4th and 7th Tank Divisions of the 6th Mechanized Corps are similar.

Another example: Major General D. D. Lelyushenko, commander of the 21st Mechanized Corps, reported the following:

> *The equipment earmarked for me on plans of the Main Armored Force Directorate and the Main Artillery Directorate and sent to me has been intercepted by the 22nd Army's commander. At Velikiye Luki I lost 1,500 self-loading rifles, 126 trucks, 15 kitchen trucks, 28 76-mm guns, 22 KV tanks, 13 T-34s, several cars of spare parts, and 800 tire sets.*[4]

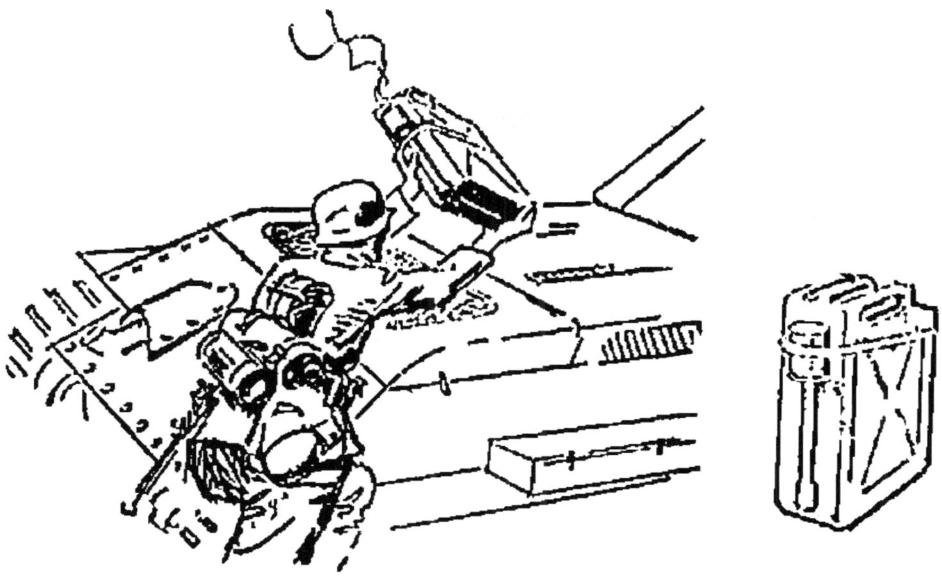

Abbildung 21.

c) Werkzeuge.

43. Für die Panzernahbekämpfung können auch schwere Hieb- und Schlaggeräte, wie Beile, Brecheisen, Montagehebel usw. bereitgelegt werden, um nicht fest verschlossene Luken und Klappen öffnen oder MG.-Läufe zerstören zu können. Für die Zerstörung von MG.-Läufen können auch dicke Steine oder Holzpfähle verwendet werden.

Rohrkrepierer können auch dadurch hervorgerufen werden, daß man Gegenstände, wie Holz, kleine Steine, Erde usw. in die Waffenmündungen steckt.

Illustrations from the German manual of anti-tank infantry tactics. How to disable a tank using a can of gasoline with a hand grenade attached.

The fate of those tanks remains unknown. At best, they went to the 48th Tank Division of the 22nd Army; at worst, they ended up in an improvised formation, about whose actions and fate nothing is known.

Meanwhile:

To: Col. Preysman, Chief, Armored Force Directorate, Northwest Axis. 11 August 1941. According to a GABTU message, 24 T-34 tanks were sent from Stalingrad to us at the Krasnoye Selo Station on July 19 on train No. 19/101. We still do not know where those vehicles went. We are in receipt of a telegram from GABTU requesting confirmation that we have received these vehicles. I hereby request that you send a query via

A T-34 of the 5th Tank Division near Alitus. This vehicle also appears in the photo on page 71.◊

the Northwestern Axis to learn when they were dispatched from the Krasnoyo Selo Station and to whom.[5]

We do not know whether he ever learned what happened to the train carrying the tanks; the recipient of the tanks remains unknown. Therefore, there is no information about the involvement of these "thirty-fours" in battles.

Available sources nevertheless allow us to shed light on actions involving "thirty-fours" during the summer of 1941.

The aggressor's illusions that his next blitzkrieg would be a "cakewalk" and that the "Russian armed forces were a clay colossus without a head"[6] started being shattered in the first hours of the war. In the Baltics on June 22, the 7th Panzer Division of the Wehrmacht's 3rd Panzer Group quickly reached the Lithuanian town of Alitus, 50 km from the border, by about noon. Despite being small, Alitus was a highly desirable objective for units of Hermann Hoth's 3rd Panzer Group—it had two bridges across the Nieman River, and capturing them could save the attackers a great deal of precious time and resources. The Germans managed to capture the bridges intact, but they failed to gain time—Hoth's tankers were met by units of Colonel F. F. Fedorov's 5th Tank Division from the 3rd Mechanized Corps. Two days before the war, it had 268 tanks, 50 of which were the new "thirty-fours."[7] If only they could reach the bridges before the Germans... An incident that occurred when German tanks crossed the northern bridge serves to illustrate what could have befallen the 7th Division's 25th Panzer Regiment: after about 20 German tanks had crossed the bridge, a Soviet tank fired on and disabled the next tank in a previously undetected ambush near the bridge. The Soviet tank that had given its position away withdrew despite fire from approximately 30 German 38(t) tanks, which made up the foundation of the 7th Panzer Division's tank fleet.[8] This episode was the Ghost Division's first encounter with a T-34.[9] Unfortunately, history does not like the subjunctive mood—instead of defending the water obstacle, the Soviet tankers were forced to attack an enemy already dug in on their side of the bridges.

If we were to go by just the tabular values of millimeters of armor that could be penetrated and armor thicknesses, the T-34s, even without the T-28s and BT-7s, should rapidly and without appreciable losses have routed the German panzer division, which, you may recall, was mainly equipped with former Czech 38(t)s. However, no "face-to-face," tank meeting engagement took place: in addition to the tanks, the 7th Panzer Division's motorized infantry and an antitank battalion equipped with twelve 50 mm antitank guns also went to Alitus. A heavy battle ensued that lasted for the remainder of the day. Attempts by the Germans to break out of their positions in front of the bridges and move further east alternated with Soviet counterattacks. The situation remained unchanged until evening, when another German panzer division—the 20th—arrived at the city. Only then were the Germans able to move forward from their position at the northern bridge, flanking the units of the 5th Tank Division engaged in the fight and pushing them towards the northeast. But that was a belated success—the "longest day of the year" came to an end, and darkness separated the opponents.

The outcome of the first battle was not reassuring for the 5th Tank Division. A total of 73 tanks were lost in the battle for Alitus. Of the 44 "thirty-fours" that took part in the fighting, 27 were lost. The German units reported a loss of 11 tanks. Their reports probably concerned irreplaceable losses—the field of battle remained in German hands; therefore, they did not need to count their "wounded pigeons" as complete losses. But the number of serviceable vehicles remaining in the 7th Panzer Division was reduced quite significantly—according to some sources, on June 27 it had no more than 150 tanks in its order of battle, and the 2nd Battalion of the 25th Panzer Regiment was disbanded as a result of heavy losses. According to German officers who took part in the Battle of Alitus, the fight with the Red Army's 5th Tank Division was the 7th Panzer Division's most complex battle since the beginning of World War II—and the Ghosts had taken part in the French campaign, during which the division participated in the breakthrough at the Meuse River and a tank engagement at Arras.

Then, at the very beginning, many people felt that little had been done, that the 5th Tank Division should have accomplished much more. Retreating under pressure from two German panzer divisions,[10] on June 24, 1941, remnants of the 5th Tank Division including 15 tanks (several of which were T-34s), 20 armored cars, and 9 guns, with a column of vehicles carrying wounded, reached the vicinity of the Western Front's 13th Army headquarters not far from Molodechno.

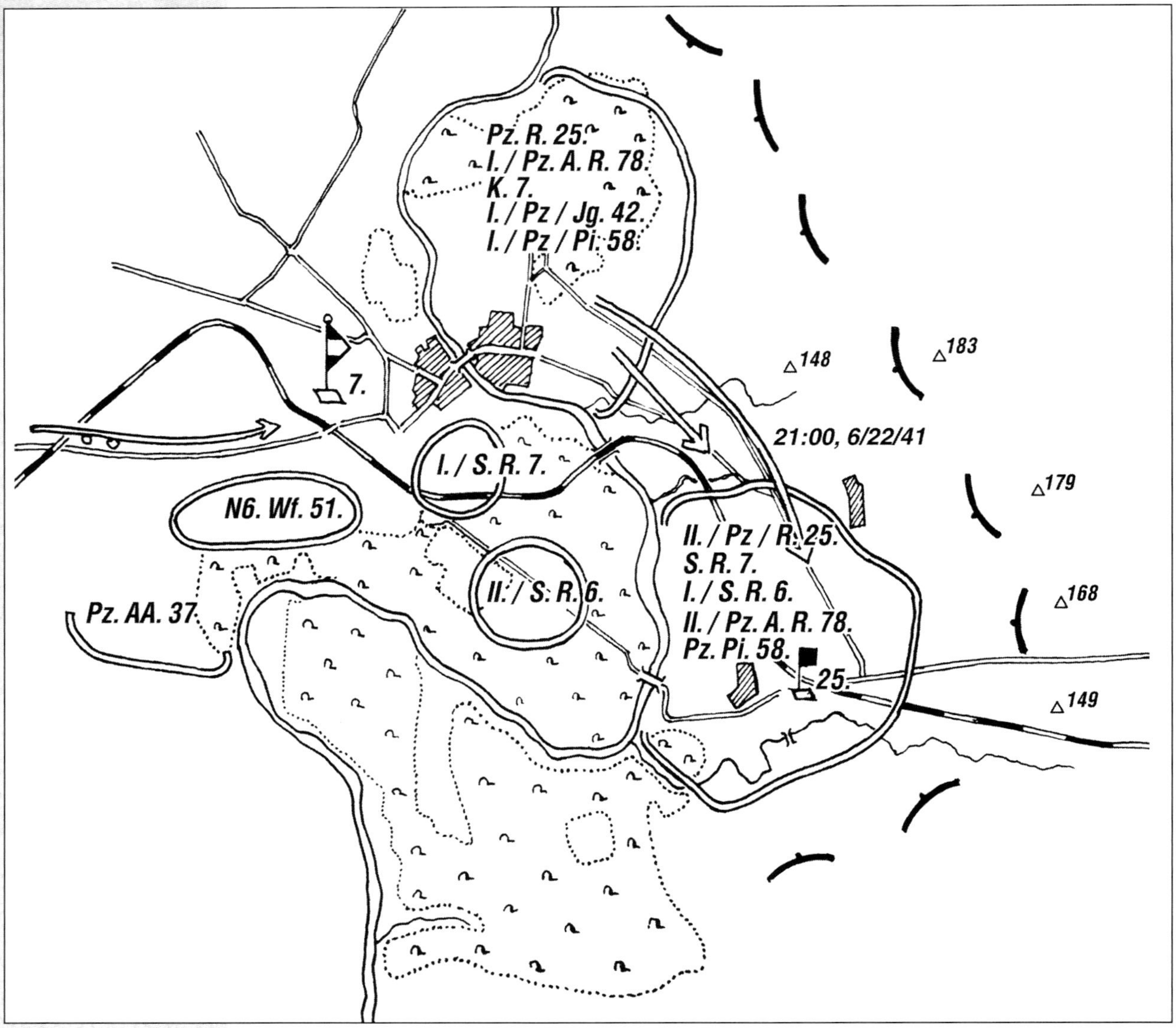

Forces deployed near Alitus the evening of June 22, 1941.

In a conversation with the army's commander, Lieutenant General P. M. Filatov, Colonel F. F. Fedorov talked in detail about the events in Lithuania. The gung ho tanker was depressed and ended by saying that he would 'have to pay with his head' for the enemy's capture of the bridges over the Nieman.[11]

Neither he nor the general knew then that the winning of 10 hours of daylight by the 5th Tank Division on the "longest day of the year," although temporary, and the reduction of an enemy panzer division's inventory by almost a half was a major accomplishment by the standards of the bloody summer of 1941. It was more than anyone else was able to accomplish in the fiery cauldron of fighting at the border.

In fairness, we should note that the 5th Tank Division had better luck with the conditions under which it fought than did others. The division had been stationed in Alitus before the war began, and the German tanks ran into Fedorov's "thirty-fours" there.

Therefore, the division's infantry and artillery took part in the battle for the bridges over the Nieman, and the 5th Tank Division did not need to travel hundreds of kilometers for the battle, leaving broken down tanks alongside of the road as they went. The situation was much worse for other Soviet tank units.

One of the clearest examples of this were the battles fought by the Western Front's 6th Mechanized Corps. We said earlier that the 6th Mechanized Corps was the most fully equipped mechanized corps; it had 322 "thirty-fours" and more than 1,000 tanks altogether.[12] That force should have been enough to greatly complicate life for Heinz Guderian's Panzer Group, which was attacking from the south of the Belostok salient, or sufficient to cut off the spearhead of Hoth's advancing 3rd Panzer Group with a powerful flanking counterattack. But that would have required what the modern reader would consider obvious, and what was dearer than gold that "fateful June"—knowledge of precisely where the German tanks were coming from, where they were going, and when they would do it.

Colonel F. F. Fedorov, 5th Tank Division commander

Unfortunately, on the first day of the war "accurate intelligence reports" stated that:

on the East Prussian axis, bounded by Suvalki and Haidenburg on the right and by Schuchen and Naidenburg on the left, the enemy attacked with five or six infantry divisions, two motorized divisions, two tank divisions, and ten artillery regiments towards Grodno and by 20:00 had captured Palnitsa, Novoselki, Novy Dvur, Guta, Grayevo, Kolno, and Staviski. Up to two panzer and two motorized divisions have broken through at the boundary with the Northwestern Front's army on the left flank on the Martsinkonis-Nacha axis.[13]

The picture was becoming very clear—the Germans would attack from the Suvalki salient toward the east and southeast, inserting a mobile group consisting of two panzer and two motorized divisions through a breakthrough near Grodno. The countermeasures were just as obvious—attack with a mobile group toward Grodno from the direction of Belostok and then move towards the northeast along the western bank of the Nieman River to defeat the German infantry providing flanking cover for the panzer spearhead moving eastward, and cut off and destroy the German mobile grouping that was breaking through. Unfortunately, the intelligence report by the Western Front was completely divorced from reality. Hoth's 3rd Panzer Group was actually advancing toward the north, in the Northwest Front's sector. Infantry divisions of the 9th Army were advancing in a dense formation from the southeast side of the Suvalki salient. Thus, instead of the proposed destruction of the panzer spearhead's covering force on the flank and disruption of maneuver operations on the western bank of the Nieman, Boldin's group was to push through the subunits of the German infantry divisions, which were supported by assault guns; fast, large-caliber, tractor-drawn artillery; and antiaircraft artillery from Luftwaffe motorized antiaircraft battalions. Frankly, the approach taken by Boldin's group, which included the 6th and 11th Mechanized Corps and the 36th Cavalry Division but no infantry or artillery, was poor. The Western Front knew virtually nothing about Guderian's 2nd Panzer Group, which was crossing the Bug River near Brest at the time.

A Pz.38(t) of the German 7th Panzer Division towing an auxilliary fuel tank trailer passing a burning T-34 of the Red Army's 5th Tank Division near Alitus, June 1941.

The 6th Mechanized Corps began having problems when Boldin's group began taking part in the counterattack. The Western Front's intelligence summary No. 1, which we quoted earlier, said, in part:

up to two enemy tank divisions reached the Bryansk-Boćki line by 17:30 and are engaged in fighting with the 6th and 13th Mechanized Corps.[14]

In order to intercept the enemy panzer division that was breaking through towards Belostok, units of the 6th Mechanized Corps were sent from their assembly areas on the west and southwest of Belostok to a staging area for a counterattack eastward from Belostok. Meanwhile, some forces were detached from the 4th Tank Division, leaving the 4th Tank Division to defend the Narew River with a motorized rifle regiment and an artillery regiment. This weakened the already modest infantry and artillery forces of Boldin's group even further. According to some reports, a motorized rifle regiment of the 7th Tank Division was also left at the Narew.

Actually, no German panzer division was breaking through toward Belostok; however, enemy aerial reconnaissance detected the movement of the Soviet mechanized units near Belostok, and columns of the 6th Mechanized Corps received heavy bombing. This is how Major General of Armor S. V. Borzilov, commander of the 7th Tank Division, described what happened in his report:[15]

At 22:00 on 22 June, the division received an order to move to a new assembly area—the Valila Station (east of Belostok) with the following mission—destroy a tank division that was breaking through in the vicinity of Belsk. In carrying out its order, the division encountered roads jammed with rear service units and citizens of Belostok retreating in disorder (everything was in chaos because no traffic control had been established). The division was constantly under attack by enemy aviation while on the march and in its assembly area from 04:00 until 09:00 and from 11:00 until 14:00 on 23 June 1941. The division took the following losses before 14:00 while on the march and while located in the assembly area: tanks—63 disabled and scattered by enemy aircraft; all regimental rear service units were crippled, especially those of the 13th Regiment. Steps have been taken to reassemble the scattered rear service units and tanks.[16]

M. G. Khatskilevich, 6th Mechanized Corps commander

German aircraft attacked columns of Soviet forces on the march virtually with impunity. The Western Front's air assets suffered heavy losses from attacks on airfields on the first day of the war, and antiaircraft battalions belonging to divisions of the 6th Mechanized Corps were located at a training range 120 km east of Minsk the day before the war started and were unable to return to their units. Only direct hits by bombs were a threat to the new T-34s and KVs, but the destruction of regimental rear service units described by Borzilov caused serious difficulties with supplying and supporting the corps. It did not bode well that the 6th Mechanized Corps had experienced a serious shortage of support equipment before the war…

There was no enemy tank division in the vicinity of Belsk; as a result, the division was not used. New information has been received: an enemy tank division has broken through between Grodno and Sokulka. At 14:00 on 23 June, the division received a new mission—move in the direction of Sokulka-Kuznitsa, destroy the tank division that has broken through, and assemble south of Grodno (approximately 140 km). In accomplishing its mission, the division concentrated on a line of attack to the south of Sokulka and Staroye Dubovoye during the morning of 24 June. Reconnaissance revealed that there was no enemy tank division, but there were small groups of tanks operating with infantry and cavalry.[17]

A 5th Tank Division T-34 tank near Alitus, June 1941.

A burned 8th Tank Division T-34 near Alitus, June 1941. The tank's turret was blown off by an internal explosion, and its road wheel tires burned..

Having lost about a day countering a nonexistent breakthrough by an imaginary enemy panzer division, the 6th Mechanized Corps units assembled in a staging area for a counterattack. However, the tank rally near Belostok greatly reduced the corps' already meager supply of fuel,[18] and the disrupted regimental rear service units inspired little optimism that more fuel would be forthcoming. According to statements by General of the Army D. G. Pavlov during the interrogation that followed his arrest and removal as commander of the Western Front, he received a message the evening of June 23 from I. V. Boldin stating that the 6th Mechanized Corps had only one quarter of the fuel it needed. The Western Front's fuel supply service sent the 6th Mechanized Corps 300 tons of fuel, but the fuel was only able to get as far as Baranovichi,[19] more than 150 km from the area where corps' units were assembled. Not surprisingly, Borzilov's report contained the wording "*...in general, we got what POL [Petroleum, Oil, Lubricants] we could.*"

Enemy aerial reconnaissance discovered a large number of Soviet tanks moving from Grodno towards Belostok. Germany's 162nd and 256th Infantry Divisions, which were located in the path of units of the 6th Mechanized Corps, had several hours to prepare their defenses, and the Soviet columns were bombed heavily by German aircraft. Tanks and motorized infantry of the 6th Mechanized Corps attacked on the afternoon[20] of June 24. The decisive attack caused panic in the ranks of the German units defending Sidra; abandoning the positions they had planned to use for an offensive the following day, the enemy's 162nd Infantry Division retreated to the north. However, the attacking Soviet tankers paid a rather high price for their success:

A disabled 5th Tank Division T-34 near Alitus, June 1941.

67 enemy tanks were destroyed in battles south of Grodno, including 20 by assault batteries, 20 by artillery, and 27 by antiaircraft guns. This information is preliminary; it is still being corrected.[21]

Early the next day,[22] June 25, 1941, units of the 6th Mechanized Corps resumed their bloody attacks in the general direction of Grodno; they lasted almost all morning. A shortage of artillery prevented suppression of enemy antitank artillery during the preparatory artillery bombardment for the attack; the attacking tanks had to take on that mission. The Germans noted that at about 10 AM attacking Soviet forces near the village of Poganitsa made a tactical breakthrough of the 162nd German Infantry Division's defenses; however, the 6th Mechanized Corps no longer had sufficient forces to exploit the breakthrough.

On 24–25 June, the division on order of the corps commander and Marshal Kulikov attacked with the 14th Tank Regiment at Stara Dubova and then Grodno, and with the 13th Tank Regiment it attacked Kuznitsa and then Grodno from the west, where up to two battalions of infantry and two artillery batteries were destroyed. After completing the mission, units of the division assembled in the vicinity of Kuznitsa and Stara Dubova, having lost 18 tanks burned and mired in swamps.[23]

S. V. Borzilov, commander of the 7th Tank Division, 6th Mechanized Corps.

Unfortunately, these 18 tanks were not the only ones lost by the 6th Mechanized Corps in general or by its 7th Tank Division. These are just the recorded losses—tanks lost before the division commander's eyes or tanks about whose loss the division headquarters was informed. German estimates of losses by attacking Red Army units were significantly higher: Soviet tanks disabled at Grodno from June 24–25 numbered as follows:

- 87 by units of the 256th Infantry Division;
- 56 by units of the 162nd Infantry Division;
- 21 by the 2nd Battalion of the Luftwaffe's 4th Antiaircraft Regiment; [24]
- 43 by aircraft of the 8th Air Corps.

In all, 207 tanks were knocked out. [25]

It is entirely possible that by that time the 6th Mechanized Corps' total losses were much higher: a battle dispatch by the Western Front's headquarters on the situation as of 16:45 on June 25 stated that, "according to the corps commander's report, losses have reached 50%." [26] It also said that "units of the 4th Tank Division report that they are out of ammunition."

Despite the losses sustained by the 6th Mechanized Corps and its shortage of fuel and ammunition, it remained a significant force, capable of continuing to hold the German infantry divisions near Grodno. [277] However… At dawn on June 24, as units of the 6th Mechanized Corps were moving towards their starting positions for an offensive, units of the Red Army's 155th Rifle Division broke up a small German vehicle column southwest of Slonim. Among other items captured, the victors got their hands on two maps, one of which was an operations map from the headquarters of the 2nd Panzer Group—it showed all three motorized corps of Guderian's Panzer Group. Another valuable day went by before the map finally reached the Western Front's headquarters. Only then could they understand and assess the real threat, and most importantly, where it was coming from. While the front's most powerful armored unit was fruitlessly battering the German infantry defenses at Grodno in a vain attempt to break through

Tank park of the 5th Tank Division in Alitus after capture by the enemy, June 1941. The photograph shows at least four T-34s.

A 5th Tank Division T-34 near Alitus, June 1941.

into a neighboring front's sector, enemy tank columns were racing almost unopposed towards Minsk. The situation needed to be corrected immediately:

To: 3rd and 10th Armies.
Commander, 6th Mechanized Corps.

Immediately discontinue battle and execute a forced march by night and day; assemble at Slonim.

Contact Golubev[288] *by radio and me directly. Initiate movement morning of the 26 and report upon arrival. Radio situation with fuel and ammunition.*

Pavlov. Fominykh. Klimovskikh.[299]

Whether Khatskilevich received the order to immediately break contact and was able to transmit his own order is unknown; meanwhile, the Western Front headquarters sent out a directive ordering a general withdrawal of the front's troops.

Figure 1. **Combat Operations in the Baltics, June 22–23, 1941**

Unit positions

— End of day, June 21, 1941

— End of day, June 22, 1941

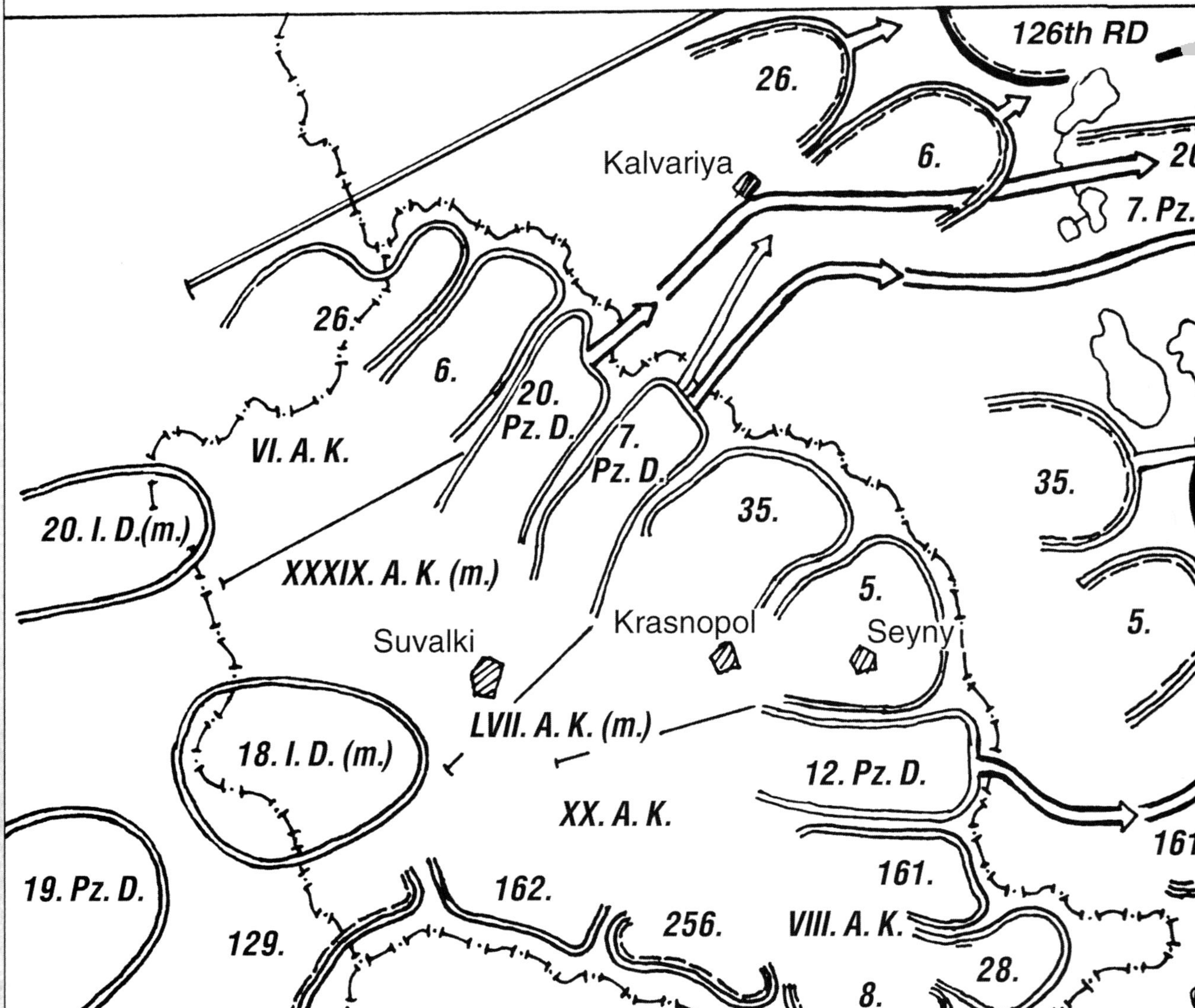

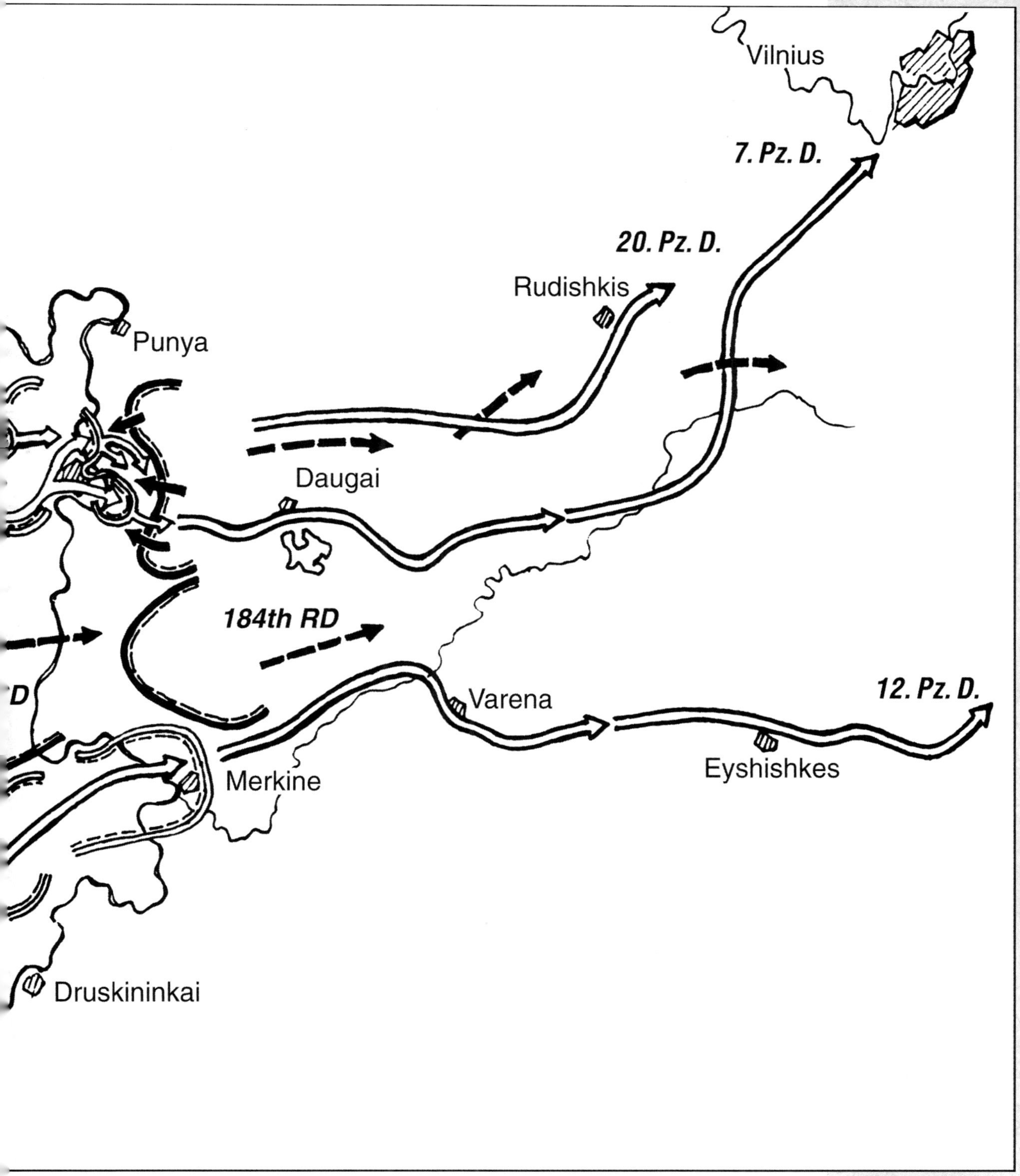
Vilnius
7. Pz. D.
20. Pz. D.
Rudishkis
Punya
Daugai
184th RD
D
Varena
12. Pz. D.
Merkine
Eyshishkes
Druskininkai

A 5th Tank Division T-34 near Alitus, June 1941.

To: Commanders, 13th, 10th, 3rd, and 4th Armies

Prepare units to begin withdrawal no later than the night of 25 June 1941. Place tanks in the vanguard and cavalry and a strong antitank defense in the rear guard. 6th Mechanized Corps to move first—to the vicinity of Slonim. Final lines of departure:. . .

10th Army—Slonim, Byten. Army headquarters—Obuz-Lesna. . .

Execute march swiftly, traveling by day and night under the cover of a strong rear guard. Break contact across broad front.

Communicate by radio; report start, routes, and milestones every two hours. Travel at least 60 km per day during first part of trip.

Allow troops to forage locally and commandeer carts as needed.

Additional instructions to follow. If no additional instructions received, proceed per this preliminary order.

Commander, Western Front
General of the Army Pavlov
Member, Western Front Military Council

A 5th Tank Division T-34 near Alitus, June 1941.

Ponomarenko
Chief Of Staff, Western Front
Major General Klimovskikh.[30]

It appears that from Borzilov's report ("Toward nightfall on 25 June, I received an order from the corps commander to withdraw beyond the Svisloch River, but we carried it out only after receiving a special signal. According to preliminary data, the 4th Tank Division of the 6th Corps was to cross the Svisloch River, which exposed the 36th Cavalry Division's flank."[31]) that a second order was sent—Borzilov wrote about a withdrawal only upon receipt of a special signal, whereas the "personal" order of Front Commander Khatskilevich gave instructions to break contact and proceed to Slonim without additional instructions.

The uncoordinated withdrawal of the corps' divisions signaled a breakdown of control and the general collapse of the 6th Mechanized Corps:

> *From 25 June until 21:00 on 26 June, the division fought a defensive battle in conjunction with the 29th Motorized Rifle Division and the 36th Cavalry Division and attacked from close range in front of the 128th Motorized Rifle Regiment of the 29th Motorized Rifle Division and the 36th Cavalry Division...*
>
> *Toward nightfall on 26 June, the enemy used his reserve to go on the offensive. At 21:00, units of the 36th Cavalry Division and the 128th Motorized Rifle Regiment of the 29th Motorized Rifle Division began retreating in disorder (in a panic). I took action to reverse the situation but was unsuccessful. I gave an order to cover the retreating units of the 29th Motorized Rifle Division and the 36th Cavalry Division, and I made*

A 5th Tank Division T-34 near Alitus, June 1941.

a second attempt to restrain the retreating units. I succeeded in holding the 128th Motorized Rifle Regiment; and during the night of the 26th I crossed the Svisloch River east of Krinki (this was the beginning of a general disorderly retreat), as a result of which communication was lost with the corps headquarters. Communication was restored by nightfall on 27 June at the crossing near Volkovysk. Units of the division fought a running battle with pursuing enemy assault units on the route Kuznitsa-Sokulki until reaching Slonim."[32]

As was common in 1941, "enemy assault units" referred to advance detachments of Wehrmacht units pursuing retreating Soviet forces.

The 6th Mechanized Corps (and the "thirty-fours" that belonged to it) actually met its end on the road from Sokulki to Slonim:

All of the equipment was abandoned in territory occupied by the enemy, from Belostok to Slonim. The remainder of the equipment was disabled. The equipment was abandoned due to the lack of POL [Petroleum, Oil, Lubricants] and repair. Their crews have joined the retreating infantry.[333]

The tanks of units that were retreating in disorder toward the east and that became separated from the main body of their units were abandoned due to breakdowns or the lack of fuel, which prompted suspicions in the headquarters intelligence department of the German 9th Army about preparations for a kind of "guerrilla warfare" using the tanks:

T-34 and BT tanks of the 5th Tank Division near Alitus, June 1941.

Sometimes the destroyed tanks had people wearing civilian clothes in them. Abandoned tanks were found in forests. Therefore, the 9th Army headquarters intelligence department concludes that the tank crews are hiding in forests in civilian clothes, and, given the opportunity, will again fight German forces. The intact tanks discovered in forests without crews lead us to conclude that they are waiting in secure hiding places for a convenient moment to attack. There are many indicators that dressing in civilian clothes is also an enemy strategem for avoiding capture.[344]

Two events that happened literally within a day of each other are representative of the 6th Mechanized Corps' collapse.

At 11:00 on 29 June, I entered the woods east of Slonim with the vehicles that remained (3 T-34s) and a detachment of infantry and cavalry, and there I fought a battle on 29 and 30 June 1941.[35]

When Major General Borzilov's detachment entered Pinsk Marsh on the evening of 30 June, it no longer had any tanks. And on the evening of July 1, three Soviet tanks—a KV and two T-34s—attempted to break out through Slonim. One of the T-34s was burned in the center of town, and the other was disabled at the entrance to the Ruzhansky Highway. The KV fell into the Shchara River when the bridge collapsed under it. All of the tankers were from various companies of the 7th Tank Division's 13th Tank Regiment.[36]

The most powerful Soviet mechanized corps of the Western Front was unable to halt the tanks of "Speedy Heinz" Guderian. They did not even reach him. Guderian's tankers were much luckier than their comrades with Hoth—the majority of their job of knocking out the new Russian tanks was accomplished by cutting communication lines, bombing munitions and POL depots, and shooting up supply trucks along highways. Future engagements with T-34s would bring them dubious satisfaction. Khatskilevich's tank-

A. G. Potaturchev, commander of the 4th Tank Division, 6th Mechanized Corps.

ers managed to slow down the advance by the German infantry divisions in support of an organized withdrawal of Western Front forces from the Belostok salient, and they then broke through the closing encirclement at Volkovysk for the retreating units of the 3rd and 10th Armies. That was a great accomplishment. However, the tanks that had been burned; abandoned when they ran out of fuel; and drowned in rivers, lakes, and marshes could no longer help break through the new encirclement at Minsk, where the deadly jaws of Hoth and Guderian's two panzer groups were closing.

Further to the south, in the former Kiev Special Military District, which had become the Southwest Front, Lieutenant General Ryabyshev's mechanized corps, which, like a baton, had been transferred from one command to another, executed a forced march to move from one assembly area to a different one. That unit holds the sad record of putting the most useless number of kilometers behind its tracks:

> *By order No. 002 of the Commander of the 26th Army, dated 17 May 1941,*[337] *units of the 8th Mechanized Corps were alerted and by the end of the day constituted the reserve of the 26th Army and assembled in the vicinity of Chishki, Raykovitse, Raytarovitse. On 22 June, the corps covered 81 km, including movement of units to assembly areas upon alert.*
>
> *At 20:40 on 22 June, the Southwest Front commander ordered the corps to shift to a new area—Kurovitse, Vinniki, Baryniche—without having completely assembled at Chishki, Raykovitse, Raytarovitse. Pursuant to that order, the corps was given the following mission: assemble by nighttime march in the vicinity of Kurovitse and be prepared to parry an attack by enemy motorized units in the direction of Broda under the command of the 6th Army. Between 23:00 and 24:00 on 22 June 1941, the corps began moving toward the new area over two routes, and by 11:00 on 23 June the lead units of the division had arrived as follows: 12th Tank Division—Kurowitse; 7th Motorized Rifle Division—Mikolayuv; and the 34th Tank Division had crossed Grudek Yagelyonsky. By then, an oral order had been received from the 6th Army Commander to turn the corps and assemble it in the vicinity of Yavoruv, Grudek, Yagelyonsky, Yarin. The corps (minus tank regiments of the 12th Tank Division and an artillery regiment of the 7th Motorized Rifle Division that had assembled in the vicinity of Kurovitse) had assembled in this region by 24:00 23 June. It executed a march from the first and second assembly areas to an area northwest of Grudek Yagelyonsky along two routes without being attacked by enemy aviation. During that time, the corps traveled 215 km on average. The number of vehicles left on that transit due to the fact that the corps had not concentrated fully and were transferred to a new area—Busk, Zadvuzhe, Ostrovchik Polny—is unknown.*
>
> *Movement to the new area began at 06:00 on June 24 by order No. 005 of the 6th Army Commander: Busk, Zadvuzhe, Ostrovchik Polny. The corps executed its march over two roads that were congested with a large number of troops. Due to the large number of traffic jams on the travel route, the corps traveled 113 km towards Busk during the afternoon of 25 June. A large amount of equipment was delayed en route as a result of the traffic jams (especially in Lvov), breakdowns, and lack of fuel.*
>
> *In accordance with order No. 0015 of the Commander of the Southwest Front, the corps executed a nighttime march to the area of Srebno, Bolduny, Stanislavchik,*

A 6th Mechanized Corps T-34, Kuznitsa, June 1941.

Razhnyuv. By 06:00 on 26 June, the 12th and 34th Tank Divisions that were operating on the right flank in the direction of the main attack had taken up their final positions for the attack. The travel distance from Busk to the tank units' final positions is 86 km.

Before the battle began, the corps had traveled an average of 495 km, leaving up to 50% of its equipment along the roads during the march.[388]

According to the equipment loss report that the 8th Mechanized Corps commander sent to the Armor Directorate of the Southwest Front, of the 100 T-34s that the 8th Mechanized Corps had when the war began, 40 vehicles were abandoned en route and lost (and another 5 were left in storage areas).[39] The 12th Tank Division failed to complete its first combat mission on 26 June 1941—cross the Slonuvka River in the vicinity of Leshnyuv and Korsuv and advance towards Berestechko. It lost 5 KVs, 18 T-34s, and 10 BT-7s.[40]

Support provided for the 8th Mechanized Corps' breakout from encirclement in the vicinity of Sitno summarizes actions by the T-34s of the 12th Tank Division:

After many units of the 34th Tank Division and the rearguard of the 7th Motorized Rifle Division passed through Sitno, the enemy stopped the rest of the units and began to surround the 7th Motorized Rifle Division. Seeing the difficult situation, the 7th Division commander requested assistance from the commander of the 8th Mechanized Corps.

The 8th Mechanized Corps commander decided to send tanks from the 12th Tank Division into the battle. About 15:00 on 28 June, up to 20 tanks from the 12th Tank Division entered Sitno, and shortly afterwards the enemy closed the road behind them. Elements of the 7th Motorized Rifle and the 12th Tank Division were now facing

A 6th Mechanized Corps T-34, Kuznitsa, June 1941.

up to 210 infantry fighting vehicles, 40–50 tanks, an antitank gun battalion, and up to a cavalry division.

By then the commander of the 8th Mechanized Corps had assessed the situation as unfavorable and gave the order to withdraw. The remaining tanks covered the right flank of the retreating column of staff and transport vehicles. Lieutenant General Mishanin's tank was knocked out and burned upon entering the battle. The 12th Tank Division commander, Lieutenant General Mishanin, and his chief of communications, Major Krutiyev, were killed in this battle. In all, the battle at Sitno resulted in the following losses: KV – 6, BT-7 – 7, T-26 – 11, T-34 – 15. . . This equipment was destroyed by antitank gun fire or aviation. It either burned or was rendered disabled by crews.

The column assembly for breaking out of the encirclement and withdrawing from battle in the vicinity of Sitno was completely non-regulation. Vehicles were arranged in the following order on the 10 m wide highway: tanks on the right, headquarters and motorized rifle regiment in the middle, and tanks on the left. Only the lead tanks were able to fire, meaning not enough fire could be brought to bear. This gave the enemy confidence to fire on the tanks from a range of 100–150 m. . . .[41]

Another page from the history of the bitter summer of 1941 that was little known until recently was a battle that took place near Senno-Lepel. Unlike the great tank battle at Prokhorovka Station [Kursk 1943], it was almost forgotten during the Soviet era, even though the two engagements were very similar. Just as in the summer of 1943, the Soviet command decided to counterattack the German panzer units that had broken through—this time they were advance divisions of Hoth's 3rd Panzer Group. And the size of the 5th Mechanized Corps coming from the Baikal region and the 7th Mecha-

A 6th Mechanized Corps T-34 destroyed 11 km from Slonim. The tank was destroyed by an internal explosion, the turret blown off, and its road wheel tires burned.

nized Corps from the Moscow Military District was also comparable with Rotmistrov's 5th Guards Tank Army and the units attached to it in 1943. For the most part, however, in 1941 they were made up of older light tanks. They had dozens, not hundreds, of the new vehicles that had been with the units destroyed at the border.

The 14th Tank Division of the 7th Mechanized Corps was luckier than the others in this respect; prior to the offensive, it had received a consolidated cadet battalion from the Kharkov Tank School, which had 29 T-34 tanks and 4 KVs. The 23rd Air Division was to cover and support the advance from the air. Two so-called special air regiments manned by test pilots had been attached to it for this purpose: the 401st Fighter Regiment, which had 19 of the new MiG-1 fighters, and the 430th Attack Regiment with 22 Il-2s "Sturmovik" ground attack aircraft.

Opposing the 14th Tank Division was the 7th Panzer Division from Hoth's group, which we are already familiar with from Alitus. Now, however, the roles were reversed—the German division took up defensive positions on the west bank of a small river and prepared to repel the Red Army's counterattack. At dawn on July 7, 1941, a motorized rifle regiment of the 14th Tank Division secured a bridgehead on the enemy's bank. Sappers immediately began constructing crossings and managed to complete three of the four they had planned before the attack got underway. Then the tanks entered the fight.

> *At 06:30 on 7 July 1941, the 27th and 28th Tank Regiments attacked from their jumping-off positions. The enemy's artillery did not fire until the tanks reached the eastern bank of the Chernogostnitsa River. The enemy laid blocking fire on the river with antiaircraft artillery. Due to damage caused to several lanes by enemy fire and our tanks, delays occurred and tanks bunched up at the three serviceable crossings in the 27th Tank Regiment's sector. Several tanks began moving parallel to the front, looking for other places to cross the river, and became stuck when they attempted to*

A T-34 of the 6th Mechanized Corps fording the Zelva River.

force the river. The enemy opened heavy artillery fire from guns of all calibers along the river bed and on the crossings, inflicting heavy losses to our tanks.

At that point, enemy dive bombers and fighters attacked the artillery positions, the artillery observation posts, the corps commander's deployed reserve on the eastern bank of the river, the 27th Tank Regiment tanks that had broken through the defensive positions in depth, and the forward echelon repair stations of the division and units in the vicinity of Ostrovno. Which bombed the tanks and infantry of the 14th Motorized Rifle Regiment again and again, inflicting heavy losses. All of the tanks of the 27th and 28th Tank Regiments penetrated the defensive positions to a depth of 3–5 km but were forced to retreat to their jumping-off positions when they encountered heavy small- and medium-caliber antitank fire both from fixed positions and in a counterattack on the flank of the 28th Tank Regiment from the south and were heavily attacked by enemy aircraft.

The tanks still in operating condition and the units they belonged to assembled on the eastern bank of the Chernogostnitsa River by 17:00, 7 July 1941. The enemy bombed the crossings and KV tanks continuously. A group of tanks from the 27th Tank Regiment led by regimental commander Major Romanovsky broke through the enemy's antitank sector and penetrated to his tactical depth. Attempts to contact the 27th Tank Regiment commander by radio were unsuccessful. The 27th Tank Regiment committed 51 tanks to the battle. Of that number, 21 tanks remained behind enemy lines.

The following tanks participated in the battle on 7 July 1941:

27th Tank Regiment—51, 28th Tank Regiment—54, reconnaissance battalion—7, division headquarters and reserve—14. Total: 126 tanks, including 11 KVs and 24 T-34s.

Losses in the battle included more than 50% of tanks and more than 200 men killed or wounded. Due to the very difficult terrain in the area from the jumping-off position

A 6th Mechanized Corps T-34 in the center of Slonim disabled by being penetrated, July 1, 1941.

A 6th Mechanized Corps T-34 on the Belostok-Minsk Road, June 1941. The same tank is visible in the photo on page 135, in the background and to the right.

A 6th Mechanized Corps T-34 3 km from Slonim, June 1941.

to the river (peat), 17 tanks became stuck (including two KVs and seven T-34s). Nine tanks were recovered under enemy fire, including one KV. The other tanks were destroyed by enemy artillery and aircraft.

Casualties included the following individuals: Senior Battalion Commissar Fedoseyev, Deputy Chief of the Political Propaganda Section; Major Romanovsky, Commander of the 27th Tank Regiment; Senior Political Instructor Romanov, Assistant Chief of the Political Section. Casualties in the T-34 cadet battalion: killed 4; wounded 113; missing in action 38; Captain Starykh, heavy tank battalion commander; Major Grishin, T-34 tank battalion commander; Commissar Shinkarenko. Losses in the 28th Tank Regiment—7 junior officers and 19 tank crewman. Division Commander Colonel Vasilyev was wounded by shrapnel in the face and arm but remained on duty.

A 6th Mechanized Corps T-34 disabled near Slonim on June 30, 1941, by the Großdeutschland Regiment.

The main reason for the unsuccessful attack was the absence of aircraft, particularly reconnaissance planes, because the division and regiments lacked knowledge of the enemy's activities in the tactical depth and lacked air cover. A shortage of artillery and unreliable communications within the division also had a negative impact on the battle. The terrain greatly hindered tank operations.[42]

The attack by the 14th Tank Division was not a "firing exercise under simulated combat conditions" for the Germans, either—the Soviet forces claimed 42 enemy tanks destroyed. One Pz. II tank was captured and taken from the field of battle as a trophy. According to 7th Panzer Division reports, German losses were 211 men killed or wounded, two tanks, one sIG 33 auf Pz. I 150 mm self-propelled gun, two 88 mm Flak 18 (Sf.) self-propelled guns, a PaK 38 50 mm antitank gun, and a 75 mm leIG.18 infantry cannon. How much disabled German equipment was left out of the dispatch on irrecoverable losses remains unknown, but the casualty numbers among the defenders are very close to the losses among the attacking forces, so we can cautiously assume that equipment losses were also comparable (not an exchange of dozens of Soviet tanks for a couple of German ones). The German 7th Panzer Division halted its advance for four days after the battle of 7 July, and thereafter it operated in the Hoth group's second echelon. On the whole, however, the course and outcome of the battle were typical for the stormy summer of 1941: without reliable reconnaissance data and adequate infantry and artillery support, even tank units armed with T-34s and KVs could only rely on their own armor, which, of course, was not infinitely strong.

Combat losses:
KV-M[43]*—1 vehicle, wheel blown off by aerial bomb; recovered to Disabled Vehicle Collection Post No. 2.*
T-34—2 vehicles burned.
T-34—2 vehicles disabled by shelling.
T-34—7 vehicles disabled and sunk while crossing the Chernogostnitsa River.
T-34—6 vehicles missing with their crews.
Vehicles remaining in good condition after the battle:
KV tanks—5 vehicles
T-34 tanks—6 vehicles...
transferred to Ostrovno. Withdrawn from Chernogostye area:
KV tanks—5 vehicles
T-34 tanks—6 vehicles, including one disabled tank sent to the forward echelon repair station and two to Rudnya Station for shipment to the factory.[44]

A 6th Mechanized Corps T-34 disabled on the Ruzhan Highway on the outskirts of Slonim, July 1, 1941.

Action by the 50th Tank Regiment of the 25th Mechanized Corps is the last combat incident involving T-34s that we would like to address in this chapter. Historians have paid little attention to actions by the 25th Mechanized Corps: this corps belonged to the "second wave" that had formed by the beginning of the war and was one of the weakest and least equipped corps. Also, the battle it took part in unfolded not far from a city that was subsequently renamed and which would be awkward to mention on a book's cover jacket: on July 5, 1941, Corps Commander Krivoshein received an order from Colonel General F. I. Kuznetsov, commander of the 21st Army, to assemble the 50th Tank Division in the vicinity of Staroselye, Aleshnya (4–6 km northeast of Dovsk) and destroy an enemy panzer group that had broken through near the city of Propoysk.

At that time, the 50th Tank Division had 149 tanks (of the 183 in the mechanized corps), and 65 of them were the new "thirty-fours" with crews from the Orlov and Kharkov Tank Schools. A comparison of the capabilities of the opponents based on the "tabular" specifications of their equipment leaves no room for doubt: the 21st Army's commander will succeed in this mission! However, the reality turned out to be considerably less rosy. To begin with, they needed to locate the enemy in general and his "breakthrough panzer group" in particular...

Report on combat operations of the 50th Tank Division from 16 to 21 July 1941.

16 and 17 July 1941: Reconnaissance group consisting of 3 T-34 tanks and 32 soldiers on trucks. One tank had an accident en route (broken idler sprocket). Enemy found by combat. Reconnaissance Chief Senior Lieutenant BULGAKOV.

17 and 18 July 1941: Reconnaissance group consisting of 6 T-34 tanks and 5 T-26 tanks in the direction of PROPOYSK. Reconnaissance Chief Major SHURENKOV. One T-26 tank broke down (blown piston).

17 July 1941: Independent reconnaissance patrol of 5 T-34 tanks in the direction of IVANISHCHEVICHI. Tanks stuck in swamp; later returned. Reconnaissance Chief Captain CHERKAS.

18–21 July 1941: Reconnaissance group of 11 T-34 tanks from the 99th Tank Regiment on the route KULCHITSA, BOVKI, TRILESINO, KRASNITSA, KUSKOVICHI. 4 tanks stuck south of KULIKOVKA; tanks not yet returned. Reconnaissance Group Chief Captain POTEKHIN has not yet returned (en route to unit lines).

18 July: Reconnaissance group of 6 T-34 tanks from the 100th Tank Regiment to vicinity of MASHEVSKAYA SLOBODA. Chief, Captain KABYSHEV. Three tanks struck mines in the vicinity of PRUDOK.

19 July 1941: tank group of 24 T-34 tanks to disrupt the enemy's rear areas on the axis KULIKOVKA, MOTISHCHE, TRILESINO, KRASNITSA, KUSKOVICHI, BYKHOV, SMILITSA, KHOCHINKI. According to incomplete data, three T-34 tanks burned, one tank destroyed by a mine, four tanks disabled; seven tanks returned. The rest are returning, but the location of two T-34s is unknown. Group chief Colonel BAKHAROV.

19 July 1941 at 17:00. Seven tanks were dispatched to repel the enemy attacking in the vicinity of KHOCHINKI (two T-34s and five T-26s). One T-34 and three T-26s were disabled.

19 July 1941 at 18:00. A group of seven T-26 tanks were dispatched to repel the enemy attacking in the vicinity of PALKI-POLYANINOVICHI. Three tanks were disabled in battle.

19 July 1941 at 19:00. Three T-34 tanks were dispatched for reconnaissance in the vicinity of PALKI ORD. One returned, disabled; one was blown up; REZNIKOV was killed.

19 July 1941: Ten T-26 tanks were dispatched to support the advance of the 219th Motorized Rifle Division. Two tanks were disabled en route by antitank artillery.

18 July 1941: Ten tanks were dispatched on order of the 151st Rifle Division's commander. One tank returned; the rest were abandoned on the field of battle. Company Commander Lieutenant AMELCHENKO was wounded.

18 July 1941: 15 T-34 and 5 T-26 tanks were dispatched on order of the army staff. On the way back, Major General NERETIN sent 5 T-26 tanks and one T-34 tank into battle at gunpoint. The fate of these tanks is being determined. Four T-34 tanks have returned to their unit.[45]

The mechanized corps headquarters summarized the outcome of the intense reconnaissance activity as follows:

Sitrep No. 8
Corps headquarters, 25th Mechanized Corps
21 July 1941 at 12:00

1. *On the night of 20–21 July, the 50th Tank Division got organized, assembled its tanks in the vicinity of BOL. ZIMNITSA, and carried out repairs.*

At 10:001 21 July, the situation with its equipment was as follows:

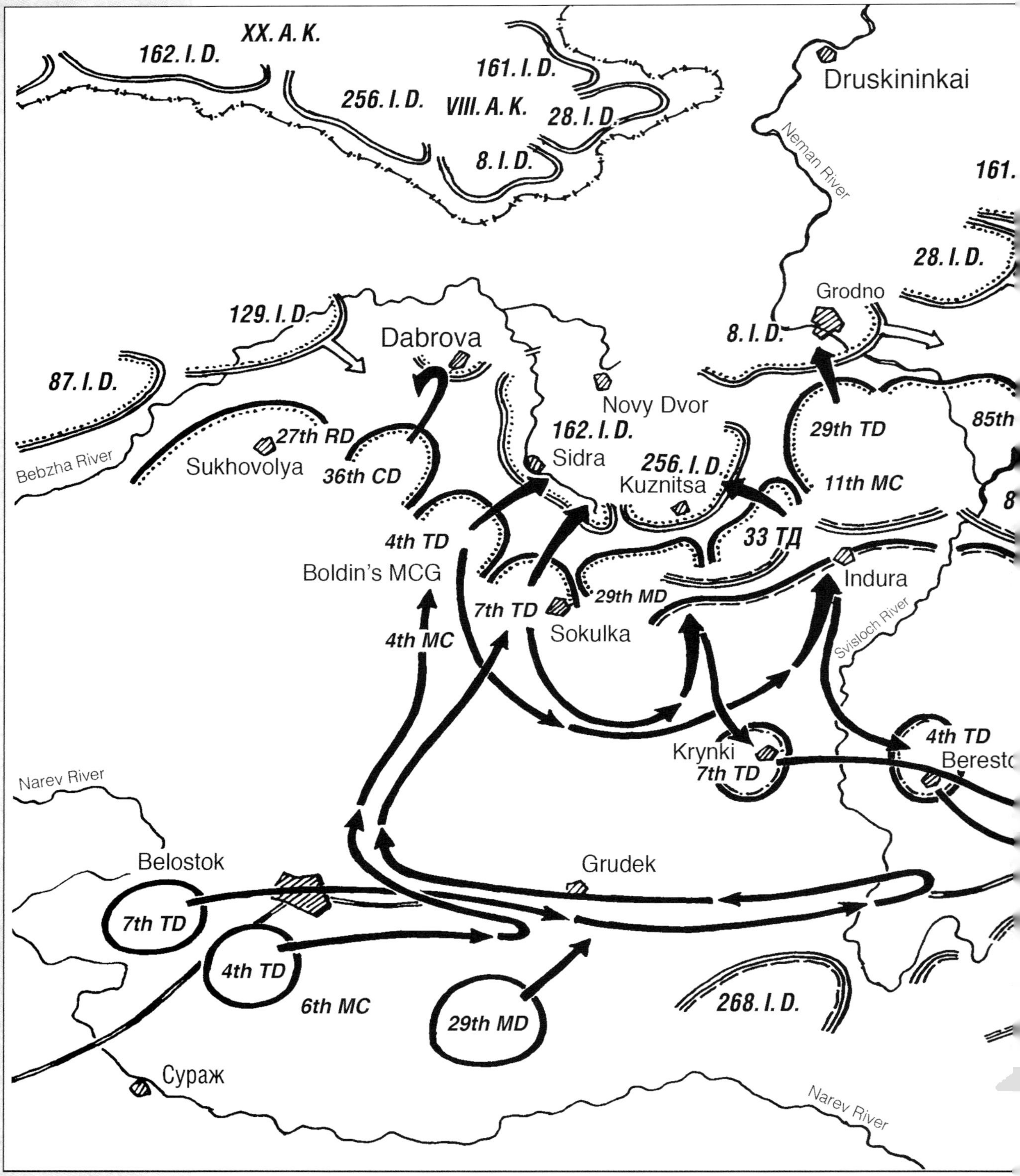
XX. A. K.
162. I. D.
161. I. D.
256. I. D.
VIII. A. K.
28. I. D.
8. I. D.
Druskininkai
Neman River
161.
28. I. D.
Grodno
8. I. D.
129. I. D.
Dabrova
87. I. D.
Novy Dvor
85th
162. I. D.
29th TD
27th RD
Sidra
256. I. D.
Bebzha River
Sukhovolya
36th CD
Kuznitsa
11th MC
33 ТД
4th TD
Boldin's MCG
Indura
29th MD
7th TD
Sokulka
Svisloch River
4th MC
4th TD
Krynki
Beresto
7th TD
Narev River
Belostok
Grudek
7th TD
4th TD
6th MC
268. I. D.
29th MD
Сураж
Narev River

Figure 2. **Actions by the 6th Mechanized Corps, June 22–30, 1941**

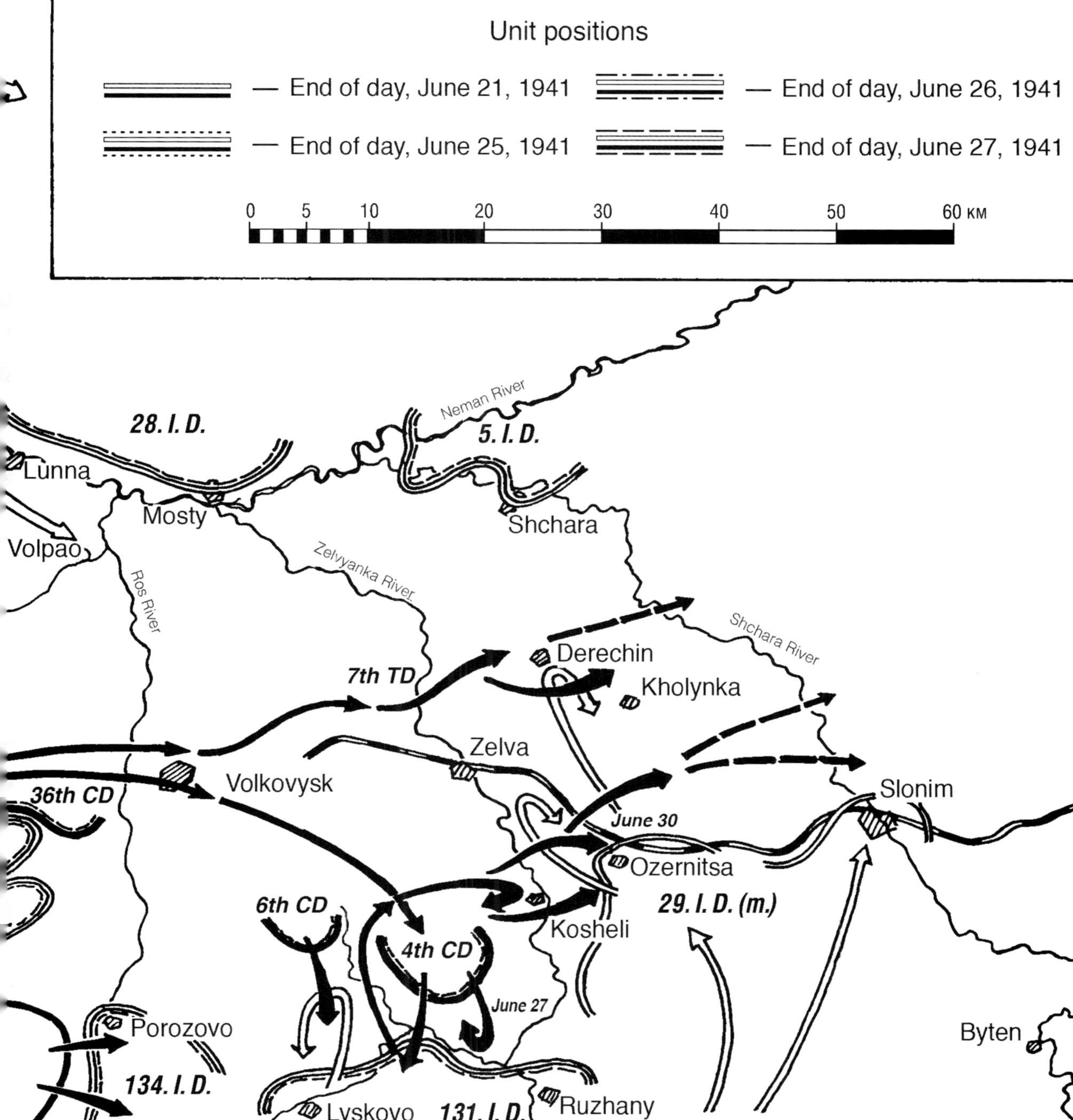

Present in unit area	T-34	T-26
In running order	15	19
Undergoing repair	4	11
In the 219th Motorized Rifle Division	—	10
In the 151st Rifle Division	—	10
With army staff	—	5
Towing other tanks	6	—
Stuck in marsh and not recovered for various reasons	29	17

[46]

Two T-34s of the 6th Mechanized Corps on the Belostok-Baranovichi Highway, June 1941.

And although some of the 29 "thirty-fours" listed on the last line of the table were later made operational, this beginning clearly demonstrates that it was not enough just to have possession of the new tanks. The results obtained by reconnaissance did not compensate for the losses incurred:

The results of the reconnaissance were as follows: 5 enemy tanks destroyed, 7 armored cars destroyed and one captured on the move; and 25 motorcycles, 3 buses, 44 trucks, 3 passenger cars, 2 storage tanks, 2 field ambulances, 2 radios, 3 antitank guns, and infantry up to a battalion destroyed. [47]

The 25th Mechanized Corps had to go into battle nevertheless, even though:

its powerful armored strikeforce was expended on trifles, and the 50th Tank Division had to fight on foot.... Its valuable cadre of tankers, motorcyclists, sappers, signalers, and other technical staff were used as infantry. [48]

The outcome of the 25th Mechanized Corps' combat operations was predictably disappointing:

To:
Comrade Lieutenant General Feorenko,
Chief, Red Army GABTU.
25th Mechanized Corps headquarters,
Terekhovka
27 July 1941

A 6th Mechanized Corps T-34 disabled on the Ruzhan Highway on the outskirts of Slonim, July 1, 1941.

It is with great indignation that I report to you about the completely improper and inappropriate use of the 25th Mechanized Corps. On 18 July, the corps assembled on the right flank of the 21st Army. The 50th Tank Division received a mission to destroy the BYKHOVSKAYA enemy grouping in conjunction with the 57th Infantry Corps, and the 219th Motorized Rifle Division was assigned to capture PROPOYSK.

For the 25th Mechanized Corps, this meant operating in two opposing directions: one division to the west, and the other to the east. Given the following additional factors:

> *An order from 21st Army commander Lieutenant General Gerasimenko to transfer two battalions of T-26 tanks to infantry corps (50 tanks that never returned);*
>
> *Repeated orders from 21st Army commander Lieutenant General Kuznetsov*[49] *to transfer T-34 and T-26 tanks to infantry corps;*
>
> *Swampy, forested terrain with narrow roads, and untrained drivers (the T-34 tank battalions from the Orlov and Stalingrad schools arrived with completely untrained drivers);*

it is clear why in five days of combat the 50th Tank Division irretrievably lost 18 T-34 tanks and 25 T-26 tanks, 18 T-34s underwent intermediate overhaul, and 40 T-26 tanks were repaired and the tanks converted into a tank battalion with 25 T-34 tanks and 20 T-26 tanks. This is from the total number of 64 T-34 tanks and 65 T-26 tanks that have not completed a single major mission to defeat the enemy.

After receiving the mission to capture PROPOYSK, the 219th Motorized Rifle Division initiated battle with battalions and without artillery, i.e., it had nowhere to get it from immediately. Fighting by itself, it incurred large losses—300 men, leaving 15–16 officers per regiment.

A 32nd Tank Division T-34 abandoned in Lvov.

Experience has shown that our great T-34 tanks, moving blindly, without reconnaissance, and through woods encounter guns at short range that fire on them. Reconnaissance by motorcycles and armored cars is needed. This is entirely true for the 50th Tank Division.

I have requested that I be given equipment and just 10 days for training in order to teach elementary combat skills. I am sure that the People's Commissar of Defense does not know about all this. I am sure that no one is allowed to give the enemy our great tanks, yet it is actually happening: inept driving is causing the main and steering clutches to burn out and the transmission adjusting rods to bend, leaving vehicles on the battlefield under enemy fire.

Some conclusions:

1) *Successful action by tanks must be immediately exploited by motorized infantry.*

2) *Tank operations must be supported by ground reconnaissance vehicles (motorcycles and armored cars), and permanently attached air reconnaissance assets must be provided; tank divisions need a reconnaissance squadron.*

3) *For tank divisions to be more successful, a tank division needs to be supported by a dive bomber regiment.*

4) *The attachment of tanks from tank divisions to rifle divisions for close cooperation results in nothing but damaged and lost tanks. Combined arms commanders*

A T-34 abandoned in Lvov. The tank was unable to move under its own power.

assign missions to tanks improperly, and when tanks are disabled or stop running in positions controlled by the enemy, they simply abandon them (as happened in the 151st and 187th Rifle Divisions).

5) *The T-34 tanks are remarkable vehicles. The following design changes are needed:*
   - ***a)*** *Make it easier to tension the tracks from outside.*
   - ***b)*** *Make the main and steering clutches stronger (they burn and warp).*
   - ***c)*** *The transmission adjusting rods bend.*
   - ***d)*** *The periscope and panoramic sight need armor protection, because most tanks leave battle with broken periscopes, panoramic sights, and triplex lenses.*

6) *Place armored shields alongside the machine guns and main gun. There have been four instances of the main gun being hit and the machine guns knocked off.*

7) *Make the tracks, idler sprockets, and drive wheels stronger.*

8) *The 71-TK radio is unsuited for the T-34 tank; it operates sporadically and malfunctions often.*

9) *The factory teams that are sent work well; they are extremely helpful with repairs.*[500]

By early August 1941, the Soviet command prepared reports about the availability and losses of combat vehicles in units in the field. The data that apply to the T-34 looked like this:

A T-34 stuck in a large crater.

Axis	Present as of June 22, 1941	Shipped from factories between June 22 and August 1, 1941	Present as of August 1, 1941	Losses
Northwestern	50	24	0	74
Western	350	428	90	688
Southwestern	485	74	50	509
Southern	50	0	18	32
Total	**935**	**526**	**158**	**1,303**

Table compiled according to data of TsAMO RF, f. 38 (GABTU) op. 11353 (Armor and mechanized force command staff), d. 909 (Reports, lists, summaries, and dispatches of the Red Army GABTU, fronts, and districts about inventory, situation, requirements, and losses of arms and other matériel), pp. 99–107.

A T-34 from an unknown unit, summer of 1941.

The number of losses is the difference between those combat vehicles present at the beginning of combat operations and those present in late July of this year, minus those evacuated to repair depots.

To this we should add that when the reports were compiled, only 66 vehicles had been sent to repair depots.

The losses look stunning—about 70% of the total Soviet total losses of "thirty-fours" for 1941 occurred during the first month and a half of the war (1,843 vehicles). The losses look doubly stunning when put next to the harmonious chorus of memoirs by Soviet generals, who describe:

the suffering of Germany's infantry in fighting Russian T-34 tanks. Why no acceptable infantry antitank weapons were developed during the three and half years between the T-34 tank's first appearance in August 1931 and April 1945 will evidently remain a mystery.[51]

We believe this question should be examined in every detail.

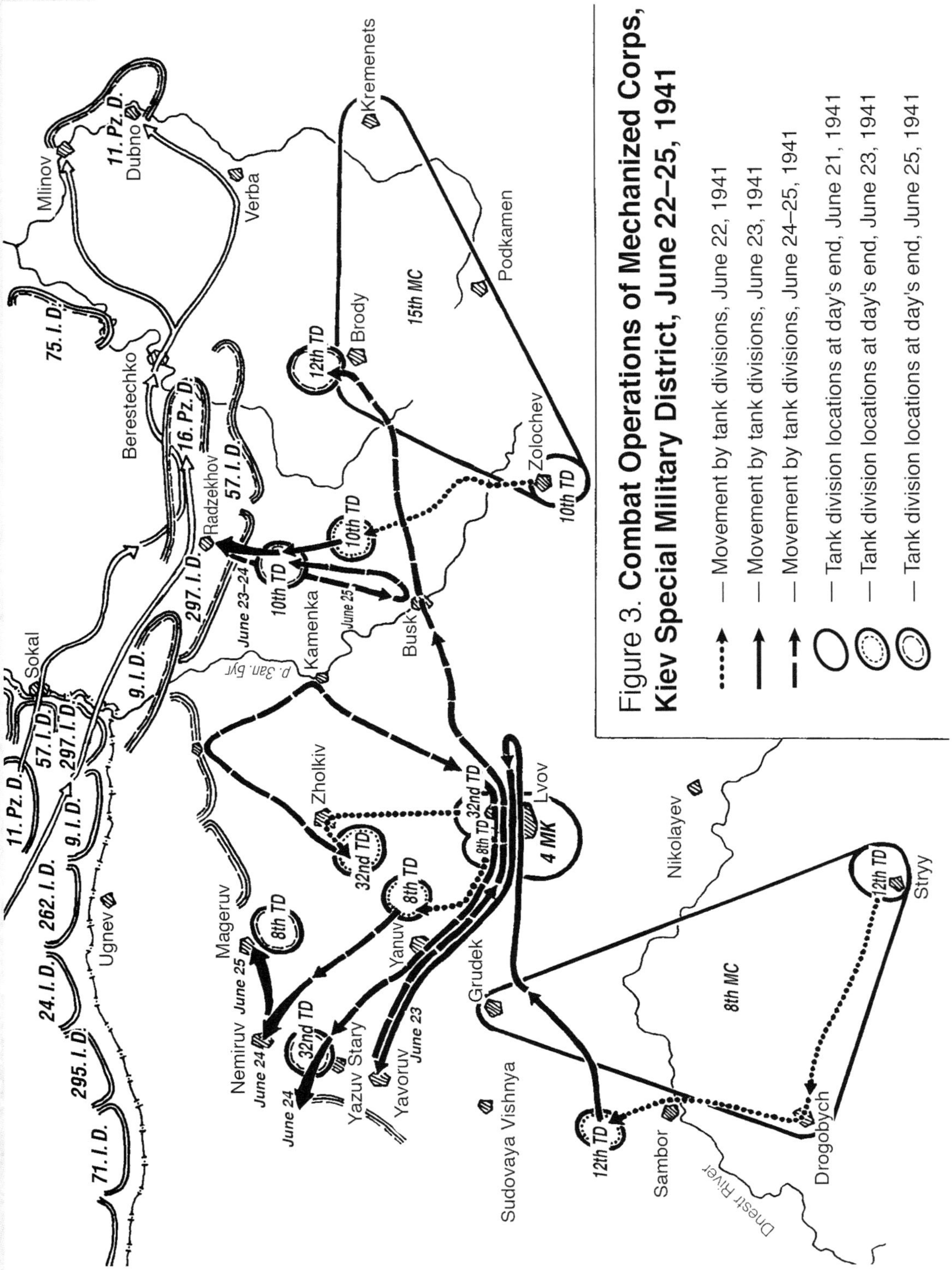

Figure 3. **Combat Operations of Mechanized Corps, Kiev Special Military District, June 22–25, 1941**

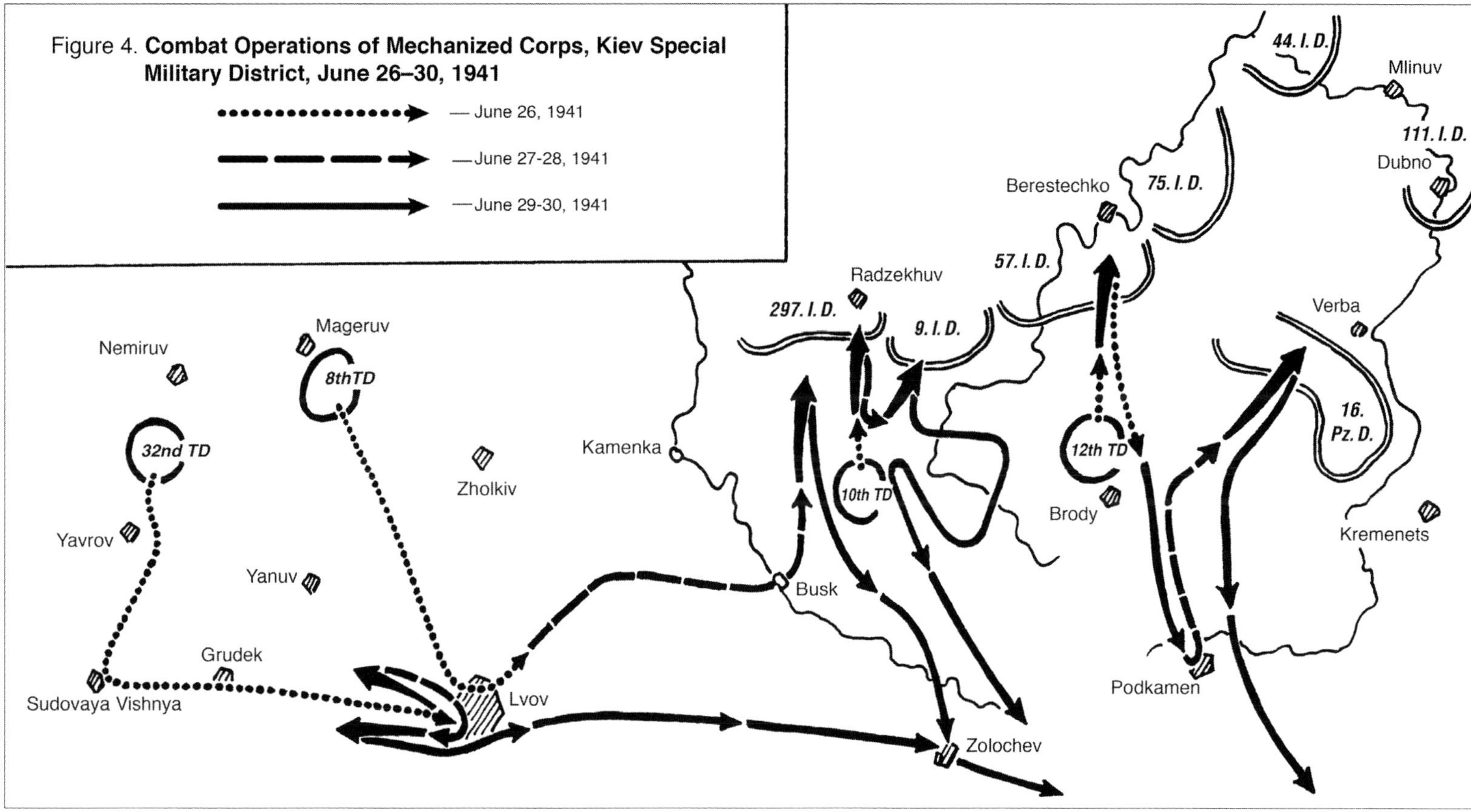

Figure 4. **Combat Operations of Mechanized Corps, Kiev Special Military District, June 26–30, 1941**

A 10th Tank Division T-34, Zolochev, June 1941. (N 49.80948, E 24.896457)◊

A T-34 of an unknown unit, summer of 1941.

NOTES

1 "The Tankers' March" (music: Pokrass brothers; lyrics: B. Laskina), 1939.

2 *"...We don't want war but will defend, ourselves / Our defenses are strong for good reason, / We'll destroy the enemy in his land / With little bloodshed and a mighty blow!"* From the song "If Tomorrow Brings War [Yesli zavtra voyna]," (music: Pokrass brothers; lyrics: V. Lebedev-Kumach), 1938.

3 Colonel Helmut Ritgen (ret.), who was in the German 6th Panzer Division when the Great Patriotic War began, remembers calculating how long the war would last from the average daily rates of advance in the Polish and French campaigns and the assumed depth of operations and resistance expected from Soviet forces. According to his calculations, the war should be over by the end of July, so he scheduled his wedding for August 2 (D. Glantz, *The Initial Period of War on the Eastern Front, 22 June–August 1941.* Portland: Frank Cass, 2001, p. 110.)

4 TsAMO RF, f. 221 (Northwest Front), op. 1376 (Armor Directorate), d. 4 (Instructions and orders of the Armor Directorate and Front Headquarters concerning use of tanks and mechanized forces with tank and truck units, prevention of combat vehicle losses, and other issues), p. 134.

5 TsAMO RF, f. 221 (Northwest Front), op. 1376 (Armor Directorate), d. 18 (Information from Armor Departments of armies, mechanized corps, and tank divisions about numbers, requirements, losses, and repairs), p. 1.

6 Transcript of a speech by Hitler at a conference in Wehrmacht headquarters, January 9, 1941. Cit. ex: V. I. Dashichev, *The Bankruptcy of the Strategy of German Fascism [Bankrotstvo strategii germanskogo fashizma], Vol. 2. Aggression Against the USSR. The Fall of the Third Reich. 1941–1945.* Moscow: Nauka, 1973, p. 93.

7 A June 20, 1941, dispatch on the mobilization readiness of the 5th Tank Division listed 50 T-34 radio tanks, 30 T-28 radio tanks, 72 DT-7 radio tanks, 39 BT-7 tanks of the line, 59 BT-7 anti-aircraft tanks, 14 T-26 single-turret tanks of the line, and 4 T-26 dual-turret tanks of the line. TsAMO RF, f. 3005 (5th Tank Division), op. 1 (Tank Directorate), d. 53 (Report on combat strength, division and unit materials regarding munitions supplies), p. 69.

8 On 22 June, the 7th Panzer Division had 11 Pz. I, 55 Pz. II, 167 Pz. 38 (t), 30 Pz. IV, and 15 Pz.Bef. (command tanks without guns), for a total of 278 tanks. (T. Jentz, *Panzertruppen, 1933–1942.* Atglen: Schiffer Military History, 1996, p. 206.

9 The Wehrmacht's 7th Panzer Division was nicknamed the "Phantom Division" during the French campaign (D. Glantz. *The Initial Period of War on the Eastern Front: 22 June – August 1941.* Portland: Frank Cass, 2001. p. 174.)

10 Documents of Army Group North mention 80 tanks in the 5th Tank Division destroyed in battles with units of the 3rd Panzer Group on June 22, and another 60 tanks destroyed on June 23. (TsAMO RF, f. 500 (Captured Documents), op. 12462 (Translations of Captured Documents), d. 606 (Intelligence reports by Army Groups Center, North, and South) p. 23). The number of enemy losses announced by the Germans on June 22 was close to friendly losses acknowledged by the Soviet side; therefore, there is reason to believe that the 5th Tank Division's June 23rd losses as reported by the Germans were not exaggerated.

11 D. N. Yegorov, *June 1941: Debacle on the Western Front [Razgrom Zapadnogo fronta].* Moscow: Yauza, Eksmo, 2008, p. 329 (with reference to: S. P. Ivanov, *Army Headquarters, Front Headquarters [Shtab armeyskiy, shtab frontovoy].* Moscow: Voyenizdat, 1990, p. 48).

12 When the war started, the 6th Mechanized Corps had 115 KVs, 322 T-34s, 58 T-28s, 470 BTUs of various types, 83 T-26s, 44 flamethrower tanks, and 93 small amphibious tanks, for a total of 1184 tanks. TsAMO RF, f. 38 (GABTU), op. 11353 (Armor and Mechanized Force Command Staff), d. 909 (Information, lists, summaries, and dispatches of the Red Army GABTU, fronts, and districts about inventory, situation, requirements, and losses of arms and other matériel), p. 103.

13 Intelligence summary No. 1 of the Western Front staff, 20:00, 22 June 1941. Cit. ex: Collection of Military Documents from the Great Patriotic War, Issue 35. Moscow: Voyenizdat, 1958, p. 19.

14 Ibid., p. 20.

15 We previously mentioned the loss of documentation from the headquarters of the 6th Mechanized Corps and its tank divisions when they were encircled. Major General Katskilevich, the 6th Corps commander, was killed during the breakout from encirclement in late June 1941. Major General A. G. Potaturchev, the 4th Tank Division commander, was taken prisoner while trying to escape the encirclement by himself. Therefore, the 7th Tank Division commander's report is the only document that addresses actions by the 6th Mechanized Corps.

16 Report by Major General of Armor S. V. Borzilov, commander of the 7th Tank Division, 6th Mechanized Corps, on the status and actions of the 7th Tank Division. TsAMO RF, f. 38 (GABTU), op. 11353 (Armor and Mechanized Force Command Staff), d. 5 (Unit reports and dispatches on unit status and combat employment, and matériel availability; Reports of the Western Front Armor Directorate and units about matériel numbers and losses, numbers of captured weapons and equipment, and correspondence with the Front Armor Directorate staff concerning operational issues and unit matériel inventories), p. 52.

17 Ibid., pp. 52–53.

18 As of 10 June, the 4th Tank Division had 125 tons of diesel fuel in the tanks of its 63 KVs, 160 T-34s, and 30 BT-7Ms and another 27 tons in tank trucks; the 7th Tank Division had 64.5 tons of fuel in the tanks of its 51 KVs and 78 T-34s and another 18.5 tons of fuel in mobile capacity. Of their authorized wartime strength of 143 tank trucks, the 4th Tank Division had 88, and the 7th had 103. TsAMO RF, f. 117 (Western Special Military District), op. 12915 (Headquarters, Departments, Divisions), d. 5 (Mobilization dispatches of mechanized formations and units on

mobilization readiness and availability of weapons, military equipment, and property), pp. 256, 268, 297, 318.

19 Central Archive of the Federal Security Service of the Russian Federation [TsA FSB]. Archive research case No. R-24000, pp. 23–53. Cit. ex: Col. "1941" in 2 vols. Vol. 2. Moscow: International Foundation "Democracy," 1998, p. 462.

20 Referencing German archives, the German researcher V. D. Heydorn states that the armor attack towards Sidra began at 21:00 on June 24, Berlin time; and an infantry attack on Dabrovo started at 01:00 on June 25, Berlin time (V. D. Heydorn, *Der sowjetische Aufmarsh im Bialystoker Balkon bis zum 22.Juni 1941 und der Kessel von Wolkowysk.* Munich: Verlag für Wehrwissenschaften, 1989, p. 233). Meanwhile, an intelligence report sent at 16:50 on June 24 by the 9th "German Army headquarters" stated that an "enemy tank unit (about 150 tanks) has attacked the 256 Infantry Division located in Kuznitsa from the direction of Indura. The battle is ongoing." (TsAMO RF, f. 500 (Captured Documents), op. 12462 (Translations of Captured Documents), d. 606 (Intelligence reports by Army Groups Center, North, and South), p. 45). The 4th Tank Division of the 6th Mechanized Corps was moving towards Indura, and the 7th Tank Division was moving towards Kuznitsa.

21 Intelligence report of the 9th Army headquarters as of 07:03 on June 25, 1941.

22 According to Heydorn, the attacks by the 6th Mechanized Corps on 25 June began between 05:00 and 06:00 Berlin time (V. D. Heydorn. *Der sowjetische Aufmarsh im Bialystoker Balkon bis zum 22.Juni 1941 und der Kessel von Wolkowysk.* Munich: Verlag für Wehrwissenschaften, 1989, p. 233). An intelligence report transmitted at 11:15 from the 9th Army headquarters stated that "major attacks from the south and southwest have been ongoing since 06:30 in the area of Sidra and Dabrovo."

23 Report by Major General of Armor S. V. Borzilov, commander of the 7th Tank Division, 6th Mechanized Corps, on the status and actions of the 7th Tank Division.

24 This number was later corrected to read 31 tanks. TsAMO RF, f. 500 (Captured Documents), op. 12462 (Translations of Captured Documents), d. 606 (Intelligence reports by Army Groups Center, North, and South), p. 81.

25 V. D. Heydorn, *Der sowjetische Aufmarsh im Bialystoker Balkon bis zum 22.Juni 1941 und der Kessel von Wolkowysk.* Munich: Verlag für Wehrwissenschaften, 1989, p. 236.

26 TsAMO RF, f. 208, op. 2454ss, d. 27, p. 57; Collection of Military Documents from the Great Patriotic War, Issue 35. Moscow: Voyenizdat, 1958, p. 45.

27 "However, the Soviet attacks were a success at the operational level. The German 20th Army Corps was so severely beaten that it was not capable of going on the offensive until June 27. Thus, it lost 3.5 days." V. D. Heydorn, *Der sowjetische Aufmarsh im Bialystoker Balkon bis zum 22.Juni 1941 und der Kessel von Wolkowysk.* Munich: Verlag für Wehrwissenschaften, 1989, p. 236.

28 Lieutenant General K. D. Golubev—Commander, 10th Army, Western Front, in whose area of responsibility Boldin's group was operating.

29 Notation on document reads: "Sent at 16:45 on 25 June 1941." TsAMO RF, f. 208, op. 2454ss, d. 27, p. 55. Cit. ex: Collection of Military Documents from the Great Patriotic War, Issue 35. Moscow: Voyenizdat, 1958, p. 43.

30 TsAMO RF, f. 208, op. 2454ss, d. 17, p. 59. Cit. ex: Collection of Military Documents from the Great Patriotic War, Issue 35. Moscow: Voyenizdat, 1958, pp. 46–47.

31 Report by Major General of Armor S. V. Borzilov, commander of the 7th Tank Division, 6th Mechanized Corps, on the status and actions of the 7th Tank Division. TsAMO RF, f. 38 (GABTU), op. 11353 (Armor and Mechanized Force Command Staff), d. 5 (Unit reports and dispatches on unit status and combat employment and matériel availability; Reports of the Western Front Armor Directorate and units about matériel numbers and losses, numbers of captured weapons and equipment, and correspondence with the Front Armor Directorate Staff concerning operational issues and unit matériel inventories), p. 53.

32 Ibid., p. 53.

33 Ibid., p. 54.

34 TsAMO RF, f. 500 (Captured Documents), op. 12462 (Translations of Captured Documents), d. 606 (Intelligence reports by Army Groups Center, North, and South) pp. 75, 84.

35 Major General of Armor S. V. Borzilov, commander of the 7th Tank Division, 6th Mechanized Corps, on the status and actions of the 7th Tank Division. TsAMO RF, f. 38 (GABTU), op. 11353 (Armor and Mechanized Force Command Staff), d. 5 (Unit reports and dispatches on unit status and combat employment and matériel availability; Reports of the Western Front Armor Directorate and units about matériel numbers and losses, numbers of captured weapons and equipment, and correspondence with the Front Armor Directorate staff concerning operational issues and unit matériel inventories), p. 53.

36 Ye. F. Drig. *Mechanized Corps of the Workers' and Peasants' Red Army in Battle [Mekhanizirovannye korpusa RKKA v boyu].* Moscow: ACT, 2005, p. 239.

37 At first glance, the order date may confuse the reader. But according to the regulations set in 1941, the actions of units and subunits at combat alert were regulated by a special order, designed in advance and approved by higher command. This order regulated the time of moving out at alarm for units and detachments, concentration areas, force apportionment by echelons, organization of intelligence activities, patrol duties, AA defense, and so on.

38 TsAMO RF, f. 38 (GABTU), op. 11360 (Department for Study and Implementation of Lessons Learned from the Patriotic War), d. 2 (Reports, accounts, and dispatches from fronts and units concerning combat operations and use of armored vehicles during June and August), p. 101.

39 TsAMO RF, f. 229 (Southwest Front), op. 157 (Armor and Mechanized Force Command Staff), d. 8 Reports to the Front Armor Directorate, Red Army GABTU, and Front Military Council regarding lessons learned from the use of armored forces and their condition), p. 220.

40 TsAMO RF, f. 38 (GABTU) op. 11360 (Department for Study and Implementation of Lessons Learned from the Patriotic War), d. 2 (Reports, accounts, and dispatches from fronts and units concerning combat operations and use of armored vehicles during June and August), p. 109.

41 Ibid., pp. 110–111.

42 TsAMO RF, f. 3014, op. 1, d. 10, pp. 10–11.

43 KV-M includes the KV-MB and the KV with small turret, i.e., the KV-1.

44 TsAMO RF, f. 3014, op. 1, d. 60, p. 11. Letter of explanation regarding losses of military matériel of the 27th Tank Regiment of the 14th Tank Division while en route and in battles between 24 June 1941 and 22 July 1941 in the vicinity of Vitebsk, Smolensk, and Yartsevo.

45 TsAMO RF, f. 3458 (25th Mechanized Corps), op. 1, d. 9 (Unit battle dispatches and situation reports), p. 178.

46 TsAMO RF, f. 3458 (25th Mechanized Corps), op. 1, d. 8 (Corps headquarters battle dispatches and situation reports. Corps commander's report on the corps' low manning level and lack of readiness), p. 25.

47 Ibid., p. 159.

48 Ibid., p. 159.

49 The Northwest Front commander was fired on July 10 and replaced by 21st Army commander F. I. Kuznetsov. Lieutenant General Gerasimenko was appointed to replace 13th Army commander Lieutenant General Remezov, who had been wounded.

50 TsAMO RF, f. 3458 (25th Mechanized Corps), op. 1, d. 8 (Corps headquarters battle dispatches and situation reports. Corps commander's report on the corps' low manning level and lack of readiness), pp. 68–69.

51 Eike Middeldorf, *The Russian Campaign: Tactics and Weapons [Russkaya kampaniya: taktika i vooruzheniye].* St. Petersburg: OOO Izdatelstvo Poligon, Moscow: OOO Firma Izdatelstvo AST, 2000, p. 15.

A T-34 stuck in a marshy meadow, summer of 1941.

CHAPTER 6. **MECHANISM OF DISASTER**

Even a mop will fire once a year.[1]

Historians are increasingly drawn to study the Great Patriotic War that began more than 70 years ago and was so destructive to the Soviet Union. Among the countless "how's?" and "why's?" not least important are two questions directly related to our story: how is it that the German forces were able to effectively combat the invulnerable "thirty-fours," and why is it that approximately 1,000 of these "newest invincible" tanks had no appreciable effect on the disastrous events of the war—to the extent that the Germans simply overlooked the tank in their memoirs?

Let us begin by examining how the enemy's forces were able to counter the T-34 and how effective the counterweapons in the hands of German troops were.

In the summer of 1942, the Artillery Committee of the Chief Artillery Directorate tasked the R&D Artillery Test Range with investigating the capability of domestic tank armor plates to resist penetration by German 37 mm and 50 mm armor-piercing hard-core projectiles, and domestic 45 mm armor-piercing and hard-core projectiles and 76.2 mm shaped-charge projectiles. Each type of projectile was at fired three angles of incidence: 90°, 30°, and 45°. Firing at a 45 mm high-hardness, homogeneous armor plate produced the following results:

MSVR—maximum stern vulnerability range: the maximum range at which the integrity of the rear surface of armor plate can be penetrated under a given set of circumstances. The armor can be defeated at this range and all shorter ranges.

MPR—maximum penetration range: the maximum range at which a projectile completely penetrates or all shrapnel from it passes through an armor plate under a given set of circumstances. A projectile is virtually guaranteed to defeat armor at this and all shorter ranges.

		Range, m					
		90 degrees		30 degrees		45 degrees	
Gun	Projectile type	MSVR Y	MPRX	MSVR	MPR	MSVR	MPR
50 mm PaK 38	Armor-piercing	1500	1500	1500	1300	950	Sub-caliber penetration when firing from 65 m
	Sub-caliber	1400	1300	850	700	280	140
37 mm PaK 36	Armor-piercing	700	65	No penetration from 65 m			
	Sub-caliber	440	350	200	150	No penetration from 65 m	

Table compiled from TsAMO RF data, f. 81 (GAU), op. 12042 (Artillery Munitions Department), d. 41 (Reports of the Gorokhovets Artillery Test Range on tank armor testing), p. 26

As the results of ballistic tests on armor plate show, only upper and lower glacis plates positioned at large angles to the vertical (the lower plates additionally being screened somewhat by the terrain) could brag of relative invulnerability against the antitank gun projectiles in the Wehrmacht's inventory. The other armor plates (45 mm plates from a welded turret, vertical 45 mm side plates, and 40 mm sloped side plates) were, unfortunately, completely vulnerable to projectiles of the enemy's main antitank calibers. The great distance from which armor-piercing projectiles of the 50 mm PaK 38 antitank gun were fired at a 45 mm armor plate (both at 90° and at an angle) approximately corresponds to the average range at which a tank type target is detected in the European theater of military operations; thus, the 50 mm antitank gun could be effective

A disabled and burned T-34.

against the T-34 at any combat range. The small number of these guns the Wehrmacht had in 1941 compensated for this somewhat.[2]

The situation was exacerbated by the hard-core projectiles in the enemy's antitank artillery inventory that were put into mass production based on lessons learned from the French campaign, where the Wehrmacht's enemies fielded French and British tanks with thick armor. During 1940, German industry produced almost 287,000 hard-core 37 mm projectiles; in 1941 it produced 885,000 hard-core 37 mm projectiles and 344,000 hard-core 50 mm projectiles.[3] For their part, the German forces were quite generous in expending the hard-core ammunition they had had since the very beginning of the Eastern campaign—from June 22 to December 31, 1941, they fired off 207,569 37-mm PaK 36 antitank gun projectiles; 17,352 37-mm KwK 36 tank gun projectiles; 45,756 50-mm PaK 38 antitank gun projectiles; 41,414 50-mm KwK 38 tank gun projectiles; and 8,353 37-mm hard-core projectiles from Czech tank guns mounted on 35(t) and 38(t) tanks.[4] We should, of course, note that the primary targets for hard-core projectiles were KV tanks. However, the ratio of shots fired to kills is still impressive—for 931 KVs and 1,843 T-34s lost in 1941, 320,444 hard-core projectiles were fired: an average of 115 hard-core projectiles for each new-type heavy/medium Soviet tank that became a total loss.

A T-34 and T-26 of the 57th Tank Division stuck in a marshy meadow near Tolochina, summer of 1941.

Thus, the "thirty-four" was not invulnerable against even the 37 mm "door knocker" PaK 36, not to mention the more powerful gun systems. Here, we would especially like to make it clear that we are specifically discussing penetration of a tank's armor—not perforated gun barrels, "apples" punched out of bow guns and driver-mechanic hatches, vision blocks ripped out along fractured welds, broken tracks, and other types of damage that disabled tanks but did not produce holes in the main armor assemblies. The T-34 was a rather difficult target for the "door knocker." To achieve reliable penetration, the gun needed to fire at the side of an attacking tank from short range (about 200 m) at almost a 90° angle of incidence; nevertheless, a variety of factors helped German antitank gunners meet this difficult challenge.

First of all, it should be noted that the Wehrmacht acquired first-hand familiarity with French and British tanks that had anti-projectile armor. The lessons learned in 1940 were analyzed and soldiers were trained on tactics to combat tanks with thick armor that could not be defeated when fired at head-on from long range; therefore, in and of itself, the appearance of well protected targets that were difficult to disable did

A 12th Tank Division T-34 disabled on the outskirts of Dubno, June 1941.

not shock German tank hunters and force them to undertake a feverish search for new tactics in the face of battlefield conditions they had not previously encountered. The German artilleryman were not surprised by the need to place division, corps, and heavy antiaircraft guns in open positions[5] for firing directly at tanks—all of these tactics had already been successfully tested in the French campaign and even earlier (88 mm antitank guns were used against tanks in Spain).

Secondly, the excellent training received by German infantry and their high morale, accompanied by the large-scale flight of Soviet infantry from the battlefield, meant that German troops were willing to let attacking Soviet tanks draw close to infantry positions and transform the fight into close-in infantry combat with tanks.

Thirdly, the T-34's design flaws that we have repeatedly mentioned—relative "blindness" and "deafness" (difficulty tuning and maintaining radio sets that frequently malfunctioned in combat)—prevented the rapid detection of antitank guns and the organization of tank group operations against antitank weapons (exchange of information on targets detected and sharing of targets among attacking tanks); in essence, each attacking "thirty-four" executed its own separate attack, independently searching for targets on the battlefield and destroying them just as independently.

Fourthly, the relatively poor training given Soviet tankers, combined with the mentioned previously difficulties in driving T-34 tanks, caused them to avoid changing direction and speed on the battlefield and instead travel in straight lines with relatively lengthy "short halts" (here, the relatively low practical rate of fire of the tank's gun system came into play),[6] all of which made things easier for the German tank killers.

Fifthly, the significant problems and shortcomings with controlling forces and organizing cooperation among the combat arms in the Red Army meant that tanks were sent directly into combat from a march piecemeal, without thorough advance reconnaissance, without artillery preparation and support for the attack, without preliminary clearance of obstacles, and without any established cooperation with the infantry. Unsuccessful attacks were frequently repeated in the same areas without reinforcement or noticeable improvement in cooperation among the attacking forces. As a result, unsuppressed enemy artillery could function almost as though it were in training, and tanks stopped by obstacles and barriers and close-in infantry attacks increased losses even further.

The following table compiled from the results of an inspection of T-34 hulls at repair facilities may serve to illustrate this.

Part name		Damage as percentage of total number of hits	Dangerous damage as percentage of total tank dangerous damage
Hull	Upper glacis	20.40	8.19
	Lower glacis	2.25	1.69
	Sides	23	33.68
	Upper side plate	27.50	17.25
	Upper stern plate	3.94	4.26
	Lower stern plate	3.58	5.3
	Engine cover	0.19	0.41
Turret	Glacis and gun mantlet	4.86	7.39
	Sides	8.61	14.28
	Stern	2.48	4.49
	Top	1.11	1.64
	Gun	1.69	1.22
	Turret skirt	0.39	0

Table compiled from TsAMO RF data, f. 38 (GABTU), op. 11355 (Tank Directorate), d. 785 (Report of Research Institute No. 48 on penetration of Red Army tanks and reasons they were disabled), p. 5

A T-34 of an unknown unit, summer of 1941.

Two captured T-34s bearing German recognition markings.

It is easy to see that more than half of all hits were to the sides of tank hulls, and the same is true for the number of dangerous hits; at the same time, less than one quarter of the total number of hits were to the front of the tank, and less than 10% of those were dangerous hits. That is, German antitank artillery fired at spots where the chances of penetrating the T-34's armor were the greatest—at the sides of the hull and turret, and the statistics clearly show that the actions of Soviet tanks on the battlefield allowed the enemy to do so.

> *The fact that the majority of hits (50.5%) were to the hull sides and side plates, which are significantly less resistant to projectiles than the front of the tank, may be due to ignorance or underestimation of the T-34's tactical properties by its crews or to an inability to take advantage of the tank's tactical properties; or it may be a result of difficulties with observation during combat for reasons associated with the tank's design and, as a result, delays in detecting enemy firing positions.*[7]

However, now that we have answered the question about the capability of German antitank defenses to relatively successfully counter the newest Soviet tanks in general and the "thirty-fours" in particular, another question comes to the fore: why is it that T-34s are not mentioned in the memoirs of German generals until August, September, or even later? We wish particularly to stress that we are talking specifically about the memoirs of generals: in the summer of 1941 numerous T-34s were photographed by German soldiers (and it is these photos that we have used to illustrate this book). The many German photos of T-34s taken near the border in the summer of 1941 in fact call the memoirs of the German generals into question—the first mention of T-34s in the memoirs of Hoth, whose tanks encountered "thirty-fours" of the 5th Tank Division in Alitus on the first day of the war, was at Borisov on July 3;[8] and Guderian wrote that:

> *the T-34 tank appeared in front of our lines in late July 1941 and was a new tank design,*[9]

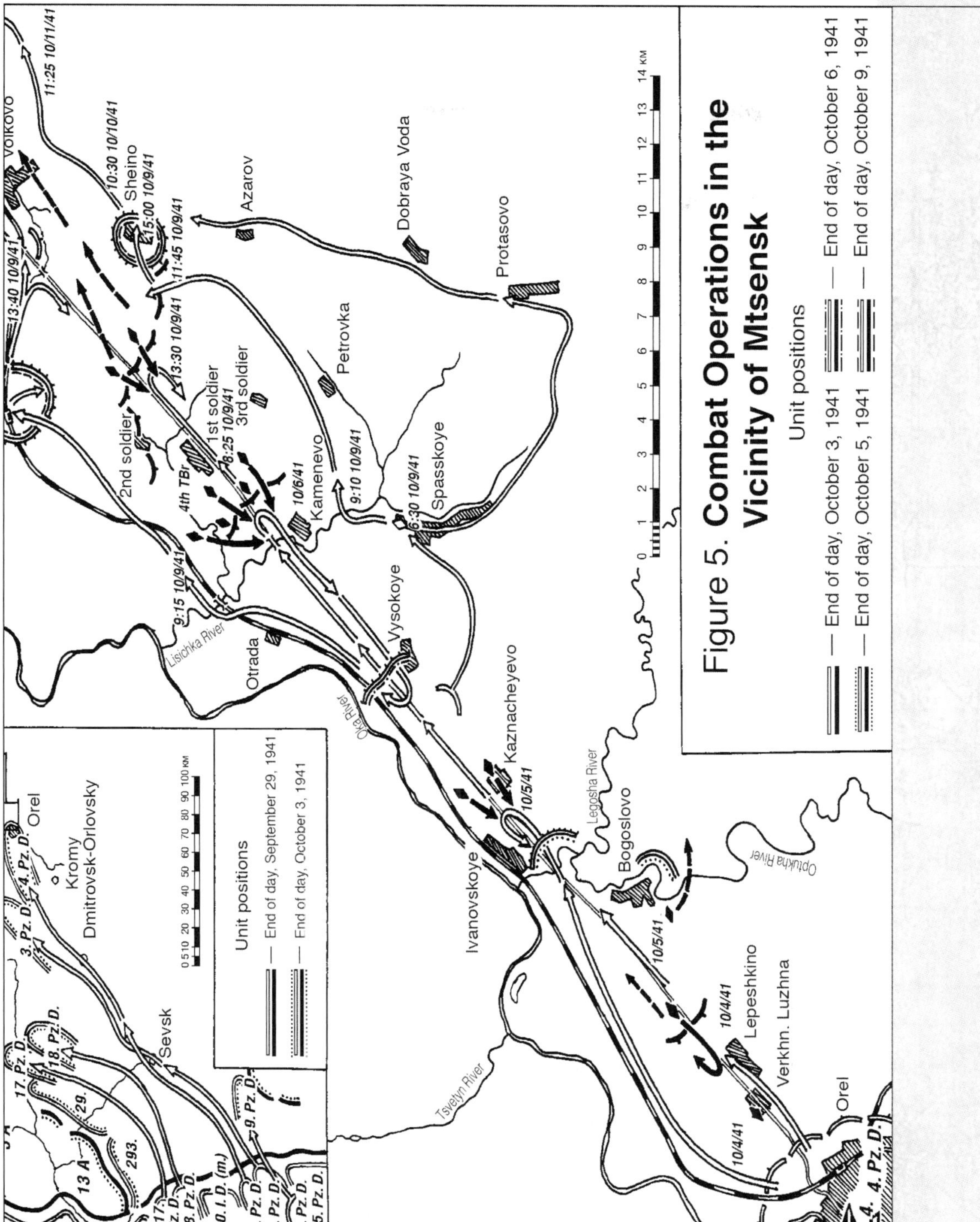

Figure 5. **Combat Operations in the Vicinity of Mtsensk**

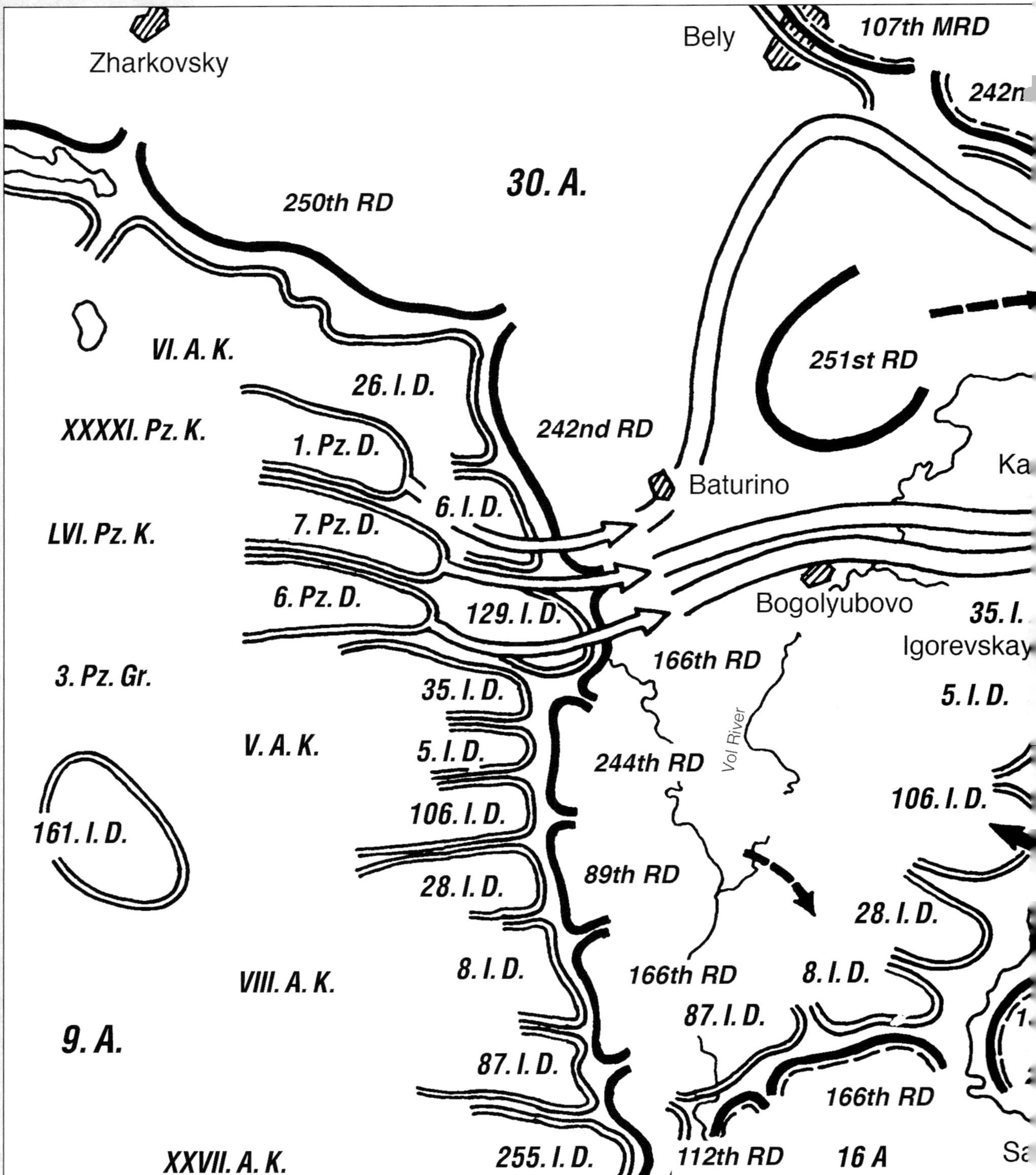
Zharkovsky
Bely
107th MRD
242n
30. A.
250th RD
251st RD
VI. A. K.
26. I. D.
XXXXI. Pz. K.
1. Pz. D.
242nd RD
Ka
Baturino
6. I. D.
LVI. Pz. K.
7. Pz. D.
6. Pz. D.
129. I. D.
Bogolyubovo
35. I.
Igorevskay
3. Pz. Gr.
166th RD
35. I. D.
5. I. D.
V. A. K.
5. I. D.
244th RD
Vol River
106. I. D.
106. I. D.
161. I. D.
89th RD
28. I. D.
28. I. D.
8. I. D.
VIII. A. K.
166th RD
8. I. D.
87. I. D.
9. A.
87. I. D.
166th RD
XXVII. A. K.
255. I. D.
112th RD
16 A
Sa

Figure 6. **Counterattack by Boldin's Group, October 4–6, 1941**

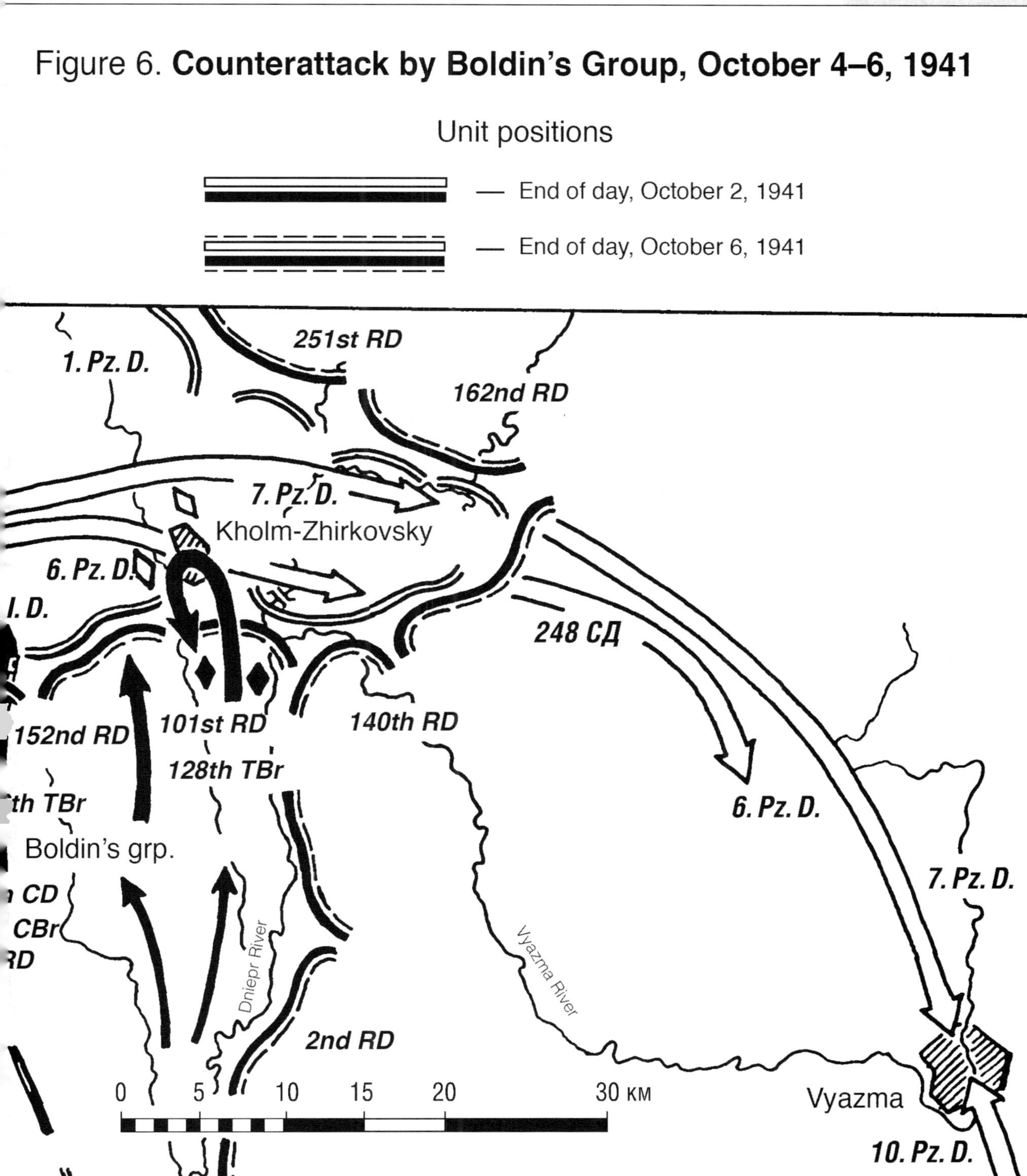

A disabled and burned T-34, summer of 1941. At first glance, the tank appears to be in good running order, but the road wheel tires on both sides have burned.

although there are photographs taken in Belarus by German forces from columns bearing the letter G (for Guderian's Panzer Group) showing soldiers examining a T-34 with interest; in Eike Middeldorf's book, T-34s first appeared in August;[10] and Friedrich von Mellenthin [who became commander of the 48th Panzer Corps] shifts the introduction of appreciable numbers of T-34s to October;[11] and so forth.

The authors have their own opinion about this issue. In discussing the memoirs of German generals, we need to consider the atmosphere in which they were written. For Nazi Germany, World War II ended with unconditional surrender, occupation by forces of the countries that won the war, dismemberment of the country, and denazification. These circumstances, particularly the last one, meant that their memoirs could not take the tragically elevated tone of "enthusiastic service in a great cause" but rather prompted memoir writers to take an overall approach of "I was a good soldier and stayed out of politics," with stress placed on the "military and technological" aspects of the memoirist's experiences on the front lines. Furthermore, the split between the former Allies and the start of the Cold War allowed them to describe their accomplishments on the Eastern Front with little fear of being subjected to public condemnation. The German memoirists approached the "1941 problem" in a uniquely German context: they needed to answer why the campaign in Russia, which had begun with record daily

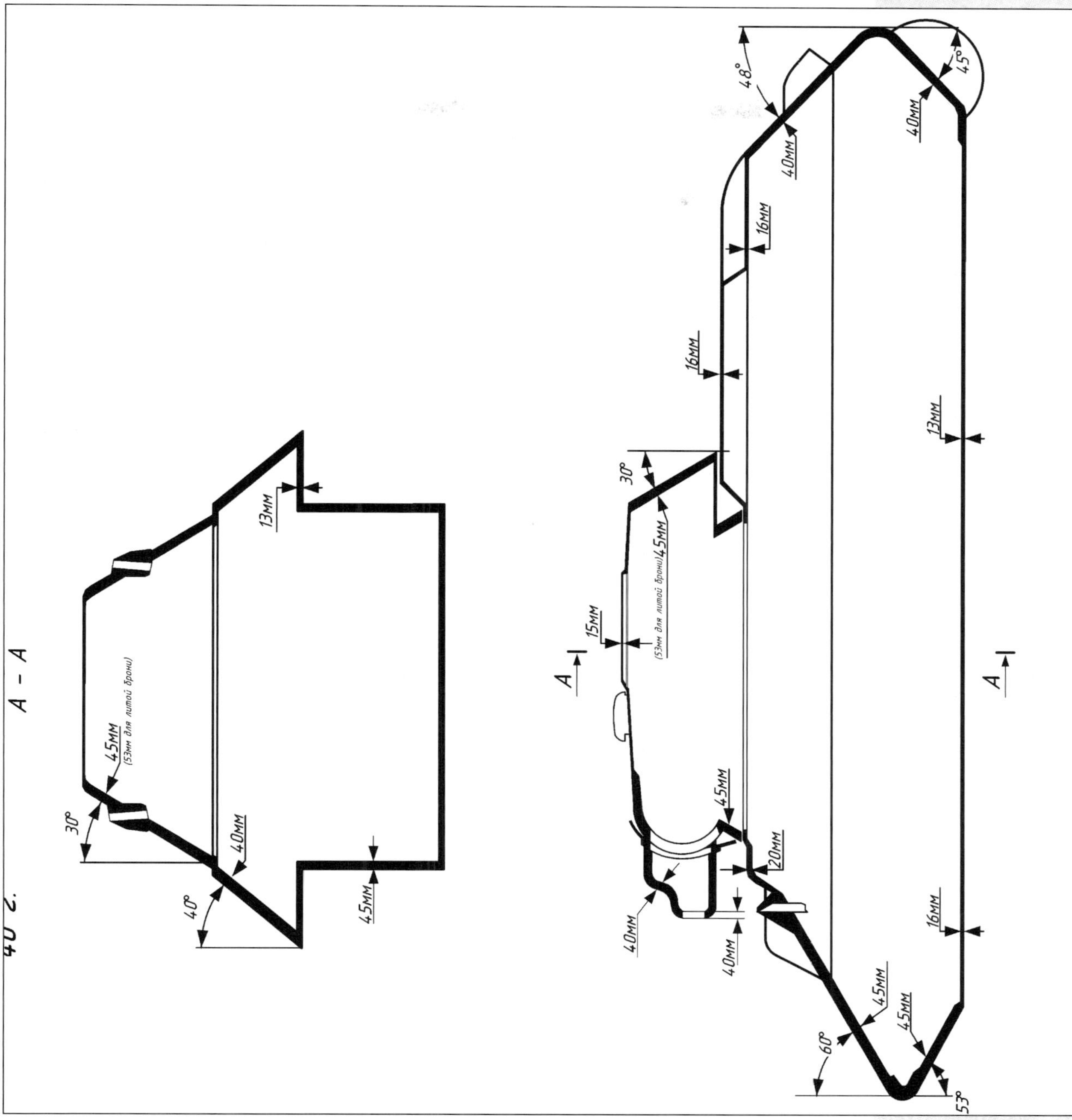

The armor scheme of a T-34 produced in the summer of 1941.

advances and the capture of astronomical numbers of prisoners, suddenly stalled outside Moscow and almost met with disaster in the winter of 1941–1942.

The obvious answer—blame everything on the military-geographic nature of the Russian theater of military operations and the large Russian population—must be discounted as unsatisfactory after a minimum of reflection. Indeed, Russian territory was no less extensive and populous in the summer of 1941 than it was in the fall and winter, but those circumstances did not prevent a successful German offensive. Furthermore, simple reflection shows that the "geography" and "climate" affected the defenders no less than the attackers—the defenders had, first of all, to use their own forces to block those "endless and vast Russian expanses" that were so difficult for the attacker to cross, and then, like the attacker, they had to supply their forces with everything they needed over the same muddy Russian roads, on which tanks and trucks bogged down, horses could not extricate their hooves, and infantrymen could not march more than a few kilometers per day.

The obvious reference to the "better adaptation of the Russian soldier, his weapons, and his equipment to the demands of the Russian theater" must also be seen as unsatisfactory: the fact that every soldier is best equipped for war in his "native" conditions is not a closely held secret of military science, but rather one of its self-evident foundations. Accordingly, a general's job is to take into account an enemy's strengths and weaknesses in advance and seek ways to neutralize his superiority and exploit his weaknesses. That is, reference to the Russian soldier's adaptation to war in geographic and climatic conditions that are typical for him on the one hand and the lack of adaptation and unsuitability of the German soldier to war in such conditions on the other is a lightly veiled admission that "I am a mediocre commander. I was unable to satisfactorily solve a fundamental problem that military leaders face." Most memoirs are not written with the intention of revealing such things.

A satisfactory explanation of the "1941 paradox" requires a factor that would be asymmetric both "temporally" (not a factor at the beginning of the campaign but in full force during the fall and winter) and "spatially" (having a negative impact on German forces without affecting Soviet forces). *New types of formidable, invincible, and highly destructive Russian tanks that appeared suddenly* and against which German antitank weapons were said to be completely powerless constituted just such a factor. It is noteworthy that this "ultimate weapon" appears in the German generals's memoirs precisely at the point where a memoirist gets into trouble and needs somehow to explain why his rate of advance has slowed or he has initiated a more or (more likely) less organized retreat. Enthusiastic praise for an enemy's weapons made it possible to show one's own actions and the achievements of one's troops in a heroic light, having done everything that was humanly possible and more, and having failed in the end only due to factors clearly beyond the memoirist's control.

The Soviet memoirists faced a similar conundrum: they also badly needed to explain the "problem of the summer of 1941"—the disaster at the beginning of the war—and they had to do it with an eye towards the "ideological" context—the message, first of all, that the Communist Party and the Soviet government had presciently identified the danger that the country would be drawn into World War II and had taken adequate actions in a timely manner and, secondly, that the Soviet people had stood up as one to resist the "rotten fascist scum." [12] And that prevented them from explaining the military failures during the summer of 1941 by pointing to the weak staying power of the poorly trained and equipped Soviet troops. Like their German counterparts, the Soviet generals had no incentive to openly describe their mistakes. Similar problems give rise to similar solutions —so the memoirs of Soviet marshals and generals say that the main problem was that there were not enough of the invulnerable and highly destructive T-34s; the production and distribution of military equipment were quite clearly beyond the control of the memoirists. The Soviet leaders that decided these issues (V. M. Molotov, Chairman of the Council of People's Commissars; J. V. Stalin; S. K. Timoshenko, People's Commissar of Defense; and later, V. A. Malyshev, People's Commissar of the Tank Industry) died without leaving memoirs that would shed light on the decisions they made. Accordingly, the fact that more "thirty-fours" were lost in the first 40 days of the war than during the next five months—a formidable tank armada that the Germans had not even noticed—was not discussed in the Soviet generals' memoirs and, therefore, not explained.

H*owever, the vulnerability of the armor of the "thirty-fours" to armor-piercing projectiles fired by the 37 mm gun (which turned out to penetrate a 47mm plate at a 90° angle of incidence from ranges of 700 m and less) was a very unpleasant surprise—when the Chief Military Council was putting together the Red Army's tank and automotive system in the spring of 1940, it included the "T-34 medium tank, which is impervious to 37–45 mm guns at any range."*

To what has been said, we would like to add that Soviet military documents contain no statements about the "invulnerability" or "highly destructive nature" of the T-34; furthermore, thorough analysis of the descriptions of battles leads us to conclude the exact opposite. For example,

> *Operating in the 348th Rifle Regiment's sector of the 51st Rifle Division, a T-34 tank platoon circumvented the enemy's artillery positions and two of its tanks reached the southern outskirts of KAKHOVKA, appearing suddenly and creating panic among in the units and, moving and maneuvering quickly, suppressed the enemy's personnel and equipment (on 4 September 1941, Political Officer Viniaminov's tank entered KAKHOVKA and, when it reached the jumping-off position, was literally covered in blood, having taken as many as 70 direct hits from enemy 37 mm and 75 mm guns,*

A burned T-34 of an unknown unit.

A disabled T-34 that had attempted to enter Minsk, which was already occupied by the Germans, summer 1941.

losing its top hatch and the driver's front hatch without being penetrated, and, as proof, it brought with it two Nazi heads and parts of the gear of an officer and enlisted personnel on its bogey brackets). [13]

At first glance it looks like this is a "positive" example—an invulnerable wonder-tank crushing everything in its path, sweeping through hordes of enemies, and returning covered in blood and glory. A closer look, however does not leave one stone of optimism unturned:

The attack by the 51st Rifle Division was set for 09:00 on 4 September 1941. A 15-minute artillery preparation was carried out before the general attack and the insertion of tanks into the battle (the artillery preparatory fire was short because there were not enough 122 mm and 152 mm shells); the artillery and infantry commanders were informed at the same time about the tanks's actions in the sectors of the 263rd in 348th Rifle Regiments. Upon receipt of the combat mission, the tank detachment's commander, Captain Borvinok, led his tanks into battle at 09:10 on 4 September 1941. During forward movement towards the enemy's firing positions located in a wooded area south of Kakhovka, infantry of our 263rd Rifle Regiment advanced forward 300–400 m; the 348th Rifle Regiment did not advance. The enemy began conducting intense mortar and artillery fire, which separated the infantry from the tanks. The attack by our rifle units bogged down, and the tanks, enveloped in smoke and dust, moved forward without returning to the infantry. Some tanks reached the southern outskirts of Kakhovka and were forced to return to their starting position. Tank losses included the following: T-34s—two burned, one missing; BT-7—one burned; T-26—two disabled. All of these tanks remained in the area held by the enemy. Actions taken to recover the tanks were unsuccessful due to the hasty retreat of our infantry units. [14]

The outcome of the battle looks much less optimistic than it seemed in the previous dispatch: of the T-34s belonging to the tank platoon that carried out the attack (5 vehicles authorized) two "thirty-fours" burned, one went missing, and one (Political Officer Viniaminov's tank) returned with serious damage (upper hatch lost, driver-mechanic's hatch lost, tank requiring repair and unable to take part in the battle until it is done)—at best (out of the platoon's full complement of T-34s before the attack began), one tank remained combat capable. The attack was a failure. This was not an attack conducted with impunity on enemy positions with tanks that "in the overwhelming majority of cases were not penetrated by projectiles fired from 37 mm German antitank guns," [15] but actually a defeat inflicted on an attacking unit of invulnerable, highly destructive tanks. The outstanding results achieved by Political Officer Viniaminov's crew only partially sweetened the bitter pill of localized damage.

Furthermore, this report clearly illustrates the reasons we have given for the heavy tank losses:

- The brief artillery preparation was insufficient to reliably suppress enemy defenses;
- The infantry and artillery were only informed about tank operations immediately before the tanks went into battle. Thus, there is no point in discussing cooperation at the "tank-rifle squad" level or artillery support for the tank attack;
- The infantry was cut off from the tanks during the attack, and the tanks broke through enemy lines alone, without infantry support.

Unfortunately, in the summer of 1941 the Red Army had neither an excess of well-trained infantrymen who knew how to cooperate with tanks nor a large, highly qualified officer corps that could quickly but thoroughly organize and then maintain cooperation among various combat arms during a battle. Many more things can be added to the list; it is much simpler to say what the Army had.

It had tanks—not the best tanks, certainly not tanks that were "invulnerable in the overwhelming majority of cases," but tanks that allowed even inexperienced crews to occasionally survive under fire from "door knockers," the Wehrmacht's main antitank gun at that time, and return from combat, sometimes with their armor scratched by several dozen projectiles, delighting friends and surprising the enemy.

Then too, there was courage, with which they tried to compensate for their lack of skill. The courage of those who went through deadly fire, penetrated enemy positions and destroyed enemy antitank guns that had not been suppressed, rammed tanks with crosses painted on their sides, and machine-gunned infantrymen in mouse-gray uniforms—and continued doing so from a disabled and burning tank until the very end. Of those who, from the very first hours of the war, caused the plan for "blitzkrieg war" against the Soviet Union to stall and fail.

A T-34 disabled between Radzekhuv and Dubno.

The personnel did not have the training needed to maneuver and fire on the battlefield, but they were loyal to the Soviet regime. Attention needs to be paid to the Bolshevist system of manning the special weapons systems (tanks, aircraft, etc.) only with proven and reliable people who are devoted to the communist regime. Soviet tanks never surrendered; they could not be captured until their crews were incapacitated.[16]

NOTES

1 Russian proverb.

2 RGASPI, f. 31811, op. 2, d. 1107, pp. 201–205. Cit. ex: "The Winter War: Correcting Mistakes (April–May 1940)." *Materials of Commissions of the Main Military Council of the Red Army on Best Practices of the Finnish Campaign.* Moscow, St. Petersburg: Letniy Sad, 2004, p. 293.

3 Fritz Hahn. *Waffen und Geheimwaffen des deutschen Heeres 1933–1945.* Bonn: Bernard & Graefe Verlag, 1998, p. 115.

4 *Kriegstagebuch des Oberkommandos der Wehrmacht. Band I,* Bonn: Bernard & Graefe Verlag, 2003. pp. 1110–1114.

5 An open firing position is a firing position located such that the weapon is not concealed from enemy ground observation or one that is revealed when it opens fire.

6 "When tanks draw even with the first echelon companies during an attack, they usually stop and open fire, and the infantrymen instinctively take cover next to the tanks. The tanks fire while stationary for about 25–30 minutes..." TsAMO RF, f. 14 (General Staff), op. 11603 (War Studies Department, Red Army General Staff), d. 2 (Servicemen's letters with proposals for tactical employment of combat arms, conclusions drawn from combat experience, and deficiencies in the training of our troops for war; correspondence with them on these issues), p. 173.

7 TsAMO RF, f. 38 (GABTU), op. 11355 (Tank Directorate), d. 785 (Report of Research Institute No. 48 on penetration of Red Army tanks and reasons they were disabled), p. 18.

8 H. Hoth. *Tank Operations.* Moscow: Voyenizdat, 1961, p. 88.

9 H. Guderian. *Memoirs of a Soldier.* Smolensk: Rusich, 1999. p. 194.

10 Eike Middeldorf, *The Russian Campaign: Tactics and Weapons [Russkaya kampaniya: taktika i vooruzheniye].* St. Petersburg: OOO Izdatelstvo Poligon, Moscow: OOO Firma Izdatelstvo AST, 2000, p. 15.

11 F. V. von Mellenthin, *Panzer Battles 1939–1945: Tactical Employment of Tanks During World War II.* Moscow: Inostrannaya literatura, 1957, p. 141.

12 "For the rotten fascist pack / We'll send a bullet to the brain. / That spawn of humanity / We'll send to the grave!" From the song "Holy War [Svyashchennaya voyna]" (music: A. Alexanderov; lyrics: Lebedev-Kumach), 1941.

13 TsAMO RF, f. 228, (Southern Front), op. 738 (Armor Directorate), d. 8 (Reports and dispatches of the armored vehicle sections of armies and units regarding actions of armored forces; Report of front military prosecutor regarding tank losses), pp. 9–10.

14 Ibid., pp. 2–3.

15 M. S. Solonin, *Screwing the Brains: The False History of the Great War [Mozgoimeniye: Fal'shivaya istoriya Velikoy voyny].* Moscow: Eksmo, Yauza, 2010.

16 TsAMO RF, f. 500, op. 12462 (Translations of Captured Documents), d. 85 (Germany's Experience in the War Against the USSR) p. 44.

A disabled T-34 that had attempted to enter Minsk, which was already occupied by the Germans, summer 1941.
This vehicle also appears in the photo on page 172.

CHAPTER 7. **UNDER OPERATION TYPHOON**

Live, brothers, live, however it may seem!
No time to grieve in this tank team.[1]

Within a month after the war began it was clear that the Soviet plan of forming 29 mechanized corps was not destined to become reality. The majority of the Red Army's prewar tank inventory had been lost in desperate attempts to delay, if not halt, the "Thousand Year Reich's" finely tuned war machine. The prospects for sharply increasing deliveries from industry looked bleak—many factories were in the process of evacuating to the East: others had yet to load onto railcars. It was clear by

A tank decorated by the Germans. This tank is also shown on pages 172 and 177.

the summer of 1941 that the Red Army not only had a shortage of the new tanks, it also had too few commanders able to properly use them.

> *... There were many shortcomings attributed directly to the commanders of mechanized units, including the following:*
>
> *The headquarters staffs of mechanized corps, tank divisions, and tank regiments had not yet mastered the skills required for an operational-tactical perspective; they were unable to draw the proper conclusions and did not fully understand the army and front commanders' concepts.*
>
> *The command staff displayed too little initiative.*
>
> *They did not employ all of the mobility systems possessed by mechanized units.*
>
> *They did not maneuver—they were lethargic and slow to execute missions.*
>
> *Most actions undertaken were frontal attacks, which resulted in unnecessary loss of matériel and personnel, and this happened because commanders at all levels neglected reconnaissance.*
>
> *They were unable to organize corps battle formations along axes and secure enemy movement routes, and the enemy moved mainly by road.*
>
> *They did not employ obstacles; cooperation with engineer forces was nonexistent.*
>
> *There was no attempt to deprive [the enemy] of the capability to transport fuel and ammunition. Ambushes were not used on the enemy's main operational axes.*
>
> *Enemy actions on flanks led to a fear of being surrounded when tank units had no reason to fear encirclement.*

Major population centers were not utilized to destroy the enemy, and the ability to fight in them was lacking.

Control was poor from the platoon level up; poor use was made of radios; poor use was made of encrypted communications; and encoding and decoding messages took too much time.

Crew training on holding onto matériel was extremely poor. There were cases where crews abandoned vehicles that had ammunition, and there were some instances where crews abandoned vehicles and retreated.

All units lacked recovery equipment, and what was available could support a mechanized corps or division only in offensive operations.

Personnel had not mastered the new equipment, especially the KV and T-34, and they were entirely untrained on how to perform field repairs. Tank division repair equipment was completely incapable of supporting repairs during a retreat.

A large percentage of the command staff did not know their missions and could not read maps, which caused entire units to go astray.

The mechanized corps did not have repair equipment even during peacetime, and therefore this training issue was given little attention.

The existing organization of logistical support was extremely cumbersome; the assistant technical officer usually remained with the logistical support elements in the second echelon. The logistical support elements should be reduced in size, leaving the mechanized corps equipment solely for transporting fuel, ammunition, and food.

The army-level disabled vehicle collection posts were disorganized as a rule. No one supervised them, and the lack of TOE recovery equipment usually meant that equipment recovery was nonexistent in the army and front rear areas.

The heads of army-level armored vehicle sections only performed supply functions, and they completely failed at that task. The army-level armored vehicle sections are seriously undermanned and unable to supervise soldiers. Personnel selection for them was done very poorly; as a result Lieutenant Colonel D. of the 6th Army's wheeled and armored vehicle section was removed from his position for inability to perform his duties.

The headquarters staffs were poorly trained and manned as a rule, with combined-arms commanders lacking experience in tank units.

The mechanized corps answered to many commanders—they received tasking from front and army, and infantry corps gave them missions, as is most clearly shown by the way the 41st Tank Division of the 22nd Mechanized Corps was employed.

Some mechanized corps commanders were not up to par and had no idea of how to command a mechanized corps.

The higher educational institutions (Academies) never taught the types of combat they would encounter, and that resulted in huge deficiencies in the operational-tactical perspective of most commanders.[2]

However, the 41st could not wait until its "*staffs possessed an operational-tactical perspective*" and its "*commanders reached the required level.*" They needed to fight in June 1941. Therefore, the remaining (existing mostly on paper) mechanized corps were "broken up" into tank divisions, and the motorized rifle divisions had to give up their many (again, existing on paper) transport vehicles to higher headquarters and become ordinary rifle divisions. However, the division structure (although weaker than the pre-war, authorized strength of July) did not become the basic structure for the armored forces. Not even dismembering the mechanized corps could solve the growing problem of equipment shortages—according to reports from the first two weeks of August, the Red Army had the following requirement for tanks and armored cars: KV tanks – 2,997, T-34 tanks – 7,541, T-50 and T-60 tanks – 5,747, armored cars – 4,303. Meanwhile, the anticipated supplies of tanks and armored cars from factories between August and the end of 1941 were as follows: 1,530 KV tanks, 3,260 T-34 tanks, 580 T-50 tanks, 10,000 T-60 tanks, and 1800 armored cars. The situation was not encouraging:

> *Thus, with the factories completely fulfilling the plan, the army's requirements for tanks and armored cars (excluding losses) can be met within the following periods (approximately):*
>
> ***a)*** *Tanks (KV and T-34)—10–11 months.*
>
> ***b)*** *Armored cars—11 months.*[3]

The backbone of the armored forces for the near future was to be brigades and independent battalions. As of August 23, 1941, the TOE of a tank brigade was that of a full-fledged mechanized unit reduced in size to be compatible with the capabilities of industry. It consisted of one tank regiment and one motorized rifle regiment, an antitank and antiaircraft artillery battalion, an independent reconnaissance company, and support units. The brigade's tank fleet, which was concentrated in a tank regiment consisting of one battalion of heavy and medium tanks and two battalions of light tanks, included 7 KVs, 20 T-34s, and 65 light tanks (or BTs and T-26s), for a total of 92 tanks. The smaller size of the proposed independent mechanized unit (in comparison with the previous mechanized corps and tank divisions) should have been easier to control.[4]

However, implementation of the plans to form lighter independent mechanized units was not in the cards—within 20 days, on September 13, a new TOE for the tank brigades had been adopted. The motorized rifle regiment was eliminated and replaced by a motorized rifle battalion. The tank regiment retained two battalions (one battalion of light tanks was eliminated), but its tank fleet had been reduced to 61 tanks (7 KVs, 22 T-34s or T-50s, 32 T-40s or T-60s). The mechanized unit, which was called a "brigade," had essentially shrunk to the size of a regiment (three battalions) and could no longer be expected to execute independent operations successfully. However, its shrinkage meant that control of the unit was simplified, something that was very important considering the acute shortage of competent officers.

But a simple "downgrading" of tank units did not solve, nor could it solve, all problems—and it gave rise to new ones. And the Soviet command would find itself learning about that very quickly.

The battle for Moscow provided the first serious test of the new "tools." Three of the Third Reich's four panzer groups took part in Operation Typhoon. Guderian's 2nd Panzer Group launched an offensive on October 30; the forces of Army Group Center

A T-34 of an unknown unit. The bodies are those of the crew.

made their move on October 2. An attempt by the Western Front's headquarters to halt the grouping of forces that had broken through with a flanking counterattack failed.

> *The breakthrough was accomplished in dry weather on October 2 with surprising ease. The 8th Aviation Corps provided effective support to ground forces. The enemy offered less resistance in the area of the armor breakthrough than we had expected. Panzer units of the 56th Panzer Corps rapidly broke through a wooded area along the Vol River, halfway between Novoselki and Kholm. Hard fighting erupted southwest of Kholm. A Russian tank brigade approached from the south and fought to the bitter end. These battles slowed our crossing of the Dniepr. On 4 October, the 6th and 7th Panzer Divisions crossed to the eastern bank over the remaining bridges, suppressed enemy resistance, and returned to Vyazma. On 6 October, the 7th Panzer Division used a highway to get behind the enemy, which had waited until too late to begin retreating to the eastern bank of the Dniepr. On 7 October, the 10th Panzer Division of the 4th Panzer Group joined up with the regiment on the left flank of the 7th Panzer Division.*[5]

The tank brigade rated so highly by Herman Hoth was actually not operating by itself: Boldin's operation group included the 126th, 128th, and 147th Tank Brigades, as well as the 15th Rifle, 45th Cavalry, and 101st Motorized Divisions. In all, these units had 241 tanks; of the new tank types there were only 16 KVs and 19 "thirty-fours." Desperate resistance by the tankers helped win valuable hours and days, but they were unable to pull off a miracle—the Germans closed a ring around units of the Western and Reserve Fronts. Now, the fate of Moscow depended on a few kilometers of autumn roads. The Soviet command had reserves and the capability to shift forces from those sections of the front where the enemy had relaxed the pressure. But that required that someone win the time needed to establish a "thin red line" in the path of the German forces. And the tank brigades were the ones capable of quickly moving in front of the new defensive line and delaying the deadly blows of German panzer spearheads aimed at Moscow.

When we speak of the fighting that October, we usually recall the actions of Katukov's 4th Tank Brigade. This brigade was renamed the 1st Guards Brigade after these battles, and it truly deserved that honor. The German 4th Panzer Division that it opposed had covered 240 km between the time the offensive began on September 30 and October 3. After the battle with the tankers of the 4th Tank Brigade began, the rate of the German advance significantly slowed—it took the Germans a week to travel the 35 km from Orel to Mtsensk. During that week, the hastily formed 1st Special Guards Rifle Corps managed to deploy on a new defensive line.

The history of the 4th Tank Brigade's battles is worthy of its own book. We hope that such a book will soon be forthcoming (or rather, re-released) in this series. But for now, we will limit ourselves to quoting from a report by 4th Panzer Division officers under Guderian.

The 4th Panzer Division has encountered heavy Russian tanks often. Initially, encounters were rare, and they could be stopped by concentrated artillery fire or bypassed. In a few particularly successful instances, individual heavy tanks were destroyed by a direct artillery hit.

The Russians first began employing heavy tanks in large numbers after the capture of Orel. Some clashes resulted in very intense tank battles, because the Russian tanks no longer allowed themselves to be stopped by artillery.

For the first time in the Eastern campaign, the absolute superiority of the Russian 26- and 52-ton tanks over our Pz.Kpfw. III and IV tanks became apparent.

The Russian tanks usually line up in a semicircle and open fire on our tanks with their 7.62 cm [caliber] guns from a range of 1,000 m; their guns combine incredible penetrating power with high accuracy.

Soviet Documents of 1941 paint a grim picture of tank combat: tanks were being thrown into battle without prior reconnaissance of the terrain and the enemy's defense system; ammunition shortages and lack of knowledge about targets limited artillery to brief periods of area fire and prevented it from supporting tank attacks; engineers did not clear obstacles; tanks and infantry did not cooperate (and the infantry was not trained to accompany attacking tanks and consolidate their gains); the infantry did not support or provide cover for recovery of damaged and inoperable tanks from the battlefield; etc.

Our 5 cm Kw.K tank guns can only penetrate vulnerable spots in very specific favorable locations from very short ranges under 50 m. They are disabling our tanks from ranges of several hundred meters. The armor of our tanks has been penetrated many times, or our Pz.Kpfw. IIIs and IVs lost their commander's cupolas after the first successful hit. This proves that the armor protection is insufficient, the placement of commander's cupolas on our tanks is flawed, and the precision and penetrating power of the Russian 7.62 cm gun are high.

In addition to the superior effectiveness of its gun and its stronger armor, the 26-ton Christie (T-34) tank is faster and more maneuverable, and its turret traversing mechanism is obviously superior. This tank's wide tracks allow it to ford rivers that our tanks cannot. Its specific ground pressure is somewhat better than that of our tanks, and, despite the Russian tank's greater weight, it can cross the same bridges that our tanks can.

Also noteworthy is its exceptional diesel engine. In traveling from Glebov to Manske, not a single Russian tank became disabled because of mechanical failure. In comparison, about 20 tanks from our 35th Panzer Regiment alone were left behind on that same section of road due to mechanical problems. It should be acknowledged, of course, that the Russian tanks were relatively new.

One specific advantage of our tanks is that their commander's cupola affords them better visibility.

These facts and, moreover, the impression that the Russians know about the technical superiority of their armored forces must be addressed as soon as possible to avoid harm to our panzer forces.

The energy and high morale that our attacks previously had are beginning to wane and will be lost due to a sense of inferiority. The crews know that they can be defeated by enemy tanks from long ranges and that they can have only a minimal effect on enemy tanks, despite having special ammunition for close-range use.

By themselves, 8.8 cm antiaircraft guns or 10 cm cannon against Russian tanks may not be sufficient. These two guns are very cumbersome in comparison with fast tanks, and most are detected, taken under fire, and destroyed as soon as they attempt to take up a firing position. In just one tank battle that occurred between Orel and Mtsensk, two 8.8 cm guns and a 10 cm cannon (all of the heavy defensive weapons used) were fired upon and suppressed. In addition, these unprotected guns, which are as big as a barn door, are too large and are easy prey.

Based on this experience, our panzer forces again must be improved as quickly as possible to prevent today's German soldiers from having to use the same primitive methods against heavy tanks that were employed in 1917 or 1918.

Judging by the fact that all of the destroyed Christie tanks were new, we can conclude that the Russians, recognizing their superiority, have already begun mass production of these heavy tanks and we can anticipate that they will possess large numbers of them by the spring of 1942.

We hereby submit the following detailed proposals for countering the heavy Russian tanks for consideration:

1) *Develop the following offensive weapons to combat the heavy tanks:*

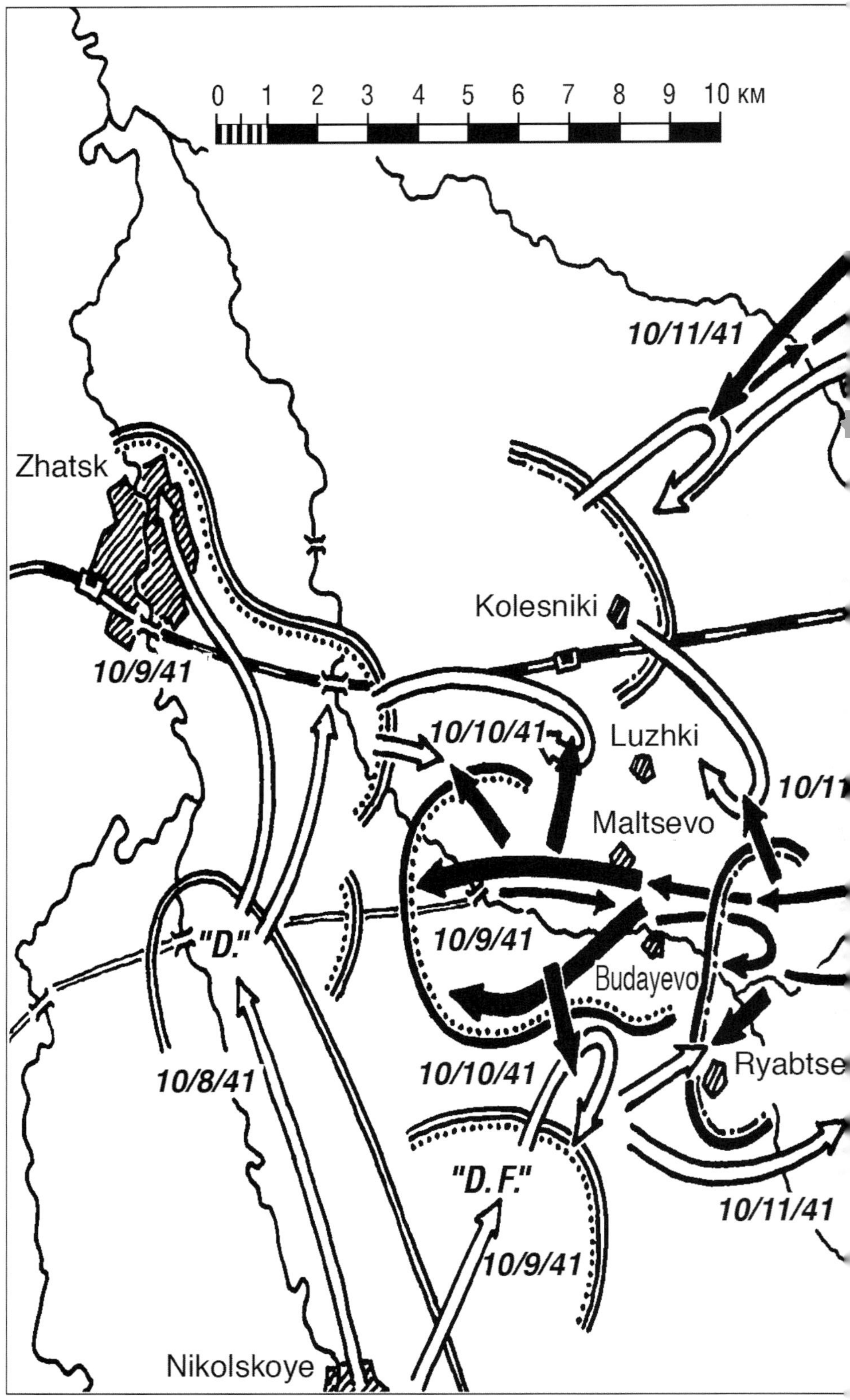
0 1 2 3 4 5 6 7 8 9 10 км
Zhatsk
10/9/41
10/11/41
Kolesniki
10/10/41
Luzhki
Maltsevo
10/9/41
Budayevo
"D."
10/8/41
10/10/41
Ryabtse
"D. F."
10/11/41
10/9/41
Nikolskoye

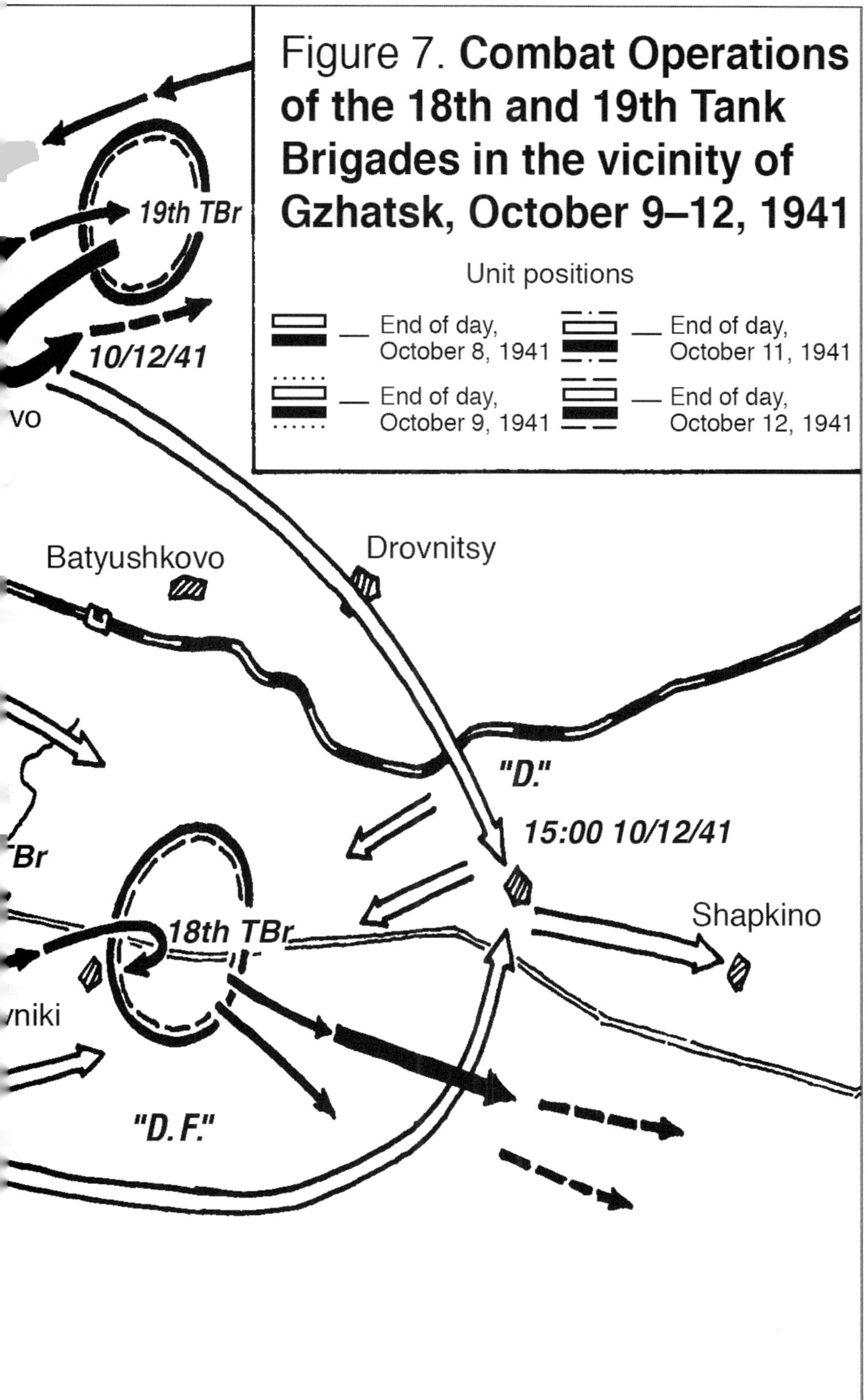
Figure 7. Combat Operations of the 18th and 19th Tank Brigades in the vicinity of Gzhatsk, October 9–12, 1941
Unit positions
— End of day, October 8, 1941
— End of day, October 9, 1941
— End of day, October 11, 1941
— End of day, October 12, 1941
19th TBr
10/12/41
vo
Batyushkovo
Drovnitsy
"D."
15:00 10/12/41
Br
18th TBr
Shapkino
rniki
"D. F."

a) *In addition to other upgrades, in order to immediately improve the situation produce copies of the Russian 26-ton tank as soon as possible and utilize undamaged 26- and 52-ton tanks that have been captured. One company is needed for each panzer regiment.*
b) *Mount the Russian 76 mm tank gun on the Pz.Kpfw. IV even if it is necessary to forgo additional armor that would increase protection for the commander and the coaxial turret-mounted machine gun.*
c) *Develop a 10 cm self-propelled antitank gun. At least six guns are needed for each panzer regiment.*
d) *Develop a new type of ammunition with greatly improved penetration.*
e) *As an immediate emergency measure before adoption of the other measures, mount a 5 cm antitank gun on the Pz.Kpfw. III even if it increases the weight at the bow.*

2) *Develop the following defensive weapons for use against heavy tanks:*
a) *Towed or self-propelled 10 cm antitank guns. Rapid fielding is very important, and their trunnion height should be as low as possible. Each antitank company needs at least two guns.*
b) *Develop a new type of improved munition.*
c) *Abandon the 37 mm antitank gun in favor of increased numbers of 50 mm antitank guns, or use Russian 76 mm antitank guns. (The 37 mm antitank gun has proven its usefulness as a small infantry gun.)*
d) *Develop a more powerful mine capable of disabling a 52-ton tank. For example, four German mines are not enough to disable a 52-ton tank.*

The troops understand that these proposals cannot be implemented immediately, especially the development of a new tank. However, they are convinced that, based on their experience and the proposals, an adequate weapon must be developed quickly in order to achieve technical superiority for destroying heavy tanks."

Thinking back to the chapter before last and considering that the authorized strength of Katukov's brigade at the beginning of the battles for Orel and Mtsensk was 7 KVs, 22 "thirty-fours," and 26 of the "light and obsolete" BTs, it is obvious that Mikhail Yefimovich could not have used larger numbers of the new tanks than the 4th Tank Division did in Alitus or the 14th Tank Division did on the Chernogostnitsa River. For some reason, however, the German commanders that had previously faced large numbers of "thirty-fours" did not write complaining letters about their absolute superiority, nor did they demand that the Russian tanks be urgently copied. They simply took them as war trophies.

The 4th Tank Division was not the only reason the victorious advance stalled. While Katukov's tankers were halting "Speedy Heinz" on the Southwest axis, soldiers of Army Group Center in the front's center sector were advancing toward Moscow. This was the shortest route to the capital: hasty fortifications had been set up here even before the German offensive—but trenches and pillboxes alone could not stop the German tanks. The mission of mining kilometers of suburban Moscow fields at the expense of burning tanks and their own lives in order to gain precious hours and days for approaching units in this section of the front fell to three tank brigades—the 17th, the 18th, and the 19th.

A 32nd Tank Division T-34 abandoned in Lvov near the St. Onufriya Monastery. This vehicle shows obvious signs of battle damage. This vehicle is also shown in the top photo on page 124. (N 49.849913, E 24.028481)◊

The reconstituted 19th Tank Brigade arrived in the vicinity of Mozhaysk on 9 and 10 October 1941.

By 13:00 on 11 October 1941, three elements of the brigade had assembled in a forested area north of Batyushkovo: its tank regiment, reconnaissance company, and motorized machine gun battalion.

At 13:00 on 11 October 1941, the brigade was ordered to capture Gzhatsk by Lieutenant General Kalinin, commander of the Mozhaysk Group.

Three other elements of the brigade, the rear services and support units, were then in the process of unloading. The brigade was given the mission of advancing on Gzhatsk together with Major General Shcherbakov's group. General Shcherbakov's group was said to have approximately 3,500 well-armed soldiers, but it turned out to be a group of a hundred soldiers detained while retreating. They retreated to the rear during the evening of 11 October.

As a result, the brigade attacked by itself without maps and intelligence, because Major General Shcherbakov had ordered it to enter the battle from the move.

The brigade began advancing on Gzhatsk at 15:00 on 11 October. After breaking enemy resistance in the forest south of Zhulevo, the brigade continued advancing towards Kurinovo-Polyaninovo-Gzhatsk; the battle lasted until 20:00 (5 hours).

At 19:00, after four hours of fighting, an order was received from Lieutenant General Kalinin to move the offensive to 8:00 on 12 October. The brigade withdrew to an assembly point in the forest northwest of Zhulevo at nightfall after the battle.

The fighting forced the enemy out of Kurinovo-Polyaninovo and inflicted the following losses: 15 medium tanks, 2 antitank guns, and about a company of infantry destroyed.

The brigade suffered the following personnel losses: 6 killed, 13 wounded, and 12 missing in action. Matériel losses: 4 T-34 tanks disabled (recovered), 2 T-34 tanks burned, and 2 T-40 tanks burned.

On 12 October 1941 at 06:00, Major General Shcherbakov ordered half of the brigade to advance in the direction of Solovyevo and the other half to capture Gzhatsk.

The advance was to begin at 08:00. The brigade's rear service units arrived before dawn on 12 October before the advance started and began replenishing ammunition and fuel. The enemy itself began an offensive at 06:30. The brigade commander ordered a counterattack, with 7 T-34 tanks attacking head on, and 10 T-34 tanks circling around the right flank and the enemy's rear area. As they approached Zhulev, the tanks were met by Major General Dreyzer, who, not knowing about the brigade commander's order to circle on the enemy's right flank and to his rear, ordered them also to attack head on.

The change of direction and frontal attack resulted in enemy fire knocking 8 T-34 tanks out of the fight (burned).

Under heavy pressure from the enemy, the brigade began retreating towards Kryukovo, where it organized a defense to cover its retreat. On the outskirts of Kryukovo, the brigade again launched a counterattack, but it was repulsed by superior enemy forces.

The enemy's forces included up to a mechanized infantry regiment, forty tanks, and two heavy artillery battalions plus a mortar and an antitank battery. The battle resulted in heavy losses to the brigade: personnel: 22 killed, 45 wounded, 253 missing in action; matériel: 11 T-34 tanks burned, 9 T-40 tanks burned, and 1 antitank gun and 1 BA-10 destroyed.

Enemy losses: 11 medium tanks, 2 antitank guns, and an infantry company destroyed; 2 medium tanks damaged.

The brigade fought no battles with the enemy on 13, 14, 15, or 16 October.

At 16:00 on 16 October, the brigade (motorized rifle regiment – 253 men, T-34 tanks – 3, T-40 tanks – 13) was given the mission of defending the western outskirts of Mozhaysk.

At 07:30 on 17 October, the brigade was ordered by the 5th Army staff to destroy the enemy that had broken through on the axis: Gudkovskaya Dacha-Psarevo-Borodino; the attack was delayed due to lack of artillery preparation.

At 11:30, units of the brigade began attacking as ordered. The commanders of a tank battalion and a tank regiment were killed in the attack, and 2 T-34 and 3 T-40 tanks were burned; the motorized rifle battalion was engaged in fighting northwest of Kurakino.

Enemy losses: 3 mortars, 3 artillery guns, 3 heavy machine guns.

At 18:10, units of the brigade on the western outskirts of Mozhaysk were bombed from the air three times, resulting in 5 men killed and 1 T-34 and 1 T-40 destroyed.

The enemy concentrated forces, conducted an attack, and occupied Mozhaysk at 18:30 on 18 October. The tank regiment was the last to withdraw from the battle and established a position on the outskirts of Teterevo, but it was forced to retreat toward Ruza under enemy fire without infantry support and without communications with its neighbors.

In the battle for Mozhaysk, the motorized machine gun battalion was surrounded and retreated in separate groups traveling in different directions, also towards Ruza; the battalion commander is missing in action.

Enemy losses: 1 medium tank, 2 antitank guns, and at least an infantry company. Brigade losses: 15 killed, 30 wounded, 150 missing in action, 1 T-34 and 3 T-40 tanks destroyed.

<...>

Conclusion.

On the Gzhatsk and Mozhaysk axes, the brigade operated independently without infantry, artillery, and aviation support.

It took the enemy's attack on these axes upon itself.

The fighting caused heavy damage to the enemy's group at Gzhatsk, thus enabling the 16th Army to escape encirclement.

<...>

Despite having personnel and matériel losses, the brigade completed its assigned mission with honor.[6]

The Mozhaysk-Gzhatsk axis was one more spot on the map where blue arrows of tank wedges striving towards Moscow were delayed when they came up against the short red stripes of defending tank brigades. Two tank brigades, the 18th and the 19th, held back two German divisions—the 10th Panzer Division and the "Das Reich" SS Motorized Division.

The October "miracle" was not the result of Soviet tankers getting their hands on some kind of new wonder-vehicle with absolutely impenetrable armor, super powerful armament, and tracks that enabled it to race across the autumn mud more rapidly than their German opponents could travel by highway. It was due to the familiar T-34s the Germans had encountered so often on the way from the border—but *for some reason* had not written panicky reports about.

In fact, many factors played a role in the battles on the approaches to Moscow.

First of all, the Germans themselves had changed since June 22. Although they had prevailed in almost every battle, and although their excellent repair services returned most disabled tanks to the fight, their overall numbers of combat-ready vehicles were slowly but surely declining.[7] They were also losing support equipment,[8] and their stretched lines of communication made the situation even worse. The advent of muddy roads in early September affected supplies for both sides—it was no easier to drag Soviet ton-and-a-half trucks loaded with artillery shells out of the autumn mud than it was German Opel Blitzes, and it may have even been harder given the many off-road vehicles the Wehrmacht had—still, the bad roads reduced the attackers's ability to maneuver. Tanks could advance through the mud, but trucks carrying infantry and artillery prime movers were left behind. Tanks could only tow them for short distances—and in any event, that meant taking tanks out of combat and using up more of their much depleted engine life on towing. Bad weather and interruptions in supply also weakened another German antitank "trump card"—aviation. And whereas during the summer of 1941 the Wehrmacht could easily beat the Russians by pitting the "rock" of their antitank defense against the "scissors" of Russian tank attacks, they found it much harder to do so in October.

Secondly, the Soviets had changed also. According to government decree No. 1749-756, dated June 25, 1941, tanks were to be shipped from factories only as companies

Mikhail Katukov, 4th Tank Brigade commander, October 1941.

that were fully-formed, manned, and equipped. To ensure this, training battalions and companies were established at the factories. The 20th Separate Tank Training Battalion trained T-34 tankers at Factory No. 183, and the 21st Separate Tank Training Battalion did the same at the Stalingrad Tractor Plant. Many of the tankers who received new vehicles had already seen combat—and now they were able to properly thank their German "teachers" for the lessons they had learned.

There was also a "secondly," a "thirdly," a "fourthly," and a "fifthly"... and together they all meant that, instead of a final victorious march to the gates of the Soviet capital, the Third Reich's panzer elite became bogged down in "*very heavy tank battles*" where the "*Russian tanks no longer let themselves be stopped by artillery.*"

This was no miracle—the enemy was still experienced and powerful, and the Soviet soldiers and commanders were seriously lacking in both qualities. "Misuse of tank units" was still a depressingly regular occurrence. Tanks attacked without intelligence and without infantry and artillery support; got stuck in marshes; blew themselves up on mines their own units had laid; and were somehow recovered, under enemy fire at times, repaired, and returned to battle.

At the time, in the fall of 1941, no one could yet tell that the worst was behind them. The Germans continued sweeping forward, breaking through the thin chain of Soviet regiments and divisions time after time. And then they were again stopped by counterattacks, and they were forced to cling to each meter of frozen and snow-covered ground.

On November 22, 1941, Field Marshal Fedor von Bock, commander of Army Group Center, said that "*the situation has reached the point where the last battalion that can be thrown into a battle may decide its outcome.*" [9] The Field Marshal was being candid—at the time, there were divisions at the front fighting with fewer soldiers than a fully manned battalion. [10] On November 30, SS soldiers from the Das Reich Motorized Division captured the Moscow suburb of Snegiri. But Operation Typhoon was blowing itself out. That was its final deadly gust—German tanks could not cross the last 20 km to Moscow.

In early November, the Soviet command was finally able to throw onto the frozen, shaky scales of the war not another handful of reinforcements, but a heavy weight of freshly formed reserve armies.

And the "thirty-fours" painted white for winter that were captured in photos and films became for all time a symbol of the Red Army's first, large-scale, strategic victory. And rightfully so.

NOTES

1 "The Tankers' March" (music: Pokrass brothers; lyrics: B. Laskina), 1939.

2 TsAMO RF, f. 38 (GABTU), op. 11360 (Department for Study and Implementation of Lessons Learned from the War), d. 2 (Reports, accounts, and dispatches from fronts and units concerning combat operations and use of armored forces during June and August), pp. 10–13.

3 TsAMO RF, f. 38 (GABTU), op. 11355, d. 231, pp. 3–10. Cit. ex: *Main Tank-Automotive Directorate: People, Events, and Facts in Documents, 1940–1942.* Moscow: GABTU, 2005, pp. 95–96.

4 "The war has demonstrated that our mechanized corps, as units that are too cumbersome, insufficiently mobile, slow, and not suited for maneuver, not to mention the fact that they are very easy targets for enemy aviation…." (TsAMO RF, f. 48a, op. 3408, d. 4, pp. 1940–42. Cit. ex: Russian archive. Great Patriotic War. Vol. 16/5(1). Moscow: Terra, 1996, pp. 72–73).

5 H . Hoth, *Tank Operations [Tankovyye operatsii].* Moscow: Voyenizdat, 1961.

6 TsAMO RF, f. 38 (GABTU), op. 11360 (War Studies Department), d. 7.

7 Suffice it to say that the 1st Panzer Regiment of the 1st Panzer Division of Hoth's 3rd Panzer Group had 145 vehicles in good condition on June 21, 1941; 79 on July 22; 72 tanks on August 23; 111 tanks on September 28; 36 vehicles on October 31; 37 tanks on November 30; and, finally, 6 tanks on December 21, 1941. T. Jentz, *Panzertruppen, 1933–1942.* Atglen: Schiffer Military History, 1996, p. 211.

8 "Out of the 500,000 vehicles currently with the ground Army in the East, 30% cannot be repaired. 40% are in need of major overhaul. 30% need minor routine maintenance or can be operated as is. 90,000 cannot be repaired by any means available. 275,000 vehicles can be returned to formation after repair." (F. Halder, *Military Diary. Daily Entries by Chief of General Staff, Ground Forces, 1939–1942.* Moscow: Voyenisdat, 1968–1971).

9 F. Halder, *Military Diary. Daily Entries by Chief of General Staff, Ground Forces, 1939–1942.* Moscow: Voyenisdat, 1968–1971.

10 For example, the November 23, 1941, report by the staff of the Soviet 30th Army contains the following statement: "107th Motorized Rifle Division (120 soldiers remaining)." Before the war, a rifle battalion had 778 soldiers. By the end of November, the German 6th Panzer Division had four combat-ready Pz. II tanks remaining.

APPENDICES **APPENDIX A**

TOP SECRET

Decree No. 443ss
of the Defense Committee of the Council of People's Commissars of the USSR

19 December 1939
The Kremlin, Moscow

On the Adoption of Tanks, Armored Cars, and Artillery Prime Movers by the Workers' and Peasants' Red Army, and Their Production in 1940.

Based on an inspection and results of tests conducted on new models of tanks, armored cars, and tractors manufactured in accordance with Defense Committee Decree No. 198ss, dated July 7, 1938, and No. 118ss, dated May 15, 1939, the DEFENSE COMMITTEE under the People's Commissariat of the USSR hereby decrees that:

1. *The following systems shall be adopted by the Workers' and Peasants' Red Army*

I. *The heavily armored "KV" tank manufactured by the Kirov Factory in accordance with the operational requirement of the People's Defense Commissariat, with the flaws identified during testing corrected. The tank shall have the following armament:*

a) *An F-32 76 mm main gun mounted coaxially with a 7.62 mm machine gun in the turret mantlet;*

b) *A separate 7.62 mm machine gun for the radio operator, and*

c) *A 7.62 mm machine gun in the turret recess.*

Provision shall be made for total visibility from the tank.

II. *The T-32 tank—a tracked vehicle with a V-2 diesel engine manufactured by Factory No. 183 of the People's Commissariat of Medium Machine Building, with the following modifications:*

a) *Increase the thickness of the main armor plates to 45 mm;*

b) *Improve visibility from the tank;*

c) *Mount the following weapons on the T-32 tank:*

1) *A 76 mm F-32 gun coaxially with a 7.62 mm machine gun;*

2) *A separate 7.62 mm machine gun for the radio operator;*

3) *A separate 7.62 mm machine gun;*

4) *A 7.62 mm antiaircraft machine gun.*

The tank shall be named the "T-34"....

III. *The BT tank manufactured by Factory No. 183 of the People's Commissariat of Medium Machine Building, with a V-2 diesel engine.*

An 8th Tank Division T-34 abandoned during a retreat, Zovka, Lvov Province. (N 50.055794 E 23.978047)◊

- ***IV.*** *The T-40 tank manufactured by Factory No. 37 of the People's Commissariat of Medium Machine Building—an amphibious tank with a torsion bar suspension and a large-caliber machine gun mounted coaxially with a 7.62 mm machine gun.*
- ***V.*** *The 450 hp V-2 diesel engine manufactured by Factory No. 75 of the People's Commissariat of Medium Machine Building.*
- ***VI.*** *The "Voroshilovets" tractor (artillery prime mover) manufactured by Factory No. 183 of the People's Commissariat of Medium Machine Building, with a V-2 diesel engine.*
- ***VII.*** *The ST-2 tractor (artillery prime mover) manufactured by the Chelyabinsk Tractor Plant of the People's Commissariat of Medium Machine Building, with a diesel engine.*
- ***VIII.*** *The STZ-5 tractor (artillery prime mover) manufactured by the Stalingrad Plant of the People's Commissariat of Medium Machine Building.*
- ***IX.*** *The BA-11 manufactured by the Izhor Factory of the People's Commissariat of the Shipbuilding Industry, with a 90 hp engine on a ZIS-6-K chassis.*

X. The GAZ-61 passenger car manufactured by the Molotov Gorky Automotive Factory of the People's Commissariat of Medium Machine Building, with two drive axles.

XI. The ZIS-5 truck—with two drive axles.

2. The following actions shall be taken to ensure the production of tanks, tractors, and armored cars in 1940 and the development of the required capacities:

1) The People's Commissar of Heavy Machine Building (Comrade V. A. Malhshev) shall:

a) Begin producing KV tanks at the Kirov Factory;

b) Begin mass production on 1 January 1940 and produce 50 KV tanks in 1940;

c) Complete work on the coaxial mount for 76 and 45 mm guns on KV tanks;

d) Prior to mass production of the F-32 gun, allow the Kirov Factory to mount the L-11 76 mm gun on the KV tank;

e) In accordance with Defense Committee Decree No. 198ss, cease production of the T-28 tank after orders for the year 1939 have been fulfilled, with the Kirov Factory continuing to perform repairs and produce spare parts for the existing fleet of T-28 vehicles.

2) The People's Commissar of Medium Machine Building (Comrade Likhachev) shall:

At Factory No. 183:

a) Begin producing T-34 tanks at the Komintern Kharkov Factory No. 183;

b) Manufacture 2 T-34 prototypes by 15 January 1940 and produce a pilot batch of 10 vehicles by 15 September 1940;

c) Produce at least 200 T-34 tanks in 1940;

d) By 1 January 1941, increase the capacity of Factory No. 183 to production of 1600 T-34 tanks;

d) Continue producing the BT tank with the V-2 diesel engine after 1 December 1939 until mass production of T-34 tanks is fully underway;

e) In 1940, manufacture at least 1,000 BT tanks with the V-2 diesel engine at Factory No. 183;

f) In 1942, cease production of the BT tank with the V-2 diesel engine and begin producing only the T-34;

g) After 1 February 1940, begin mass production of the Voroshilovets tractor with the V-2 diesel engine at Factory No. 183 and produce 600 in 1940;

h) After 1 January 1940, cease production of the KIN tractor at Factory No. 183, but continue producing spare parts for the existing fleet of KIN tractors until production begins at other factories.

At Factory No. 37:

a) Begin producing the T-40 tank at the Ordzhonikidze Factory No. 37;

b) By 1 March 1940, manufacture three prototypes of the T-40 and produce a pilot batch of 15 vehicles by 1 August 1940;

c) Initiate mass production of the T-40 tank by 1 October 1940 and produce at least 100 T-40 tanks in 1940;

d) Increase the capacity of Factory No. 37 to produce 2,000 T-40 tanks by 1 January 1941;

e) Until production of the new tractor based on the T-40 is underway, leave the Komsomolets tractor in production at Factory No. 37 and produce 2070 vehicles in 1940.

At the Stalingrad Tractor Plant:

a) *In 1940, establish production capacity at the Stalingrad Tractor Plant for annual production of 2,000 tanks;*

b) *Produce 20 T-34 tanks in 1940;*

c) *Set up a production line at the Stalingrad Tractor Plant to produce 1,000 T-34 tanks in 1941;*

Cease production engineering for T-26 tanks at the Stalingrad Tractor Plant.

The People's Commissar of Medium Machine Building (Comrade I. A. Likhachev) shall utilize the existing capacity, tools, and dies at Factory No. 174 to produce T-26s.

Provide the Defense Committee of the People's Council of Commissars of the USSR a reasonable calculation of the cost of begining production of the T-26 at the Stalingrad Tractor Plant for coverage from the reserve fund of the People's Council of Commissars.

At Factory No. 75:

a) *Devote Factory No. 75 entirely to production of V-2 tank engines;*

b) *In 1940, produce 2700 V-2 diesel engines and spare parts equivalent to 300 diesel engines;*

c) *Increase the capacity of diesel engine Factory No. 75 to produce 8,000 engines annually by 1 January 1941;*

d) *In 1939, complete efforts to increase the horsepower of the V-2 diesel engine to 650–700 hp.*

At Factory No. 48: In 1939, began installing V-2 diesel engines in BT-2-5-7 tanks currently in the Red Army's inventory and produce at least 50 upgraded vehicles in 1940.

At Factory No. 174:

a) *As of 1 January 1941, cease production of the T-26 tank at Factory No. 174;*

b) *In 1940, produce 1550 tanks at Factory No. 174;*

c) *Retain Factory No. 174 as the main base for production of T-26 spare parts and assemblies for the current T-26 tank fleet in the Workers' and Peasants' Red Army.*

At the Chelyabinsk Tractor Plant:

a) *Begin producing the ST-2 tractor (artillery prime mover) at the Chelyabinsk Tractor Plant;*

b) *By 1 January 1940, produce 10 prototypes of the ST-2, and manufacture 1,500 ST-2 tractors in 1940.*

At the Kharkov Tractor Plant:

a) *In 1940, shift production of STZ-5 tractors (artillery prime mover) from the Stalingrad Tractor Plant to the Kharkov Tractor Plant;*

b) *In 1940, manufacture 4,000 STZ-5 tractors (artillery prime mover);*

c) *Jointly with the People's Defense Commissariat, test the STZ transport prime movers with diesel engines by 1 February 1940 and submit the results for Defense Committee approval.*

At the Stalin Factory:

a) *Begin producing the ZIS-6-K chassis for the BA-11 armored car at the Stalin Automotive Factory;*

b) *By 15 March 1940, manufacture and provide 15 chassis to the Izhor Factory (People's Commissariat of Shipbuilding);*

c) *Prepare the Stalin Factory for mass production of the ZIS-6-K chassis by 1 June 1940;*

d) *Begin mass producing the ZIS-5 truck with dual drive axles by 1 October 1940. Beginning on 1 October 1940, begin mass producing GAZ-61 passenger cars at the Molotov Automotive Factory.*

3) *The People's Commissar of Shipbuilding (Comrade TEBOSYAN) shall:*

At the Izhor Factory:

a) *Facilitate the manufacture of armored hulls and turrets for the Kirov Factory at the Izhor Factory: in 1940, produce armored hulls and turrets for 50 KV tanks;*

b) *In coordination with the People's Commissariat of the Shipbuilding Industry, place hulls and turrets sufficient for production of 1600 T-26 tanks on the schedule of the People's Commissariat of Medium Machine Building for Factory No. 174 of the People's Commissariat of Medium Machine Building;*

c) *Produce armor parts for repair facilities of the People's Commissariat of Medium Machine Building, the People's Commissariat of Heavy Industry, and the People's Commissariats of Automotive Transportation of the union republics in satisfaction of planned orders of the People's Defense Commissariat;*

d) *By 15 April 1940, produce a pilot batch of 15 BA-11 armored cars after correcting all flaws identified during testing and provide for full visibility from the vehicles;*

e) *Complete tooling up for mass production of BA-11 armored cars by 1 June 1940 and, after fully mastering the technology, produce the BA-11 as a replacement for the BA-10 in accordance with planned orders of the People's Defense Commissariat for 1940.*

At the Mariupol Factory:

a) *Manufacture and deliver the following from the Mariupol Factory for Factory No. 183 of the People's Commissariat of Medium Machine Building:*

1) *Armor for hulls and turrets for the diesel-engined BT in quantities sufficient for BT tank production in 1940 according to the schedule of the People's Commissariat of Medium Machine Building as coordinated with the People's Commissariat of Shipbuilding;*

2) *Provide armor parts for repair facilities of the People's Defense Commissariat, the People's Commissariat of Medium Machine Building, the People's Commissariat of Heavy Industry, and the People's Commissariat of General Machine Building in satisfaction of the planned orders of the People's Defense Commissariat for 1940.*

3. *To provide armor for production of the new tank models, Comrade SABUROV (Gosplan, USSR), Comrade TEBOSYAN (People's Commissariat of Shipbuiding), Comrade MERKULOV (People's Commissariat of Ferrous Metallurgy), and Comrade LIKHACHEV (People's Commissariat of Medium Machine Building) shall by 10 January 1940 submit proposals to the defense committee for initiating production of armor in thicknesses up to 90 mm for the following tanks: KV, T-34, T-40, and armored cars.*

The proposals shall support full production of tanks and armored cars in both peacetime and wartime using the existing armor and steel plants.

4. *In accordance with the current decree, the following tank types shall be established and shall remain in production after 1 January 1941:*
   1) *The KV heavy tank;*
   2) *The T-34 tank;*
   3) *The T-40 tank.*
5. *Establish the vehicle produced on 1 November 1939 for each type of tank and armored car as the standard for mass production in 1940.*
   Changes to vehicles during the year shall only be made with the approval of two people's commissars—the People's Defense Commissar and the people's commissar of the appropriate industry.
6. *To improve vehicle mobility the People's Commissariat of Medium Machine Building and the People's Defense Commissariat shall, by 29 December 1939, submit proposals to the Defense Committee concerning the procedure and manufacturing dates for off-road equipment for ZIS-5 vehicles of the type manufactured by Factory No. 183 (People's Commissariat of Medium Machine Building) (by order of Comrade Khrushchev).*
7. *The People's Defense Commissariat, the People's Commissariat of Medium Machine Building, the People's Commissariat of General Machine Building, and the People's Commissariat of Automotive Transportation of the RSFSR shall, by 29 December 1939, provide specific proposals to the Defense Committee for initiating production of spare parts at factories belonging to the commissariats in quantities that support the Red Army's existing fleet of tanks and other vehicles.*
8. *The People's Commissariat of Medium Machine Building, the People's Commissariat of Shipbuilding, and the People's Commissariat of the Oil Industry shall, by 29 December 1939, provide the following to the Economic Council of the People's Council of Commissars of the USSR:*
   a) *Additional orders for equipment and the construction required for production of the new types of armored systems, and*
   b) *A plan for approval whereby the lead factories will cooperate to produce the systems approved for service.*
9. *Gosplan under the People's Council of Commissars of the USSR shall, within two weeks, review the orders and provide funding for production with due consideration to meeting the dates set for production of the systems in 1940.*
10. *To provide incentives for the engineers, technicians, and other workers engaged in producing the new armored equipment, the bonus system implemented for the People's Commissariat of the Aviation Industry in accordance with Decree No. 25, dated 27 April 1939, of the People's Council of Commissars of the USSR shall be extended to factories of the People's Commissariat of Medium Machine Building, People's Commissariat of Shipbuilding, People's Commissariat of the Oil Industry, and People's Commissariat of Medium Machine Building.*
    The People's Commissariat of Finance shall allocate the following sums from the reserve fund of the People's Council of Commissars for use in rewarding outstanding engineers, technicians, and other workers engaged in developing prototypes of armored systems:
    The People's Commissariat of Medium Machine Building – 1,500,000 rubles
    The People's Commissariat of Shipbuilding – 300,000 rubles
    The People's Commissariat of the Oil Industry – 75,000 rubles

People's Commissariat of Heavy Machine Building — 300,000 rubles

11. *In accordance with this decree, approve the planned orders for armored systems issued by the People's Defense Commissariat, the People's Commissariat of the Navy, and the People's Commissariat of Internal Affairs for 1940 per Annex No. 1.*

CHAIRMAN, DEFENSE COMMITTEE
of the COUNCIL OF PEOPLE'S COMMISSARS OF THE USSR
V. MOLOTOV

SECRETARY, DEFENSE COMMITTEE
of the COUNCIL OF PEOPLE'S COMMISSARS OF THE USSR
I. SAFONOV[1]

CHIEF, RED ARMY GABTU
LIEUTENANT GENERAL OF THE ARMORED FORCES
Comrade FEDORENKO

Defense Committee Decree No. 428 calls for increasing the size of the T-34 tank turret without increasing the size of the race ring. This upgrade does not improve the tank's overall effectiveness. Increasing the size of only the upper part of the turret slightly improves crew accommodation in the travel configuration (by providing more convenient seating). There is no improvement when in firing configuration, because the race ring is not changed, leaving a narrow space between the spent case catcher and the race ring, which will make it difficult for the crew to work during firing (especially the loader). Work of the crew is hampered even more with the F-34 gun installed, because the back of the spent case catcher almost touches the race ring, which prevents the gun crew from being switched without lowering the spent case catcher or accommodating a fifth crew member—a commander with a commander's cupola installed.

Expansion of the turret without increasing the size of the race ring is actually being done to facilitate transfer of production; this is not a proper or necessary solution.

The designers would have to adopt a temporary solution that would do little to improve work in the turret, and would interupt turret production in February and then again after some time for conversion to the needed turret option; in other words, it would cause many problems for production.

The existing T-34 tank turret is cramped, uncomfortable, and has poor visibility, but the recent field driving tests with three live fires reaffirmed that aimed fire from the tank is possible. The maximum rate of fire was 2–3 rounds per minute.

Can the size of the T-34 tank's turret race ring be increased? Yes, it can. According to preliminary estimates, the turret race ring can be increased by approximately 200 mm.

Is the increase feasible from a production standpoint? It is, because the increase would not affect the Mariupol Factory, and Factory No. 183 has the machine tools for producing a larger race ring.

Expansion of the turret and race ring by 200 mm would enable a more convenient placement of the gun crew and meet the requirement placed on industry of providing six aimed shots from the move.

It would allow the placement of a 5th crew member (the tank unit commander) with equipment to observe the battlefield and command a tank unit, which would significantly improve the combat characteristics of the tanks.

Increasing the combat load without fundamentally changing the tank's suspension would result in significant changes to the tank's interior. The fuel and oil systems would be radically altered. The coil spring suspension would be modified and the electrical wires relocated slightly, and that still would not completely resolve the issue. All of these changes would have to be made during production without performing tests in advance to check them.

Defense Committee Decree No. 428 does not provide for equipping the T-34 with a torsion-bar suspension during 1941, probably because of the difficulty Factory No. 183 would have manufacturing torsion bars.

I have learned that the machine tools at Factory No. 183 could not be used to machine torsion bars.

The factory has developed a torsion-bar suspension design using the existing road wheels and suspension arms.

What advantages does a torsion-bar suspension offer according to preliminary estimates?

- **a)** *It would increase the tank's fighting compartment volume by 20%, making it possible to increase the basic load; we will address that in a draft Decree regarding installation of a torsion-bar suspension.*
- **b)** *A larger fighting compartment would allow more convenient placement of the crew and facilitate its work under combat conditions.*
- **c)** *The capacity of the fuel tank would be increased to 750 L instead of 465 L, which would increase the tank's range by 60–100 km, and the fuel tanks would be moved from the fighting compartment to the transmission compartment.*
- **d)** *The weight of the suspension itself would be reduced by 300–400 kg.*
- **e)** *Assembly and disassembly would be made easier.*
- **f)** *Cutouts in the sides of the tank for passage of the suspension arms would be eliminated.*

The tank's weight could not be significantly reduced without a torsion-bar suspension and the reconfiguration it would entail.

Installation of the V-2-K engine without first checking the transmission is undesirable, because the transmission was designed for a tank weighing 18 t and a 500 hp engine with 240 kg-m of torque and 1800 RPM.

The V-2-K engine develops 600 hp with a torque of 265 kg-m and 2100 RPM, and the tank would weigh approximately 27 tons. Increasing all of these parameters could increase transmission part wear and lead to premature breakdowns.

CONCLUSION: As a supplement to Defense Committee Decree No. 428, we hereby request that the Defense Committee be petitioned to have Factory No. 183 of the People's Commissariat of Medium Machine Building build two improved T-34 tank models with the following modifications by 1 April 1941:

- **a)** *An enlarged turret and race ring with a commander's cupola with all-round vision.*
- **b)** *A torsion-bar suspension.*
- **c)** *A larger basic load.*
- **d)** *A stronger transmission.*
- **e)** *Increased maximum speed to 70 km/h.*
- **f)** *A crew working area enlarged as much as possible to provide for convenient placement and good visibility.*

Testing shall be performed during April and May.

Changes based on the test results shall be incorporated in June.

Follow-up testing of prototypes incorporating the changes shall be done during July.

The manufacturing process shall be developed during August and September. Mass production of the improved T-34 tank shall begin in October.

This will allow the improvements to be made without rushing, test inspections to be performed, and the transition to production of the improved vehicle to be accomplished painlessly.

Factory No. 183 is willing to undertake this work and believes that these measures to improve the tank are entirely correct.

Manufacture of the production T-34 with the existing turret shall continue without changing the suspension. Interoperability of the internal equipment shall be maintained, and the emphasis shall be on maximizing tank production.

Factory No. 183 and the People's Commissariat of Medium Machine Building shall only work on the following issues in fulfillment of Decree No. 428:

a) *The main clutch*
b) *The fan*
c) *The track*
d) *Visibility*
e) *The ammunition storage rack*

I believe it necessary to arm T-34 tanks having the same turret with 45 mm and 76 mm guns as follows:

Arm two tanks in a battalion with 45 mm guns mounted coaxially with the Degtyarev machine guns and one company with 76 mm guns coaxially with the Degtyarev machine gun, or two platoons in a company with 45 mm guns and one with 76 mm guns.

What will this accomplish? Tanks armed with the 45 mm gun will carry up to 250 projectiles (in the enlarged turret), or up to 200 projectiles in the existing turret, i.e., double the number of 76 mm projectiles. Considering the weight of the round during loading, the rate of fire with the 45 mm gun will also be doubled, which will not reduce the effectiveness of fire on enemy gun positions (machine gun placements, antitank guns) and lightly armored tanks.

When obstacles requiring more firepower are encountered, the (company or battalion) commander will have it and will deploy his forces as needed to carry out his mission.

I hereby submit the above report and request that a petition be submitted.

ENGINEER LIEUTENANT COLONEL PANOV, LEAD
13 December 1940

A T-34 with German recognition markings, 1941.

TOP SECRET

To: Comrade Khrushchev
Comrade Kobulov

MEMORANDUM

Concerning design flaws and delay in production of new A-34 tanks at Factory No. 183 in Kharkov

A number of flaws have been identified in the design for the A-34 tank prepared under the leadership of Factory No. 183's chief designer, Engineer KOSHKIN, that affect the vehicle's combat characteristics.

The driver's compartment in the first prototype was designed to provide a wide field of view forward and to the sides, as a result of which there was no exit hatch for the driver and the gunner located next to him. The intent was for them to exit the vehicle through the turret hatch.

In addition to the inconvenience, the lack of a driver's hatch will increase crew fatigue prior to a battle. In addition, if the turret hatch becomes jammed during combat, the entire crew will be trapped in the vehicle and unable to exit.

Armored Force Directorate representative PANOV was aware of the issue, but still agreed to the design of the compartment without a hatch and failed to ask KOSHKIN pointedly about a design that would provide both a lateral field of view and a hatch in the driver's compartment.

Instead of working to develop a design that had a hatch and vision to the side, KOSHKIN and his deputy, MOROZOV, stated that there would either be a hatch without a lateral field of view or a lateral field of view without a hatch.

This design for the driver's compartment was rejected by the Red Army Armored Force Directorate chief, Corps Commander Comrade PAVLOV, after the armor parts were constructed.

KOSHKIN assigned design of the second version of the driver's compartment with a hatch to BARON, designer of the transmission group, who had never worked with armor parts and considers himself unqualified in this area. The design of the driver's compartment with a hatch lacked strength and was unable to withstand projectile impacts.

In addition, in BARON'S compartment design the hatch can only be opened when the gun barrel is moved out of the way, and the driver needs to turn it 90 degrees.

All of the design flaws of the driver's compartment were pointed out in a timely fashion by the hull section chief, Design Engineer TARSHINOV, who considered the design unsuitable for mass-produced vehicles.

Instead of accepting these comments and assigning an experienced hull designer to develop a design without these flaws, Koshkin directed that BARON's design be used as the basis for working out the driver's compartment in detail.

When Engineer TARSHINOV pointed out the compartment's design flaws, he offered to produce his own design, but KOSHKIN sent him to Mariupol even though he did not need to be the one to make the trip.

When he returned, Engineer TARSHINOV developed and submitted a driver's compartment design with a lateral field of view and a hatch that could be opened without turning the turret. In addition, the entire compartment was capable of withstanding projectile impacts.

Assembly of second prototype's hull was delayed by two weeks because the armor parts of the driver's compartment were changed. All of these changes and the additional parts cost approximately 100,000 rubles.

In order to cover the squandering of funds, KOSHKIN is getting ready to begin mass production of the driver's compartment as designed by Designer BARON, and Engineer TARSHINOV's design will be manufactured as a prototype for some reason.

In addition, according to data in our possession, a large flaw in the tank's design is that the vehicle carries only 38 cartridge cases, which significantly reduces its combat capability.

KOSHKIN believes that places will be found in the final vehicle where additional cartridge cases can be stored even though the design data shows no such space.

The People's Commissar of Internal Affairs (NKVD) of the USSR has been informed in order that the appropriate actions may be taken through the People's Commissariat of Medium Machine Building and the Armored Force Directorate of the Workers' and Peasants' Red Army.

Deputy Peoples Commissar of Internal Affairs of the Ukrainian SSR
Gorlinsky
7 February 1940[2]

TOP SECRET

To: Chief
Main Economic Directorate of the NKVD of the USSR
Commissar of State Security 3rd Class
Comrade B. V. Kobulov
Moscow

MEMORANDUM

Concerning production of A-34 tanks at Factory No. 183 in Kharkov

By decree of the Central Committee of the All-Union Communist Party (Bolshevik) and the People's Council of Commissars of the USSR dated 7 June 1940, the Kharkov Factory No. 183 must manufacture and transfer 500 of the new A-34 tanks to the military in 1940.

This Government order has been obstructed. AS OF 19 December of this year, only 32 tanks, or 6.4% of the annual plan, have been manufactured and transferred to the military representative.

Factory No. 183 manufactured prototypes of the A-34 tank in early 1940.

In deciding to begin production of these tanks, the state commission pointed to the need for a number of design improvements and modifications, which were not done in a timely fashion, as a result of which the majority of changes were made during production without prior testing.

Among other changes, an enlarged turret with rolled armor and a cast turret were put directly into production, and a 45 mm gun mount was prepared.

This resulted in several changes and corrections being made to the vehicle drawings while it was in production, as well as changes to the manufacturing process and tooling, etc.

Production engineering was carried out with the expectation that the L-11 76 mm gun would be mounted on the A-34, and parts for the turrets were produced at Factory No. 183 and the Ilyich Mariupol Factory for mass production of tanks mounting that gun system.

Based on letter No. 346-3536-s of the Chief Directorate of Special Machine Building of the People's Commissariat of Medium Machine Building dated 20 August 1940 and the report of an engineering conference held by the director of Factory No. 183 and approved by the chief of the Armor Directorate of the Workers' and Peasants' Red Army, Lieutenant General Comrade FEDORENKO, the L-11 76 mm gun will be mounted on just 200 tanks, and thereafter the 45 mm gun will be installed.

Thus, a portion of the parts manufactured for mounting the 76 mm guns will have to be discarded. Some 300–400 part sets have already been made.

The Ilyich Mariupol Factory is now tooled up for production of armor parts for the 45 mm gun system.

On 10 June 1940, MAKHONIN, chief engineer of Factory No. 183 (who is under investigation on suspicion of sabotage) from Moscow, sent a telegram to the ILYICH Mariupol Factory telling it to stop production of turrets for the 45 mm artillery system and resume production of turrets for the 76 mm gun.

On this issue, the informant LINEYNY learned in a conversation with MAKHONIN that no special decision had been made to replace the 45 mm gun with the 76 mm gun after producing 200 tanks, but that the L-11 76 mm gun would be installed on tanks through the end of 1940 on the basis of a resolution issued by AFONIN, chief of the 3rd Department of the Armored Force Directorate.

Because Factory No. 183 has mastered production of the L-11 76 mm system, and the 45 mm gun has not yet been tested even on prototypes, MAKHONIN gave the order to switch from producing parts for the 45 mm system to the 76 mm system.

This "switch" from producing one system to producing another may mean that the ILYICH Mariupol Factory will be unable to support Factory No. 183 with armor parts in a timely manner.

Because the proper manufacturing process and interdepartmental planning had not been done at Factory No. 183, RATINOV, CHINOV, AND MELNIKOV (under investigation on suspicion of sabotage) were supplied with couplings that had not undergone thermal treatment and required replacement. However, the Red Army GABTU military representative, Military Engineer 2nd Class KOZYREV, agreed that these couplings could remain on the combat vehicles.

In addition, KOZYREV and POPOV, the Red Army Armored Force Directorate's representative, agreed to accept lower quality tanks and also to ship old tracks for the tanks sent to military units due to the poor quality of track shoes delivered by the Stalingrad Tractor Plant that did not provide the guaranteed kilometerage.

The supplier factories consistently provide fewer than the required quantity of parts and assemblies.

The ILYICH Mariupol Factory is not implementing the decree of the Central Committee of the All-Union Communist Party (Bolshevik) and the People's Council of Commissars of the USSR dated 7 June 1940 as regards complete shipments of armor parts; the Kharkov Factory No. 75 is not providing enough engines; the Stalingrad Tractor Plant is not supplying the needed number and quality of track shoes; the Yaroslav Rubber-Asbestos Combine is not delivering tires of the required quality on time; and the Stalin Automotive Plant is not providing radiators; etc.

The issue of extending the service life of the A-34 tank from 3,000 km to 7,000 km is currently being resolved.

As instructed by the People's Commissariat of Medium Machine Building and the Red Army's GABTU, on 16 June of this year a 3,000-kilometer road test was conducted on 3 A-34 vehicles at Factory No. 183.

The test run revealed several design flaws in the vehicles tested that caused the tanks to break down.

The main clutch plates experienced excessive wear, causing the ring gear and fan bolts to break; the main clutch adjustment cone became weakened, and the fan blades broke. This required repeated clutch overhaul and complete replacement of several parts and assemblies, since the vehicles would not move. The cast track shoes broke quickly. Three tracks were replaced during the test run.

It should be noted that the tracks on the tanks tested by the state commission were comprised of drop-forged track shoes that lasted for the 3,000 km test run. After the tank went into production, however, the drop-forged track shoes were replaced with cast track shoes that, at the initiative of Factory No. 183 and with the agreement of the People's Commissariat of Medium Machine Building and the Red Army's GABTU, had not been tested for the guaranteed kilometerage.

The rubber on all wheels broke down and came off. The Yaroslav Rubber-Asbestos Combine manufactured high-quality rubber tires good for 6,000 km for the tanks tested by the state commission, but the mass production tires only held up for 2,000 km.

The design of the track tensioning mechanism is flawed, and the worm gear jams. Excessive force is required to tension the tracks.

The locks on the front access hatches are poorly designed. When the front hatch is accidentally closed with the top turret hatch locked, it is impossible to enter the tank. When this happens, the machine gun must be removed and the lock knocked off. In addition, the front hatch is difficult to open from inside the tank, because the lock must be pulled downward and the hatch opens upward. Under combat conditions, this access hatch lock design could prove fatal for the crew.

The vision blocks quickly become covered with mud. It is impossible to clean the side vision blocks from inside the tank.

The pins that retain the rubber attachment lug spacers abrade through the oil tanks, and oil leaks into the tank hull.

Road tests for the guaranteed kilometerage were not conducted on the first A-34 prototype tanks, and these serious flaws were not detected during the brief acceptance tests, although some of the design flaws became known after the prototypes were tested.

Informant BEYEV had this to say about that issue: "Significant flaws in the A-34 design have been identified." Section "100" chief BRYANSKY told me that Designer KALENDIN had informed him (BRYANSKY) that many of the defects that have now been corrected were known to be present in the prototypes and the pilot batch vehicles. However, an order was issued at the time that no changes should be made to the vehicle and, therefore, no flaws were corrected, although it was obvious that they needed to be.

Despite the fact that production engineering for the A-34 tank is incomplete and serious design flaws have not been corrected, by order of the People's Commissariat of Medium Machine Building, Factory No. 183 must undertake to upgrade the tank by enlarging the turret, changing the armament (increasing the firepower), relocating the radio, etc.

I hereby request through the People's Commissariat of Medium Machine Building and the Red Army's GABTU an explanation for why mass production of A-34 tanks was begun without corrections being made to a number of significant design flaws.

Deputy People's Commissar of Internal Affairs of the Ukrainian SSR
Major of State Security
Tkachenko

No. 4850/sn
26 December 1940

SECRET

5/4249
15 May 1941
DEPUTY PEOPLE'S COMMISSAR OF DEFENSE
OF THE USSR
Comrade G. I. KULIK

Subject: Improved T-34 tank

As a result of constant efforts by Factory No. 183 to improve the T-34 tank, the tank currently in production is significantly superior to the 3 tanks that were built during the first months of mass production (July–September 1940), which were subjected to a long road test and which led to incorrect conclusions about the T-34's quality in general.

The factory implemented up to 200 design changes between February 1940 and April 1941, in accordance with instructions both from the field trial commission and the Red Army's GABTU, as well as on its own initiative.

The following actions were taken to correct the vehicle's main flaws:

New cast tracks from the Stalingrad Tractor Plant provided 2,200–2,900 km during testing and began mass production in March 1941. Efforts to further improve the track are ongoing.

Warping of the main clutch was eliminated by introducing steel plates with slots. The plates on all vehicles issued to the Army have been replaced.

A new driver's hatch with triplex lenses giving the driver excellent visibility from the tank has been built, tested, and accepted for mass production. Work is underway to introduce vision blocks with prisms.

An ammunition storage rack that supports a rate of fire of up to 4 rounds per minute was introduced beginning with tank number 751.

The service life of the fan has been increased to 1,500 km. An effort to further increase the guaranteed kilometerage to 3,000 km is underway. Individual prototypes have already lasted 2,800 km.

During the same period, several hundred technological measures have been implemented to improve the assembly and handling of individual units.

A great deal of work has been done to reduce cracking, as a result of which the percentage of hulls with fractures was down from 90% in October 1940 to 50% in March 1941. A particularly sharp reduction was noted in the sides: there were 68 fractures in October 1940, and there have been none at all since January.

The T-34 tank today has a guaranteed kilometerage of 2,500–3,000 km (except for the fan), and the figure for some mechanisms is significantly greater, as confirmed by the fact that two tanks operating (in the experimental workshop) under difficult winter and spring road conditions at an average travel speed of 26–30 km/h traveled 5,000–6,000 km without replacement of the main mechanisms.

The excessive vilification of the T-34 tank needs to stop.

DEPUTY PEOPLE'S COMMISSAR
OF MEDIUM MACHINE BUILDING OF THE USSR
A. GOREGLYAD[3]

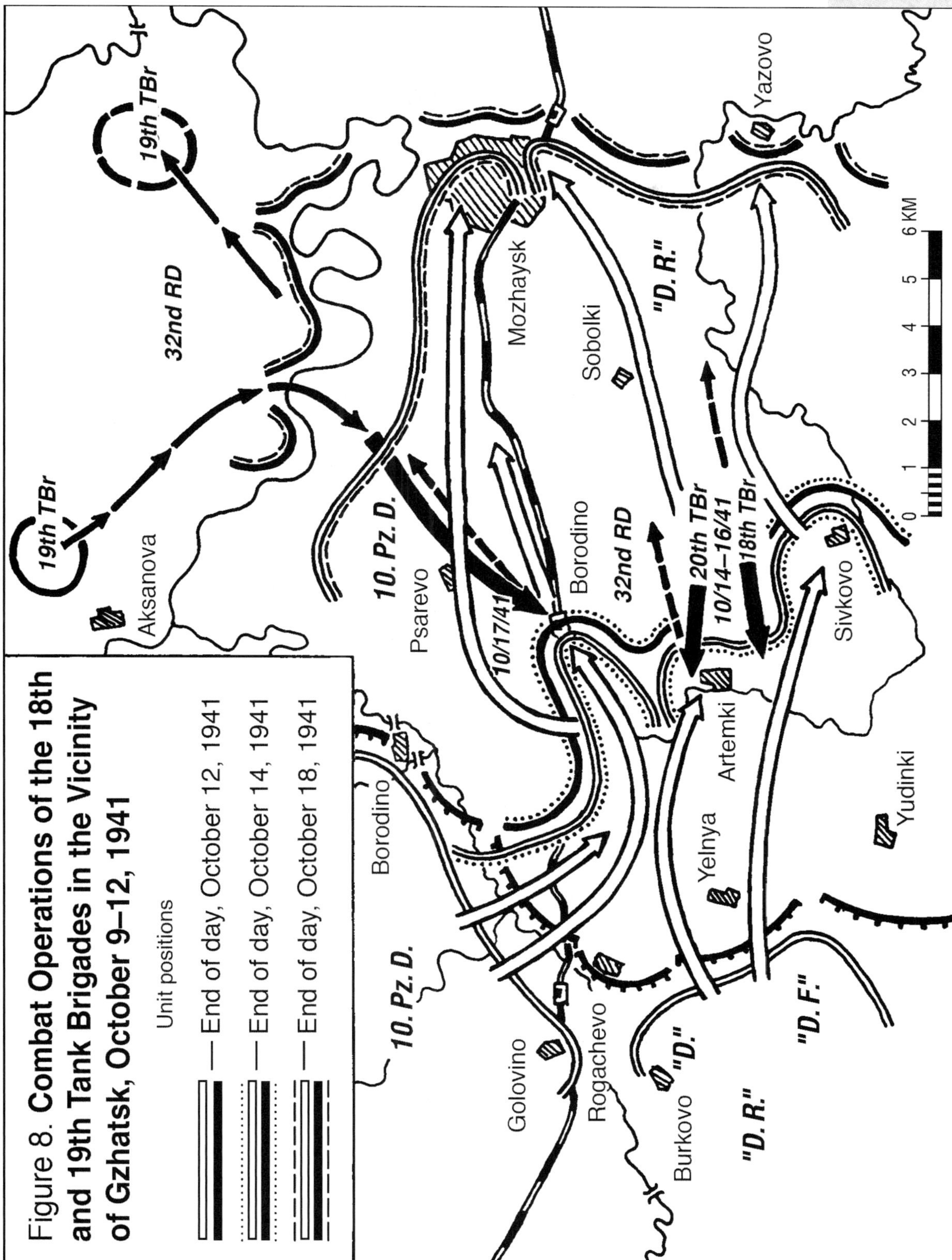

Figure 8. **Combat Operations of the 18th and 19th Tank Brigades in the Vicinity of Gzhatsk, October 9–12, 1941**

Memorandum

on correction of the main flaws in the T-34 tank of Factory 183 re. the letter from Comrade Goreglyad, Deputy People's Commissar of Medium Machine Building

The Stalingrad Tractor Plant initiated mass production of its new track shoes beginning with the 51st vehicle. Factory 183 began using them on 15 June 1941.

Warpage of the main clutch plates has been corrected. The plates on vehicles provided to the army have been replaced. There have been a few cases of plates fracturing in units that have vehicles with the new plates.

Mass production of the new driver's hatch has not begun, because Factory 183 has declined to manufacture the hatch with a triplex lens and has stopped development of the version of the hatch with a prismatic vision block.

Mass production of the improved ammunition storage rack has not yet begun. The factory did not provide the new ammunition storage rack beginning with vehicle No. 751.

The guaranteed service life of the fan has been increased to 1,500 km. A new fan (drawing 34.07.7SB-11) that will give better results has been developed, tested, and approved for production (the fan was tested on T-34 tank No. 811-28 between 27 April and 27 May 1941. The tank was driven 3070 km).

The percentage of hulls with fractures has been reduced, but weld quality remains low.

Senior Engineer, Section 1, Branch 3, Armor Directorate of the Red Army,
Military Engineer 2nd Class
(signature illegible) [4]

TOP SECRET

To: PEOPLE'S COMMISSAR OF
MEDIUM MACHINE BUILDING
Comrade MALYSHEV

According to a report dated 21 February 1941 and a supplementary agreement dated 8 March 1941, Factory No. 183 has consented to install a new driver's hatch, transmission gears, and vision blocks in the T-34 tank turret on tanks it produces and to replace these assemblies on tanks in unit hands.

The Red Army's GABTU approved the drawings during April–May of this year.

Factory No. 183 has not yet began installing them.

These assemblies will improve the tank's combat characteristics, and they must be installed as quickly as possible, especially given the current situation.

I hereby request that you issue a categorical order to the directors of Factory No. 183 and the Stalingrad Tractor Plant to immediately begin installing these assemblies on all tanks in production.

Please inform me of your decision.

CHIEF, RED ARMY GABTU
Lieutenant General of the Armor Forces
(FEDORENKO)

Chief, Armor Directorate, Red Army GABTU
Military Engineer 1st Class
(KOROBKOV)
24 June 1941[5]

To: DIRECTOR, FACTORY NO. 183, COMRADE MAKSAREV
GABTU REGIONAL ENGINEER AT FACTORY NO. 183, COMRADE
CC:
DEPUTY PEOPLE'S COMMISSAR OF STATE CONTROL OF THE USSR, COMRADE POPOV
Chief, Tank Department, People's Commissar of Medium Machine Building, Comrade
15 August 1941
No. 147965 s

Battlefield operation of T-34 tanks again confirms that the transmissions are of poor quality. The transmissions have a very short service life. Of the tanks that broke down due to transmission failure, none had traveled as much as 1,000 km.

According to unsatisfactory equipment report 102 t.d. No. 036, dated 2 August of this year, during 10 days of combat operations, 7 of 15 tanks broke down as a result of transmission failures.

Transmissions of such poor quality fail to support combat operations using T-34 tanks. There have also been a large number of main clutch failures (due to warpage, plate breakage, and excessive/preliminary release mechanism wear), steering clutch bearing failure, and bent idler sprocket cranks.

The Red Army's Armor Directorate categorically demands that Factory No. 183 take immediate steps to correct these defects and expedite installation of improved driver's hatches on the tanks this August.

To: Regional Engineer, Red Army GABTU—Military Engineer 2nd Class Comrade KOZYREV

a) *Improve quality control of tanks.*
b) *Correct the listed defects by all means possible.*
c) *Repairs on tanks coming from the front involving parts and assemblies that have not exceeded the warranty kilometerage under the contract must be done at factory expense.*

I hereby request that the Red Army's Armor Directorate be informed of actions taken to correct production defects and the dates of such actions no later than 25 August 1941.

Deputy Chief, Red Army GABTU Armor Directorate, Military Engineer 1st Class
Alymov

Military Commissar, Red Army GABTU Armor Directorate, Regimental Commissar
(Name not given)[6]

TOP SECRET

To: CHIEF, 1ST DEPARTMENT, PEOPLE'S COMMISSARIAT OF MEDIUM MACHINE BUILDING, COMRADE GNESIN
CC:
DIRECTOR, FACTORY NO. 183,
COMRADE MAKSAREV
GABTU REGIONAL ENGINEER AT FACTORY NO. 183, MILITARY ENGINEER 2ND CLASS
COMRADE KOZYREV
SENIOR RED ARMY GABTU MILITARY REPRESENTATIVE AT THE STALINGRAD TRACTOR PLANT, MILITARY ENGINEER 2ND CLASS
COMRADE LEVIN

7 September 1941
No. 148453ss

According to a dispatch by Chief, Western Front Armored Force Directorate, the following defects have been identified in the T-34 tank:

1. *The system's armor protection is weak; it is easily penetrated by enemy projectiles, and the system jams.*
2. *The fighting compartment fan does not clean the air, which partially poisons the crew.*
3. *A projectile hit on the driver's hatch cover causes it to come off its hinges and drop inside the tank. The turret hatch cover is not securely attached to its hinges.*
4. *The air shut-off valve leaks. There have been instances of fire in tanks due to this leakage.*

Request that you instruct the factories to undertake urgent measures to correct these tank defects.

Please inform me of decisions taken.

Chief, Department 1, Armor Directorate, Red Army GABTU
Military Engineer 1st Class
PAVLOV

Chief, Branch 1, Department 1, Red Army Armor Directorate
Military Engineer 2nd Class
CHIKOV[7]

TOP SECRET

CHIEF, RED ARMY GABTU,
LIEUTENANT GENERAL FEDORENKO
Moscow
18 Jun 1941

During use of KV and T-34 vehicles in military unit 5427,[8] *a number of significant design flaws were identified, especially among the vehicles that were produced first.*

The following T-34 breakdowns occurred:

Bolts attaching the fan to the flywheel sheared because there were too few bolts and they were too small in diameter. Vehicles from the first production run had 15 bolts; those from later production runs had 27 bolts.

Transmission forks break when the nuts connecting the forks and shafts come loose. The nuts come loose when the lock washer straightens.

Track shoes on vehicles from the first production run wear quickly and break.

On KV tanks:

The tubing that carries lubricant to the fan bushing breaks. The tubing breaks as a result of a large bend in the tube and the difference in speed between the two halves of the fan.

The fan blades break because the attachment of the fixed blades weakens and both blades come in contact with each other.

The turret traversing mechanism pinion breaks while the vehicle is in motion. The travel lock bends when the vehicle is moving and does not lock the turret.

The manufacturers are in receipt of unsatisfactory equipment reports on all of these breakages and are working to correct the defects. The manufacturers are doing nothing to prevent possible damage occurring on vehicles that are in mothballs and not being operated.

I hereby request that you instruct the Kirov Factory and Factory No. 183 to take the steps necessary to prevent the above indicated damage from occurring on the KV and T-34 tanks that were produced first. The numbers of vehicles needing an upgrade in military unit 5427 are as follows: KV – 52, and T-34 – 100.

CHIEF: ARMORED FORCE DIRECTORATE, KIEV SPECIAL MILITARY DISTRICT, MAJOR GENERAL OF ARMOR
MORGUNOV

CHIEF, DEPARTMENT THREE, ARMORED FORCE DIRECTORATE, KIEV SPECIAL MILITARY DISTRICT, MILITARY ENGINEER 2ND CLASS
GANOPOLSKY[9]

To: Chiefs of Military District Armored Force Directorates
Tank Corps and Separate Tank Division Commanders
16 April 1941
No. 140385ss

Take the following steps to maintain secrecy on the KV and T-34 vehicles:

Prohibit travel by these vehicles in cities and towns during the hours of daylight. Travel to training grounds and back only during hours of darkness. Do not drive tanks to and from firing ranges; leave them at the training ground and take steps to protect them.

Only give personnel undergoing training or servicing the vehicles access to them.

When vehicles are no longer used, they must be placed under seal and protected.

The vehicles must be completely canvas covered during shipment by rail, and they must be under guard while en route and on site.

To the extent possible, unload from railcars at night. If the dictates of time require unloading during daylight hours, move vehicles to units at night.

Store vehicles under roof if possible; otherwise store under canvas.

Correspondence about these vehicles must be classified "SECRET."

Do not mention the vehicle types in telephone conversations.

Pay particular attention to maintaining secrecy about the "vehicle operational characteristics," which must be known only to the command staff and the crews that work on the vehicles.

Make this clear to all personnel and require that they protect information about these vehicles.

Chief, Main Armored Force Directorate, Red Army,
Lieutenant General of Armor
Fedorenko [10]

A T-34 with German recognition markings, 1941

To: Factory No. 75 Chief Engineer Comrade Nevyazhsky
From: Sergeant Andrey Grigoryevich
Dudnik
Military Unit 4141, Zlochev

Comrade Engineer Nevyazhsky, I am reporting to you concerning the operating conditions of the V-2 diesel engine in the KV vehicles with military units.

The silk that the Kirov Factory includes in the vehicle for filtering gas oil fuel doesn't do what it's supposed to. The silk that the factory includes is very thin; I'm sending you a piece of it.

I fold the silk in eight layers when I put fuel in the vehicle, and even then it catches little dirt; also, the fuel tanks in the units are very dirty. I started getting involved in this problem although I am an enlisted soldier in the Red Army, because I worked as a driver-mechanic in the experimental shop of Factory No. 183 and had a lot of experience with factory tests on the engine. I started telling people that the silk isn't right for fueling because it's folded in two or four layers, but the technical people told me I should mind my own business and laughed at me.

Refueling through this kind of silk goes faster, of course, but it affects vehicle operation—the fuel injectors stop working. You are probably already aware of the unsatisfactory equipment report written by your representative, Comrade Stepanenko. But that isn't all. I went to see how they fuel A-34 vehicles and saw that they do it without using any silk at all. I asked why, and they said that they're following factory instructions, and when I asked to see the instructions, they clearly said that fueling should be done through a screen and two layers of silk fabric. There's no silk in the vehicle; it's shut up in the warehouse like the special nozzle.

Comrade Engineer, please provide military units with the appropriate instructions for refueling V-2 engines, because the engines won't last their full warranty period, and you will have a lot of trouble and hassle with unsatisfactory equipment reports coming from all over. And tell the Kirov Factory to include silk fabric that is right for the job.[11]

SECRET
27 September 1941

INSTRUCTIONS FOR USE OF THE TANK BRIGADE IN THE MAIN TYPES OF COMBAT

I. *March and meeting engagement*

1. *When preparing for a march in anticipation of a meeting engagement, the commander and his staff must focus on establishing a proper march formation and on organizing reconnaissance and security.*

2. *In a march, the main forces of the tank brigade proceed along one or two routes. The movement zone should not exceed 4–5 km.*

The brigade's order of march may differ depending on the situation:

- *Move the tank regiment along one route and the motorized rifle battalion along another;*
- *Distribute the motorized rifle regiment among the tank battalions, forming separate, completely independent columns;*
- *Travel in a single column with tanks (on open terrain) or infantry in the lead;*
- *The column should always be separated into echelons. An echelon should be of battalion strength. The distance between echelons should be 1–1.5 km.*

3. *Organize reconnaissance such that:*

- *All routes in the tank brigade's zone of movement are reconnoitered;*
- *The commander receives needed intelligence on the enemy (direction of travel, force, and composition of columns) to support timely decisions.*

4. *The normal makeup of a reconnaissance group (RG) operating along the main axis in a 2–3 km zone should be as follows: a platoon or company of armored cars or tanks, a motorized infantry platoon, 1–2 guns, and 5–10 motorcycles.*

The reconnaissance group should be separated from the main column by 15–20 km.

Separate reconnaissance patrols consisting of an armored car platoon with motorcycles and one or two infantry squads should be sent along secondary axes or towards an open flank; the interval between the separate reconnaissance patrol and the main column should be as much as 10–15 km.

5. *The reconnaissance units should report by radio using a code chart and simple signals previously established by the headquarters. When the enemy is encountered, messages should also be sent by messenger.*

6. *March security should be accomplished by sending out the point unit (GPZ) in strength up to a tank company reinforced by a motorized infantry company with antitank guns and mortars.*

7. *Antiaircraft defense for a brigade tank column should be provided by:*

- *Distribution of anti-aircraft machine guns along the column to repel attacks by dive bombers.*
- *Coverage of chokepoints and open spaces by antiaircraft guns, for which an antiaircraft battalion either moves by bounds from line to line along independent routes or covers the most dangerous areas subject to aerial attack and rejoins the main column upon completing a mission;*

- *Assignment of squads in a motorized rifle battalion to fire by groups on diving aircraft;*
- *Strict observance of regulation intervals between vehicles in a march. Do not allow these intervals to close up during a halt.*

8. *Stopping a column during an enemy air attack in an open field is prohibited; no increase in interval or speed is permitted, the column must continue moving in the same order. During an attack by enemy aircraft in terrain with natural concealment, the column must disperse and camouflage itself.*

9. *The depot forward echelon (GEP) should, as a rule, follow the brigade along the most convenient route.*
The depot forward echelon should have at least enough fuel to top up fuel tanks when half empty and half a basic load of ammunition.

10. *Tanks must not be driven until their fuel tanks are empty. Each vehicle must retain at least enough fuel for three hours of engine operation. When unit commanders reports that this point has been reached, the brigade commander must do everything possible to carry out refueling.*

11. *Supply and evacuation routes must be assigned to combined arms units, and subunits of the motorized rifle battalion must be used for that purpose only in extreme cases, and then they must be reinforced with tanks.*
On axes where the enemy can cut the supply lines, the brigade must have everything it needs to fight without receiving supplies from the rear or transport aircraft.

12. *March control should be implemented by indicating in order the times when phase lines are to be crossed and by establishing communications between columns and within columns. Communication should be by motorcycle and by brief radio signals according to a previously established table.*
The tank brigade headquarters should be accompanied by two communications officers each from the tank regiment and the motorized rifle battalion.
When deploying for battle, the brigade headquarters must communicate with the tank regiment and motorized rifle battalion headquarters by wire.

13. *The reconnaissance aircraft supporting the brigade should drop a message about the enemy and neighboring units when the air observation, warning, and communications post issues a prearranged codeword.*
The tank brigade commander should be accompanied by an air liaison with a radio. The brigade commander uses the air liaison to request bombers and fighters.

14. *In order that friendly tanks can be recognized from the air, their turrets must have 25 cm-wide white stripes applied in the shape of a cross.*

15. *In anticipation of a meeting engagement, the commander and his command staff travel in the first echelon of the main column during a march. When the lead units engage in battle, the commander moves forward under cover of the point unit together with his unit commanders or communications officers from the tank regiment and motorized rifle battalion in order to assign missions on the ground.*

16. *The tank brigade's main force attacks the enemy from the move, deploying directly from column formation, or crosses the deployment line and attacks upon receipt of a general signal.*

17. The motorized rifle battalion should deploy quickly with its antitank guns and mortars and attack following the tanks or, occupying a favorable position, establish an antitank defense to support the tank regiment's deployment, maneuver, and attack.

18. A tank attack should be preceded by an airstrike on the enemy columns.

II. Offensive battle

19. A tank brigade may conduct an offensive battle in close coordination with the motorized rifle regiment (division) or independently. An independent attack may only be carried out during a mobile battle and against an enemy that has assumed a hasty defense.

20. When organizing an offensive battle, the brigade staff must organize reconnaissance jointly with the combined arms staff in order to determine the following:

- *Location of the forward edge of the battlefield (FEBA) and identification of antitank obstacles to the front;*
- *Location of the main grouping of enemy antitank guns (tank kill zones);*
- *Antitank obstacles located in the depth of defense;*
- *Locations of the enemy's main artillery groupings and reserves.*

21. A tank brigade will normally be attached to one of the infantry regiments of an infantry division's assault group. Splitting up tanks when assigning to infantry units into groups smaller than a tank battalion is not permitted. A tank battalion must include heavy, medium and light tanks, or medium and light tanks. The tank brigade's motorized rifle battalion is used for attacking as part of the infantry unit to which the tank brigade has been assigned, or it is held in the tank brigade commander's reserve. A tank brigade commander must always be prepared to consolidate the brigade's actions in his hands to repel counterattacks or pursue a retreating enemy. When pursuing a retreating enemy, the motorized rifle battalion should move behind the tank regiment in vehicles.

Based on the decision of the combined arms commander to which a tank brigade is attached, the brigade commander assigns a mission to the tank units, allocates them to units of the maneuvering forces, and issues instructions for logistical support. The tank brigade commander's command post must be located at or near the command post of the combined arms commander.

22. The tank brigade commander should direct the battle by radio and by dispatching couriers on combat vehicles from his command post.

23. In accordance with the commander's decision, his staff coordinates actions by tanks, infantry, artillery, and aviation. The time and locations of artillery and air preparaton, allocation of targets for suppression among the artillery and aviation, and signals used to request artillery fire and airstrikes are established by a coordination table. The supporting aviation unit must have a liaison officer at the brigade command post. Forward artillery observers travel on tanks with radios in the first echelon and adjust fire. Tank crew commanders must be assigned to the artillery and infantry units cooperating with the tank brigade.

24. Tank company and battalion commanders must be given at least 3–5 hours of daylight to organize cooperation on the ground.

In organizing cooperation, a tank commander must establish the following precisely:

a) With the infantry commanders:

- *Where the FEBA is located and what antitank obstacles are located in front of it;*
- *The locations and types of firing positions;*

- *The most suitable locations for starting positions and routes from them to the FEBA;*
- *How and by what means the infantry will provide passages through antitank obstacles;*
- *The locations and numbers of antipersonnel obstacles through which passages must be cleared;*
- *The locations and types of high-priority firing positions that must be suppressed;*
- *What antitank guns (1 gun per 250 m of front) and machine guns the infantry allocates to support the tank attack;*
- *Lines for reconnecting with the infantry.*

b) *with the artillery commanders:*

- *The firing positions to be suppressed during artillery preparation;*
- *Where to shift fires during the tank attack on the FEBA;*
- *The areas to be fired upon in support of the tank attack;*
- *The directions from which enemy tank counterattacks are to be prevented.*

25. Signals between the infantry and tanks (designating targets, tanks returning to the infantry, etc.) and signals between tanks and artillery (calling for and shifting fire) are established by the tank brigade staff jointly with the combined arms staff.

26. Success in an offensive battle will be determined by the proper organization of cooperation, which should lead to continuous forward movement of the tank and infantry battle formation supported by artillery fire.

The infantry must never become separated from the tanks and must employ all of its firepower to destroy enemy antitank guns discovered during the attack.

27. If there is sufficient time to prepare for an offensive, joint exercises between tanks and infantry must be organized.

28. ***THE FOLLOWING ACTIONS ARE STRICTLY PROHIBITED:***

- *A tank attack without arranging infantry and artillery support;*
- *An attack on enemy defenses unsupported by artillery and aviation;*
- *Employment of tanks in groups of 3–5 vehicles.*

29. The combat formation of a tank brigade must meet the requirements for a mass tank attack, offer an opportunity for scaling up an assault from the rear, and be capable of maneuvering on the battlefield.

A tank attack must be sudden, massive, and continuous.

A brigade usually attacks on a front of 1.5–2 km, with heavy and medium tanks in the first echelon and light tanks in the second.

The interval between echelons is 200–300 m.

Echeloning is practiced only when there are enough tanks in the first echelon. A reserve can be established when there is a sufficient number of tanks in the first and second echelons.

The infantry advances behind the second tank echelon. The mission of the heavy and medium tanks is suppression of antitank guns and artillery to support actions by light tanks accompanied by infantry.

Light tanks not only suppress defensive firing positions to support infantry penetration throughout the depth of the defenses, some light tanks also provide fire support for the first echelon of tanks.

The area designated for assembly after completion of the mission of the day should be behind friendly infantry.

Combat experience has shown that when our attacking tanks appear German tanks retreat behind infantry formations that have organized an antitank defense. When this happens, friendly artillery fire must be directed on the infantry's defensive area, and the attack executed only after this has been done. Fire from friendly tanks prior to an attack is conducted from the halt and from cover, while changing the positions of the tanks.

The situation sometimes allows pursuit of retreating enemy tanks while simultaneously breaking through the enemy's defenses.

30. *In maneuver combat, a tank brigade may encounter an enemy that has assumed a hasty defense.*

If the defending enemy cannot be bypassed, the commander should attack independently.

31. *Aerial reconnaissance should give advance warning that an enemy has gone on the defensive and provide an approximate sketch. Ground reconnaissance means are used to determine the location of the FEBA and the antitank defense plan.*

A T-34 in winter camouflage paint, winter 1941.

32. *After stopping the main force 3–4 km from the FEBA, the headquarters should organize a commander's reconnaissance under cover of the reconnaissance elements and the point unit to establish the defense plan, direction of the main assault, and the starting line for the attack.*

33. *The brigade should attack independently on a front of 1,000–1,500 m, with heavy and medium tanks in the lead. The motorized rifle battalion should attack immediately behind the light tanks.*

The depth of the attack should encompass the enemy's artillery firing positions. As soon as the enemy's defenses are penetrated, the tanks should act boldly and courageously on the enemy's flanks and in his rear areas.

The brigade commander must have a tank reserve during independent offensive operations.

34. *The lack of artillery in the tank brigade requires preparation for an airstrike.*

The brigade headquarters must have an air liaison officer through which the staff assigns missions for air preparation and support for tank attacks.

35. *The depot forward echelon (GEP) must carry half a basic load of ammunition and sufficient POL for one refueling.*

The depot forward echelon should be located 10–15 km from the FEBA, and after the immediate mission is completed, it should move to the assembly area in order to resupply the combat vehicles.

III. *Defensive battle*

36. *A tank brigade usually does not conduct a defensive battle independently; it does so as part of an assault group and may counterattack jointly with infantry units or independently.*

37. *The tank brigade should be deployed 8–10 km from the FEBA in a waiting area and remain ready to counterattack along designated axes.*

The brigade staff should organize and reconnoiter the likely directions of counterattack assigned to the brigade and indicate starting positions (deployment lines).

If a tank brigade joins an combined arms unit's assault group, the reconnaissance should be done under the direction of the combined arms commander with the involvement of the commanders of the units included in the assault group and the artillery units supporting the counterattack.

38. *The reconnaissance should provide the following information:*

- *How the tanks will operate along a given axis during counterattacks:*
- *How the artillery will support the counterattack on each axis;*
- *What fire means will be attached to support the tank counterattack and where they will come from;*
- *Where the passages through the antitank obstacles will be, and how they will be designated.*

39. *If the enemy breaks through the defensive zone, tanks should counterattack with the mission of destroying the breakthrough enemy units. Enemy tanks must be destroyed as a first priority.*

The combined arms assault group may counterattack immediately behind the tanks or on the flank from a different direction, taking advantage of the enemy's confusion following the tank counterattack.

40. *In some instances, the situation may require that the tank brigade go on the defensive.*

41. *When defending independently, the brigade's motorized rifle battalion should take separate defensive positions along a front of 2–3 km. The spaces between the defensive positions must be covered by effective machine gun fire.*

42. *A tank regiment should comprise an assault group (one or two) and be employed for counterattacks on an enemy preparing for an offensive, with counterattacks coming around the flanks of friendly infantry or through gaps in order to destroy enemy infantry and tanks that have crossed the FEBA.*

It is best to designate the starting positions as the assembly area following a counterattack.

43. *To enhance the defense, the motorized rifle battalion should have tanks attached that are dug in or positioned in terrain folds in order to fire from stationary positions along pre-sighted lines.*

Assistant Armored Force Commander,
Western Front
(signed)[12]

SECRET
SUPREME HIGH COMMAND GENERAL HEADQUARTERS ORDER No. 057

22 January 1942,
Moscow

On the Combat Employment of Tank Units

Lessons learned in the war have shown that serious shortcomings remain in the way tank forces are being employed in combat, as a result of which our units are suffering heavy losses of tanks and personnel.

The excessive and completely unjustified and ineffective losses in the tank forces are occurring for the following reasons:

1. *Infantry coordination with tank units is still poorly organized; the missions assigned by infantry commanders are not specific and are done in haste; the infantry lags behind tanks during offensives and does not secure lines captured by tanks; on the defensive, it does not provide cover for tanks waiting in ambush; and during a retreat, it does not even warn tank unit commanders about the changing situation and abandons tanks to fend for themselves.*
2. *Attacking tanks are not supported by friendly artillery fire; guns do not accompany tanks, and, as a result, combat vehicles are destroyed by enemy antitank artillery.*
3. *Combined arms commanders are hasty in their use of tank units—they throw them piecemeal directly into battle from the move without giving them time to carry out even basic reconnaissance of the enemy and the terrain.*
4. *Tank units are used as small subunits, sometimes one tank at a time, which results in a dissipation of force, causes the detached tanks to lose contact with the brigade, and makes it impossible to support them logistically during battle; and infantry commanders carrying out their unit's narrow mission use these small groups of tanks in frontal attacks without the ability to maneuver, and that increases vehicle and personnel losses.*
5. *Combined arms commanders pay little attention to the technical condition of the tank units under them—they move them long distances under their own power, are dismissive of problems involved in recovering damaged equipment from the battlefield, and assign missions without considering the length of time tanks spend in battle without preventive maintenance, which further increases the already heavy tank losses.*

The Supreme High Command General Headquarters hereby orders the following:

1. *As a rule, tank brigades and separate tank battalions are to be used in battle as complete units and in close coordination with infantry, artillery, and aviation; and tanks are not to be put into battle without advance reconnaissance and personal reconnaissance by infantry, artillery, and tank commanders.*
2. *Each instance of improper use of tank forces, abandonment of tanks in enemy territory, and failure to recover them is to be investigated and those responsible prosecuted.*
3. *To increase the authority and responsibility of the armor chiefs of armies and fronts, the Supreme High Command General Headquarters is designating the former as deputy army*

commanders for tank forces, and the latter as deputy front commanders. Axis commanders shall have a deputy for wheeled and armored forces and three liaison officers who are armor specialists.

4. *Front headquarters shall have an armor section, and army staffs shall include two deputies: one for the combat use and employment of tank forces, the other for the supply, maintenance, and operation of combat and support vehicles.*

5. *The institution of assistant front commanders for armor forces shall be eliminated from staffs.*

Promulgate this order down to battalion level.

Supreme High Command General Headquarters:
J. Stalin
A. Vasilevsky[13]

NOTES

1 RGAE [Russian State Archive of the Economy], f. 8418 op. 28 d. 92 pp. 121-129. Original. Annex No. 1 not published

2 State Archives of the Security Service of Ukraine, f. 16, op. 33 (1951 r.), d. 90, pp. 213-217. Carbon copy. Cit. ex: *Soviet Organs of State Security, 1939 – June 1941 (Documents of the State Archives of the Security Service of Ukraine).* Kyiv: Kiev-Mohyla Academy, 2009.

3 TsAMO RF, f. 38, op. 11355, d. 279, pp. 7–8. Original. Letterhead of the People's Commissariat of Medium Machine Building. Authentication: "T. Fedorenko. I concur with Goreglyad. Take action. 16 May 1941" G. I. Kulik.

4 TsAMO RF, f. 38, op. 11355, d. 279, p. 8a. Handwritten original.

5 TsAMO RF, f. 38, op. 11355, d. 279, p. 93. Typewritten manuscript, copy

6 TsAMO RF, f. 38, op. 11355, d. 235, p. 23. Typewritten manuscript, copy.

7 TsAMO RF, f. 38, op. 11355, d. 235, p. 44. Typewritten manuscript, copy.

8 Military Unit 5427—8th Tank Division, 4th Mechanized Corps, Kiev Special Military District.

9 TsAMO RF, f. 38, op. 11355, d. 279, p. 92. Typewritten manuscript, original.

10 TsAMO RF, f. 38, op. 11353, d. 883, p. 4. Typewritten manuscript, original.

11 TsAMO RF, f. 38, op. 11355, d. 138, p. 115. Typewritten manuscript, exact copy.

12 TsAMO RF, f. 208, op. 33783ss, d. 1, pp. 51–60. Cit. ex: *Collection of Military Documents from the Great Patriotic War [Sbornik boyevykh dokumentov Velikoy Otechestvennoy Voyny]*, Issue 21.

13 Cit. ex: *Collection of Military Documents from the Great Patriotic War,* Issue 5. Moscow: Voyenizdat, 1958.

APPENDIX B

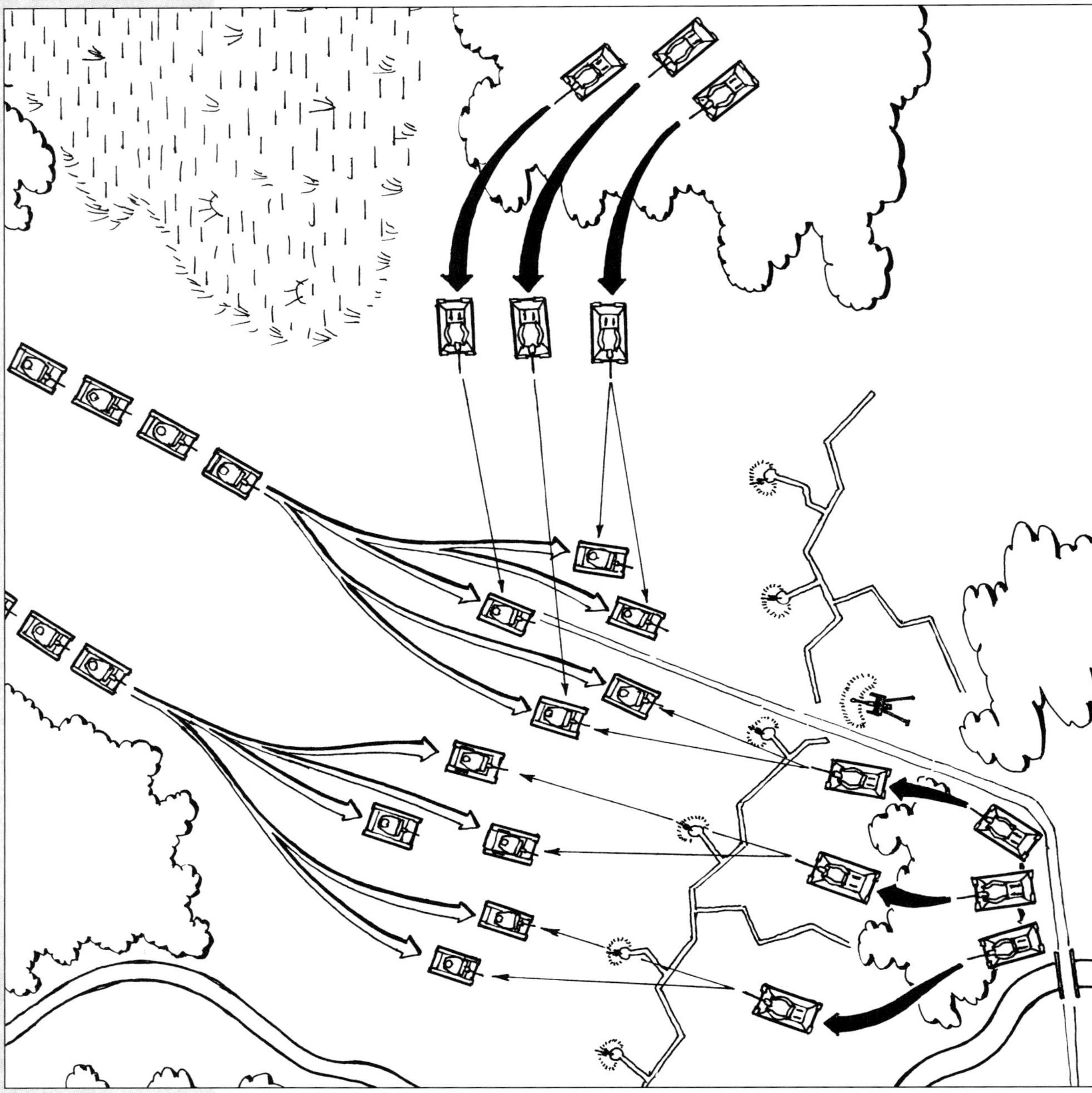

"In a mobile defense, tanks achieve their greatest impact with tank ambushes. The advantage of ambushes is that they provide an opportunity for catching the enemy in a location where he cannot advantageously deploy his fire weapons and where he can be engaged with organized fire. Such fire has a stunning effect on the enemy, deprives him of the time needed to take appropriate countermeasures, and forces him to do everything hastily and under unfavorable conditions of time and terrain. In addition, the heavy losses that always occur in an ambush have an extremely negative impact on his morale and cause his soldiers to become depressed and confused. This all means that even an ambush that is minor in its composition but tactically sound can defeat a large enemy force." T. P. Kuznetsov, *Armor Tactics [Taktika tankovykh voysk]*, 1940.

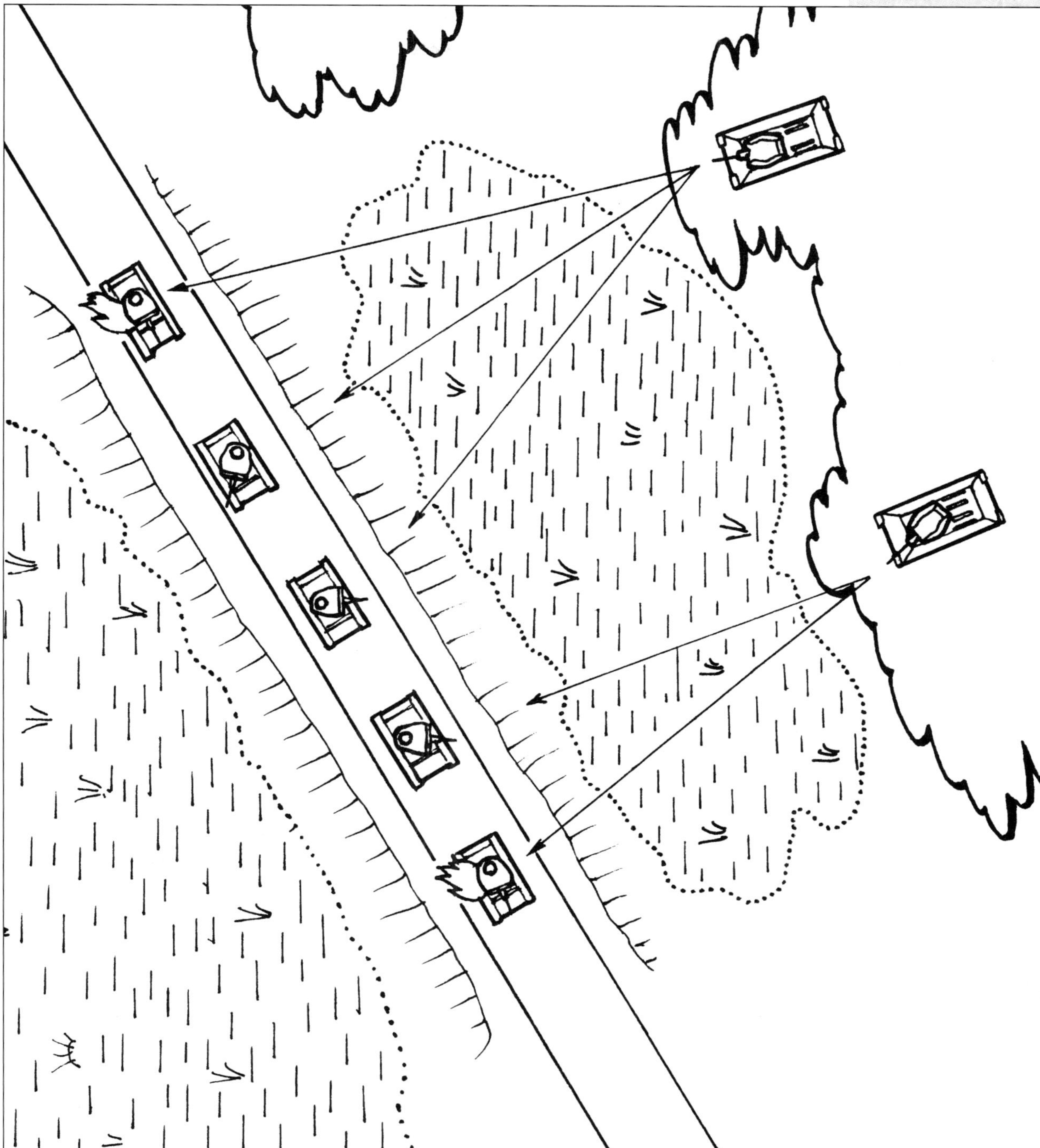

In the fall of 1941, when muddy conditions limited the maneuverability of Germany's mobile forces, tank ambushes proved to be a successful tactic for Red Army tankers. The ambush tactics employed by the 4th Tank Brigade commanded by M. Ye Katukov are the most famous.

Index

Note: *Page numbers in italics indicate production drawings or photographs.*

Index

Index

U

V

W

Y

Z

BATTALION OF HEAVY & MEDIUM TANKS

Organization Chart 010/87 of September 13, 1941

HQ

MAINTENANCE & RECOVERY SQUAD

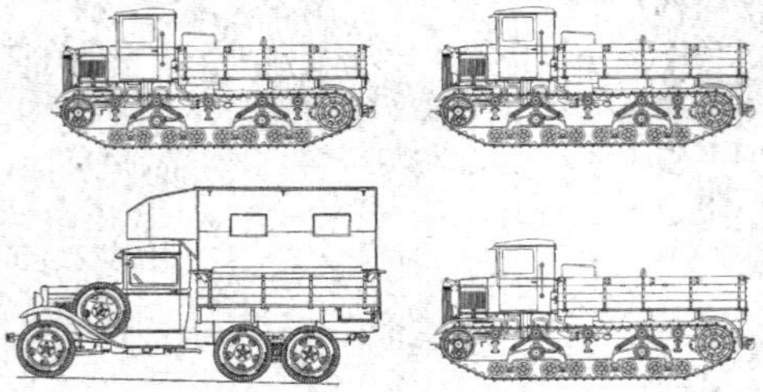

HEAVY TANK COMPANY

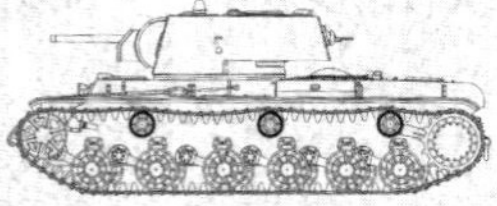

Company Commander's Tank

TANK PLATOON

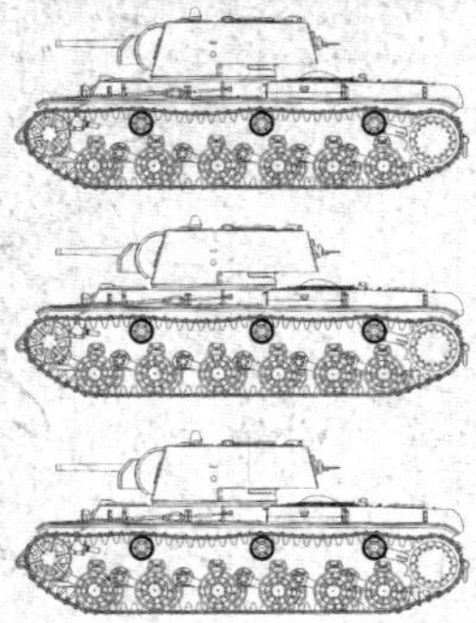

TANK PLATOON

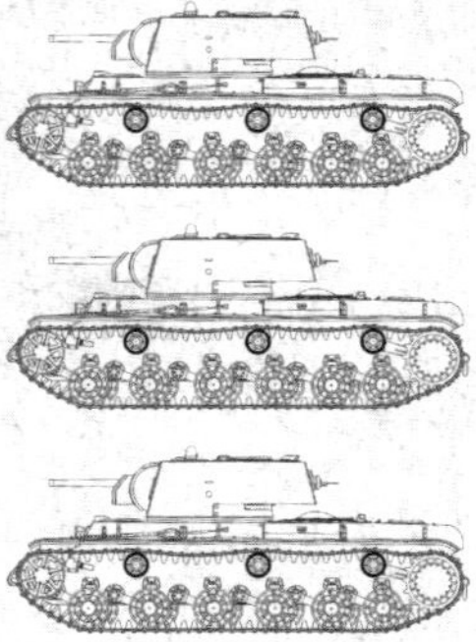

MEDIUM TANK COMPANY (3 PER BATTALION)

T-34

Company Commander's Tank

TANK PLATOON

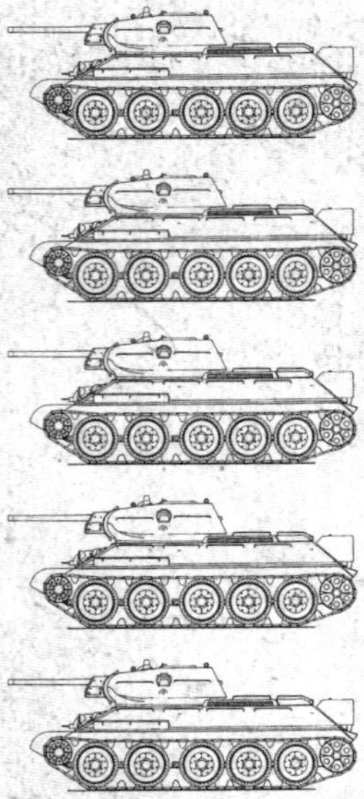

TANK PLATOON

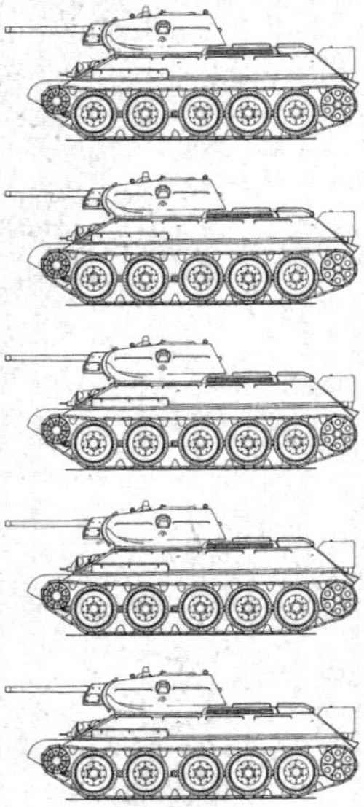

TANK PLATOON

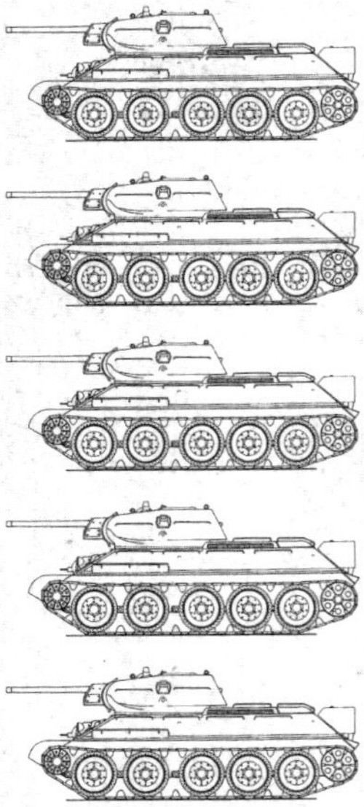

❶ ❷